"There are three huge strengths that set this book apart from anything else available on the transition to adulthood. First, it is written in a lively and jargon-free style by two rare social scientists who are familiar with the English language. Second, its scope is stunning, including challenges to becoming an adult created by dramatic changes in education, relations between young adults and parents, marriage and its precursors, civic life, and the world of work. Third, the tone is relentlessly upbeat about the advantages these changes are opening up for young people. This book proves that it is possible to write an interesting book about a big social problem that reflects research knowledge while nonetheless being accessible to the American public."

—RON HASKINS, co-director of the Brookings Institution's
Center on Children and Families

"One of the most important functions of social science research is to raise the quality of public debate by challenging myth, conjecture, and sensationalism with empirical realities. This book does just that by presenting an integrated social map of young adulthood in twenty-first-century America that is grounded in a diverse body of research."

—JAMES GARBARINO, PH.D., Loyola University Chicago, author of
Children and the Dark Side of Human Experience

"Amid all the outcry over young people stuck in adultolescence and failing to launch comes this sensible portrait of a generation of almost-adults. Based on empirical research, and not hand-wringing punditry, Settersten and Ray reveal a new stage of development that slows the clock, but does not stop it, making slower, but steady progress to more durable relationships and stable

—MICHAEL KIMMEL, profe   k,
author of *Guyland: The F   en*

"The rulebook has changed; the good ol' days of a universally accepted school-work-family-retirement fast track are gone. Despite mainstream media's attempt to portray 20-somethings as a group of lazy, no-good slackers, *Not Quite Adults* uncovers the real story—how a slower, more calculated transition into adulthood often makes more sense and leads to a better future for us all."

—SEAN AIKEN, author of *The One-Week Job Project*

"A provocative look at how a changing reality is transforming the transition to adulthood for a generation of Americans, and the implications of this transformation in today's competitive world." —*Kirkus Reviews*

"Aside from enjoying a panoramic perspective on one generation, readers will be able to glean tips on everything from dating to parenting from this admirably lucid and fair-minded study that, in describing what is happening, reveals what is working."   —*Publishers Weekly*

"*Not Quite Adults* is perhaps the most important contribution to date about the strange new life of America's twenty-somethings. Settersten and Ray are able to combine a deep grasp of the research with commonsense advice for 'not quite adults' and their parents. The slower path to adulthood is here to stay; thanks to the authors, we are now much wiser about what that means for all of us."

—KAY HYMOWITZ, author of *Manning Up: How the Rise of Women Has Turned Men Into Boys* and contributing editor for *City Journal*

"Based on interviews with 500 young adults and extensive research, this outstanding book offers a fresh and compelling view of why it is taking this generation longer to make career and family decisions. The message here is about the value of 'slowing down,' and it makes sense not just for young adults, but also for their parents and educators, who are 'fast-tracking children' into a lengthy period of being nearly, but not quite, adults. Learn about today's young adults, why they are making the life choices they are, and why we should feel good about it."

—BARBARA SCHNEIDER, author of *The Ambitious Generation,* John A. Hannah Distinguished Professor, Michigan State University

NOT QUITE ADULTS

NOT QUITE ADULTS

Why 20-Somethings Are Choosing a Slower Path
to Adulthood, and Why It's Good for Everyone

Richard Settersten, Ph.D.,
and
Barbara E. Ray

BANTAM BOOKS TRADE PAPERBACKS / NEW YORK

A Bantam Books Trade Paperback Original

Copyright © 2010 by Richard Settersten, Jr., and Barbara Ray

Published in the United States by Bantam Books, an imprint of
The Random House Publishing Group, a division of
Random House, Inc., New York.

BANTAM BOOKS and the rooster colophon are registered trademarks of Random House, Inc.

ISBN 978-0-553-80740-0

Printed in the United States of America

www.bantamdell.com

2 4 6 8 9 7 5 3 1

FIRST EDITION

Book design by Casey Hampton

Contents

MacArthur Research Network
on Transitions to Adulthood and Public Policy

Introduction

There was a time not so long ago when a popular high school graduation gift was a suitcase. Not for nothing, this gift. It marked the young person as a newly minted member of the adult clan, bound for independence and autonomy. Armed with a wallet full of small bills from family, friends, and neighbors, and either a dictionary for college or a pair of new work boots for the factory floor, high school graduates set off to conquer the world with their suitcases in tow.

Young adults once hit the road on a clearly marked path. The first stop was college, some training, or the military. Next up was a job. Marriage followed, and then children. Between marriage and kids, the new family bought a home. All of this was accomplished by age twenty-five—and often in that order. There would be exceptions and a few detours for some, but for the majority, the gap between the end of adolescence and the embrace of adulthood was short and sweet. This sprint was not confined to the halcyon days of the 1950s. The suitcase and the quick ticket to independence were alive and well for the high school class of 1980.

From the vantage point of parents and eighteen-year-olds today, this beeline to adulthood is unfathomable. Move out? Who can afford it? A college degree and a job by age twenty-one—no way. Marriage and kids by twenty-five? Unheard of. Today, one-half of those between eighteen and twenty-four have not left their childhood bedrooms, let alone landed a job, married, or had children of their own. This is a 37 percent increase over 1970. And an even bigger jump in living at home has occurred for those ages twenty-five through thirty-four—a 139 percent increase since 1970. Some of these young people never left the nest, and others have boomeranged back. Regardless, this sizable increase is a strong clue to how much the transition into adulthood is stretching. Today's graduation gift might as well be a GPS device, because the signposts on the road to adulthood seem to have all but vanished.

What happened? If we're to believe the media, these changes are the result of too much coddling and too few hard knocks. Spoiled and indulged at every turn, today's young adults are a generation of stunted Peter Pans dodging the serious business of adulthood. Fifteen years ago, you couldn't pay twenty-somethings to live at home with their parents, even if it meant renting roach-infested apartments and eating ramen noodles every day. They sucked it up, cut corners, and survived. Today, some young people are staying at home past their thirtieth birthdays.

But a peek under the rug of easy anecdote reveals a much more complex story, a story we tell in this book. The media and others may paint today's young adults as spoiled slackers, implicitly blaming parents for their children's failure to launch. But the real story lies largely elsewhere, in a host of changes that today affect how young adults think about education, work, love, home, and country. Like the butterfly that flaps its wings in Indonesia, causing a thunderstorm to erupt in New York, the events and upheavals of the past few decades have unleashed a perfect storm just as this generation's high school graduates were poised to launch themselves onto the tried-and-true road to adulthood. These forces have shredded the old rule book for when to leave home, how long to spend in college, and when to marry and settle down. The new rule book, meanwhile, is still being written, leaving much ambiguity and uncertainty for young people and their families as they try to make their way. It is a particularly perilous time for those least prepared to compete in this high-stakes world.

In the pages that follow, we dispel many misperceptions about young adults, and in so doing we hope to change the conversations we have with our children and one another about these longer and less direct routes to adulthood. Many parents privately feel a sense of failure as they are bombarded with the negative news stories and stereotypes about their children's generation. They feel as if they have somehow failed in a critical role of parenting—preparing their children to leave the nest. They look inward at their parenting styles, wondering if they have been too indulgent, feeling guilty that they still have such close relationships with their adult children, or that their adult children feel no compunction about returning home. Books such as *The Death of the Grown-Up: How America's Arrested Development Is Bringing Down Western Civilization* by Diana West have only fueled this sense by setting their sights directly on parents, accusing them of abdicating adulthood in favor of their own perpetual youth, and for making child rearing a "no bad guy" experience. The result, these books argue, is a generation of young people—and parents—who refuse to grow up.

What the actual research shows, however, may ease some of the guilt and shame parents may feel and open their eyes to the new world of the twenties that their children are attempting to navigate. With new insights, we hope parents can begin to shape new strategies for helping their children, or at least better understand why their children are doing adulthood so differently today. We hope, too, to offer guidance to young people, who are themselves anxious about their futures and the heaviness of their choices.

We also want to bring to focus another little-remarked but alarming trend: the sharply diverging destinies among young people. One group of young adults is taking their time launching into adulthood, but doing so in a careful and calculated way. They are gaining a good education, getting the building blocks in place for a successful career, and putting off marriage and children until they get their lives in order. They may be doing a leisurely backstroke, but they are headed in the right direction.

A second and much larger group is in a more worrisome position.

This group of young adults is treading water instead of swimming because they have embraced the responsibilities of adulthood too quickly, without being adequately prepared for today's competitive world. These treaders often skip or struggle with the most crucial step in the transition to adulthood: education. To give a sense of the size of this group: Approximately 70 percent of those ages eighteen through thirty-four in 2005 had less than an associate's degree. Treaders may try to go on for some additional schooling, but, lacking the skills or direction, their stuttering course through higher education takes much longer than normal or ends in failure. With few credentials, they quickly find that the workforce has little to offer them. They often start families early and find they must defer or abandon important life dreams once children arrive. These young people may have tried to mimic their parents' quick paths to adulthood, only to find that following these models today makes it much harder to get a secure start in life.

This is not a group confined to the ranks of the poor; these kids are from both middle-class and working-class families. They are the kids in our classrooms and offices. They are the kids who live next door. They are the children of our friends. They are our own children. Their well-being, and our country's, is at stake. If too many treaders ultimately sink rather than swim, the nation's progress will be severely compromised. When approximately two-thirds of the next generation of workers, parents, and taxpayers is, because of a lack of higher education, at risk of not finding a secure foothold into the middle class, we will all pay the price. The future rests on the fates of these young people. We shine a spotlight on this large and overlooked group, and explain how the starkly divergent destinies between swimmers and treaders come about and the serious consequences they bring for young people, our families, and our nation.

Slaying Misperceptions

We follow these new paths into adulthood by looking at how the traditional milestones of "adulthood" have changed and why. We shadow this generation at college and at work. We examine their debts and finances and their road to relationships, cohabitation, and marriage. We underscore the increasing significance of friends as young people delay marriage and live independently for longer. Finally, we look at their civic lives as they become the next generation of voters, community volunteers, and citizens. Along the way, we slay the many myths about this generation.

Take work: A common misperception about young adults is that they have lost their work ethic; they want to make it big without paying their dues. It is true that in this world of tenuous jobs, where brains have replaced brawn and loyalty is defunct, young adults are leery of promising their futures to one employer. They are also wary of sinking their entire lives into a job. As a result, they change jobs frequently. Yet where some see a self-indulged, entitled worker, we see an adaptive response (with a small dose of self-entitlement) to a gutted workforce. In this downsized and globalized economy, job-hopping is not necessarily a sign of restlessness or fickleness. It is a smart professional strategy for the well credentialed. It is job-*shopping*. However, in a knowledge economy, swimmers are better positioned to negotiate than treaders. For those without credentials, job-hopping is done less by choice than by force. This group's moves are often not to higher-paying jobs, and they are in no position to bargain. The economy makes that choice for them.

Those with the luxury of choice in the workforce are those with education. Never before has education so determined the destinies of young people. College is for all, our society tells us, and we harbor the (mistaken) perception that most children are college-bound—or, more accurately, college-prepared. While nearly everyone today aspires to a college degree, nearly half of those who do manage to enroll drop out within six years. This generation has heard the message that college is a must, but many walk through college doors with plans that are surprisingly half-baked or without the necessary skills to make it. A select minority has been cultivated from day one to succeed in college, and succeed they do. Yet the majority flounders badly on the path through higher education, and more often than not they drop out or flunk out— a critical misstep in this high-stakes knowledge economy.

The lack of education often leads these young people along a path of financial insecurity. Before the current financial crisis, which put everyone's spending on display, young adults were often singled out by the media for their profligate ways. If it wasn't their shopping habits that felled them, it was their crushing college debt, or so the story went. Yet we have uncovered a different story, one that once again underscores the diverging destinies of swimmers and treaders. Debt is not the main reason young adults are failing to launch. In fact, *not* taking on debt is sinking the futures of many young adults. Fearful of the burden of college loans, they are underinvesting in themselves at this critical time, letting their immediate worries compromise their long-term security. The average college debt today is the equivalent of a car loan, and yet the return to that degree has rarely been greater. Not taking on college debt in this knowledge economy is a costly decision. That is not to say that debt should be taken on willy-nilly. Being strategic is key to getting ahead. Some young adults are actually going overboard in their quest for a gold-plated degree when a public university offers a fine education. Indeed, there is little evidence that lifetime earnings are as significantly affected by *where* one goes to college as much as having the degree in hand.

Another misperception about this generation is that they are afraid of commitment and are abandoning marriage. Marriage is definitely on hold for this generation, but it is delayed, not abandoned. The majority of young people eventually marry. They are just getting their ducks in a row before they do. It is in getting married and having children where we see the starkest divide between swimmers and treaders. Swimmers are delaying marriage and children, while treaders are often delaying marriage but not children. Children are a significant source of meaning and even salvation for many young people, but having a child too early becomes one of the costliest barriers to getting ahead—interrupting and often severing college plans and progress, and seriously restricting opportunities in the labor market.

One frequently overlooked aspect of the delay in marriage is the role of friends. As marriage is delayed, friends are playing a bigger part for a longer time. Where once young people made critical life decisions with the help of their spouses, today they are more often consulting with their friends. Friends are an important source of contacts for jobs, networks, introductions, and just getting around in a new city. Indeed, our connections shape our destinies in ways both large and small. The people in our networks, where we sit within them, the network's size and shape can affect everything from our job opportunities to our health. When networks are small, tight, and more exclusively family-based, as the networks of treaders often are, they can impede life chances and cement disadvantages. The much-maligned digital age might be a panacea for this narrow set of ties. While many tag this generation as loners addicted to video games, their online lives are hardly solitary. In fact, online social networking is an important tool for expanding the contacts and horizons of those who are treading. The portals of the digital world are open to everyone.

Parents are playing an even larger and longer role in young adults' lives. Indeed, strong and continued support from parents is often the biggest factor that separates those who swim from those who tread. Involved parents, and even the helicopter parents of media fame, it turns out, aren't so bad after all—especially in contrast with parents who give no support at all. It's far worse to have uninvolved parents than it is to have super-involved ones. Rather than a sign of weakness, involved parents provide young people with advantages, including advice, funds, a roof and a bed, and connections. It can be as simple as making sure that their daughter doesn't take unnecessary classes in college or the bigger step of allowing her to move home after she graduates so that she can take her time in finding the right job. Parents of treaders are not necessarily uninvolved. Many of these parents simply believe that the paths they took are the right ones for their children, too. Even if their intentions are good, many lack the money, time, or connections to help their kids navigate the early-adult years in our high-stakes world. Between their young adulthood and their children's, the world did an about-face. Rushing headlong into adulthood no longer makes sense and can put kids at risk.

And then there is politics. We've all heard the story: This generation does not vote, they do not read a newspaper, they do not write to their elected officials, and they do not join community groups. The Obama election may just have reinvigorated this famously skeptical generation. Yet even here we see stark disparities—the twenty-three million young voters who went to the polls in 2008 were overwhelmingly the college-educated. These disparities are evident in all aspects of civic life, which raises serious concerns about entrenched inequalities and the fate of democracy. Voters typically vote with their own interests in mind. How will a country in which only the elite vote and participate manage to stay truly democratic?

Finally, we offer some ideas and solutions that may help alleviate financial and other pressures on families during their children's protracted path to independence. Our story is not just about privileged youth versus underprivileged youth—between those who have the luxury to use the transition to adulthood for exploration versus those who have limited opportunities, are lacking personal resources, or live in fragile circumstances. It is also the story of the middle class, which has now been left out in the cold institutionally, and which increasingly shoulders the burden of supporting young people in the face of dwindling public resources. Indeed, middle-class families are now, more than at any other time in recent history, offering extraordinary amounts of support to help their children get ahead—but they are unprepared to do so for such a long period of time and at such a high level. Families on the low end of middle income are particularly vulnerable—they have some, but not ample, resources, and their incomes are just enough to render them ineligible for government support, such as college grants or other supports. This is even more problematic in the wake of the recession, as middle-class families have found themselves on even shakier ground. They are no longer able to offer the same set of resources to their children they had once planned to.

But Don't Just Take Our Word for It

Many authors, of course, have come before us writing about the Millennials, Generation X, Twixters, and the many other names this generation has been tagged with. We don't want to add yet another ungrounded opinion to the heap. What we are adding instead is the culmination of eight years of research by a network of leading scholars who came together at the behest of the John D. and Catherine T. MacArthur Foundation in Chicago. The charge was to study how the twenties have changed and what that means for families and for the country.

The MacArthur Foundation's "network" model was designed with the understanding that the world is complex and that social change does not happen in a vacuum. It also takes into account that researchers in academia specialize. Psychologists do not often talk to economists, and sociologists do not often talk with neurologists, even though they are studying related facets of the same topic. The foundation's network model brings scholars from different disciplines together in a "research without walls" format to drill down deeply and explore a specific topic from many different directions. As the number of "failure to launch" stories began to grow, and researchers began to wonder whether a new "period" of life was budding (much as adolescence had emerged a century earlier), the MacArthur Foundation recognized an opportunity to look more deeply at the changing passage to adulthood.

The foundation funded a core group of twelve leading researchers from a variety of fields, including sociology, economics, psychology, and criminology. This group became the MacArthur Research Network on Transitions to Adulthood and Public Policy. The Network also invited other experts to participate so that special topics could be researched in greater depth. Most of the Network's research has focused on young people between ages eighteen and thirty-four, a time span that encompasses all the traditional milestones of adulthood: leaving home, employment, education, marriage and relationships, childbearing. Because so much of the relevant action continues into the thirties, we deliberately took a long view of the process. We wanted to not only understand the early part, as young people make their way through these experiences, but also the later part, once they've come through them. How things shake out in this decade of life has a profound impact on the many decades of adult life that follow.

The sociologists in the Network examined the broad changes in society that have impacted us all. Is it becoming more acceptable to live at home longer? If so, how did that happen? When social norms change, there is often an economic reason behind that change. Therefore, the economists in the Network, along with many of their colleagues, examined how the workforce, wages, cost of living, and other economic factors have influenced the path to adulthood. This group mined the large data sets that several government agencies collect to answer these questions, typically using advanced statistical methods to zero in on the main reasons for a particular outcome.

The outcomes of these broad social and economic forces alter how people think and act, so the Network included psychologists to examine how young adults perceive these changes and the paths before them. Do they perceive a distinct order to achieving adulthood—and if so, how does it make them feel if their lives aren't following that order? What exactly is adulthood in their estimation? The researchers compared their findings with other periods of life, wondering how the early twenties might differ from life in the thirties, or in midlife. Were they looking at an extended adolescence or a distinct period in the life course? They also designed a set of questions to insert in large ongoing surveys so that future scholars can begin to gain a fuller understanding of this important period of life.

Not all young people are lucky enough to have close families and middle-class comforts. The criminologists and social welfare experts in the Network traced how the most vulnerable young people make their way into adulthood—including those who have disabilities or special needs, those who are aging out of foster care, and those who have prison records. They examined what happens when government programs that support these vulnerable youth suddenly diminish—and are often terminated—at age eighteen or twenty-one, and what it means for their transition into adulthood.

An often overlooked aspect of this extended stretch to adulthood is what it means for our country's civic culture. The Network took a broad look at the changing civic character of this generation, ranging from young adults' trust in government and their fellow man, to their willingness to pitch in to solve problems, to their voting trends.

Finally, the Network looked at how we might make the transition smoother for those who need the most help. As this "gap" time stretches out for an additional decade, parents are often called upon to shoulder the costs of supporting their young adult children, and our social institutions have been slow to catch up to this changing period. The Network collaborated with MDRC (formerly Manpower Demonstration Research Corporation), a renowned social policy research firm in New York, to help us contemplate and evaluate social programs that might improve the success of young adults.

The Basis for Our Story

To explore all of these issues, the Network tracked trends in the lives of young adults, sometimes over a full century, using nearly two dozen large and representative data sets. These data sets, many of which were commissioned or underwritten by research divisions of the federal government, are the nation's best sources of information on young people and their families. These data sets range in size, design, and focus. Some surveys, such as the decennial census or other regular population supplements like the Current Population Surveys, capture the circumstances of millions of people on topics like education, work, and family status. Other surveys (such as High School and Beyond, Monitoring the Future, and the National Longitudinal Survey of Youth) capture thousands of people but nonetheless provide comprehensive windows into households, families, and the lives of young people. Still others are smaller and more regional (such as the Youth Development Study or the Michigan Study of Adolescent and Adult Life Transitions), intensively tracking hundreds of young people and their families as they move through childhood, adolescence, and into adult life. Some of these are longitudinal studies, which follow the same people over time, while others are panel studies that occur regularly but ask the same questions of new people on each occasion. By simultaneously mining these and many other data sets, the research of the Network has produced a foundation for our story that is unparalleled in its breadth and depth.[1]

To gain a more nuanced understanding of the results of these large surveys, the Network conducted nearly five hundred in-depth interviews with young people between the ages of eighteen and thirty-four from five sites across the country—San Diego, California; New York City, New York; Minneapolis–St. Paul, Minnesota; Detroit, Michigan; and a community in rural Iowa. These sites were chosen for two primary reasons. First, it was important for the Network to sample in ways that would produce data of high scientific integrity, and members or associates of the Network had served as principal investigators on projects with sound samples in four of the five locations: the Children of Immigrants Longitudinal Study in San Diego, the New York Second Generation Study in New York City, the Youth Development Study in

Minneapolis–St. Paul, and the Michigan Study of Adolescent and Adult Life Transitions in Detroit.[2] A sample of young people who had been interviewed on the phone or by mail for these larger studies were contacted by Network researchers and interviewed in person in taped conversations.

Second, this particular combination of sites provided a highly diverse sample. This was critical for understanding the full range of young people's experiences, especially because it allowed us to hear from men and women who were moving into adulthood in such diverse local settings— that bring with them unique opportunities and challenges for schooling, jobs, housing and cost of living, dating and marriage, and raising children. San Diego and New York City on the two coasts have large but very different immigrant populations. Minneapolis–St. Paul is a midsized, thriving city in the country's midsection, and Detroit has been ground zero in the shift away from manufacturing to the knowledge economy. And, because the Network needed a site that would incorporate the experiences of young people who grow up in non-metropolitan small-town America, a new study was commissioned in a small community in Iowa. This study provided a lens for understanding what it is like to come of age in the many small farming and factory towns that pepper our country's heartland. The social and economic fabric of these communities is radically different from that of the other sites.

This constellation of research sites allows us to understand the experiences of young people from a wide array of ethnic and racial backgrounds, including immigrant youth. The ages of the young people in each of the samples are also such that we are able to examine the full process of moving into, through, and out of the twenties. The wide spectrum of topics covered in the nearly five hundred in-person interviews, which ranged between two and four hours, also provides a textured and multifaceted look at early-adult life, including living situations, education, employment, the formation of families, military service, civic participation and politics, the justice system, self-identity, and the future.

Throughout the book, you will hear the voices of these young people and follow their stories. (Their names have been changed to protect their identities.) They will provide a firsthand view into the successes and struggles that young people are experiencing as they make their way into adult life. Facts and quantitative trends are important, but it is the lives of the young people that make these facts come alive.

The Future Demands Our Attention

Not Quite Adults brings all of this together in the first comprehensive and in-depth look at the dramatic changes to this period of life. More important, it brings the forgotten majority into focus and shows how sharply the destinies of young adults today are diverging, and what we might do about it. Some might ask, *What's so new about that? Some kids make it, others don't.* But what's different today is that the stakes on all fronts are much higher. Poor judgments and small mistakes on the road to adulthood are all substantially more perilous than they were just a decade ago. In an increasingly winner-takes-all society, there is little room for missteps. With missteps, the opportunity to succeed—the bedrock of America—fades. The result: a world that opens up widely to some while narrowing for others, with a shrinking middle in between.

The tale of this generation and its diverging destinies is one that should concern us all. For the swimmers, the problem is that as the first step on the path to adulthood is delayed, all of the steps that follow are also delayed. When young adults take longer to gain an education, the job search is delayed. When they take longer to find the perfect job, their relationships are often on hold. Although taking care in each of these steps is by itself a commendable approach in a high-stakes world, there is the danger of taking too long to assemble the package. For society's sake, there is such a thing as waiting too long. Take marriage. Long delays in walking down the aisle mean fewer children, and fewer children mean there are more grandparents than grandchildren—never good for an economy.

Behind the longer passage to adulthood is another problem. The search for the best degree, the ideal job, the perfect mate all hint at a growing pattern among young people today: They live in a world of elevated expectations. This does not mean they are spoiled or coddled; it simply means they have been raised to believe in themselves. But couple that strong self-esteem with a society that cherishes only winners, and there begins the collision course. Not everyone can be a winner. Expectations for a stellar life can all too easily lead to disappointment, if not outright paralysis in moving ahead.

These high expectations are not entirely of this generation's own making. Parents, teachers, other adults, and society have all promoted these expectations. Parents in particular realize the need in this competitive, shrinking world for their children to shine brighter than the rest. Yet parents have paid, often dearly as we'll show, for the efforts they've made to boost their children's chances. These anxious efforts have created an arms race that leaves parents constantly scrambling to measure up. It is a race that has them buying homes they can barely afford in better school districts and commuting long hours to ever-more-demanding jobs. They do it so they can give their children a shot at the top tier. These often extreme efforts are costly for families in terms of time and money, leaving many at financial risk, and even more so in hard economic times like these. It is a race, as we show, that is unsustainable.

The second and larger group of young adults—the treaders—face a different set of dangers, which some may chalk up as simply bad personal decisions.[3] But there is more to their struggles than meets the eye. It is difficult in an individualist society such as the United States to think about the fates of individuals as being tied to a collective fate. By definition, individualism is anathema to that kind of thinking. Yet, the fates of this large group of young adults *do* matter to everyone. One of the more obvious examples of this is retirement. If young adults cannot get started on a path to solid earnings by their thirties, the prospects for their lifetime earnings narrow considerably, which, in turn, means less money in the tax coffers for the Baby Boomers' retirement years. And if we let this group continue to stumble their way through education, we will lose the race with China and India for the world's most innovative and powerful economy. The costs to society are potentially enormous. To give one example: The costs of childhood poverty—which the children of many treaders will be at risk for—are about $500 billion per year, or the equivalent of nearly 4 percent of our gross domestic product.[4]

Remarkable changes have occurred in what feels like the blink of an eye, changes that have intertwined and overlapped in just such a way as to create a new rule book on what it means to be an adult. These changes—cultural, social, and economic—are playing out in myriad ways. We can talk until we're blue in the face about how things used to be, lamenting a world that is lost or romanticizing a past that is selectively remembered. Real or imagined, however, we cannot go back.

NOT QUITE ADULTS

1

Education, Education, Education

Higher education is the most important first step on the road to adulthood. Deciding whether to pursue a four-year college degree, and where to do it, is stressful. It is a time filled with both hope and anxiety: *Can I get into college? Will I get into my dream school? What will I study? Will I be able to afford it? How much will my parents be able to help?* Both young people and their parents feel the weight of these questions, and parents in particular may feel under the gun. They have invested their lives in guiding their children toward this very moment. A lot is on the line. And it's not just a diploma. Parents today recognize the importance of a college degree, particularly those who have a degree themselves and have reaped its rewards. They also know that a college degree is no longer a luxury but a necessity. It is the passport to a good job and a shot at a successful life. Parents across the spectrum realize this, yet not all parents are equally equipped to guide their children into and through college. Some are breaking their backs, and their banks, to get their children into the very best schools, while others don't even know where to start.

Ask any veteran undergraduate advisers or admissions officers what the single biggest change has been in working with prospective and incoming students, and they'll quickly answer: "Parents!" No need to even think about it. "Sixteen years ago, when I started advising, parents just dropped their kids off in orientation," says Kim McAlexander, a longtime adviser at Oregon State University whom we interviewed in the winter of 2008. "They'd do the driving and be here in the opening session, and we didn't hear from them again. Now we can't get a room big enough because of the parents." While some may shake their heads at these parents' hyperinvolvement, this change signals a fundamental shift in the parenting strategies of middle-class families. Parents have recognized that they are necessary for preparing their children for college, and for guiding them through tough decisions such as school choice, majors, and post-college plans, and they are acting accordingly. Unfortunately, the intense parenting today also creates an escalating arms race from which no one can afford to back down. As one parent said, "I know this is madness, but I don't want my kid to lose out."

What has this madness wrought exactly? Family stress, financial strain, and high expectations that kids often have a hard time living up to, to name a few. This overreach has been building for decades. Parents put it all on the line to move to neighborhoods with better primary schools, leading many to overextend on mortgages. The financial strain is also exacerbated when parents and their children strive for elite colleges over more affordable state universities. As a result, families today are working more, commuting longer hours, and saving less. The education arms race has led to a rat race. Perhaps this is one reason why, according to recent surveys by the Pew Research Center, the middle class is an increasingly anxious and unhappy class.

The insidious thing about the education arms race is that it may be "smart for one, but dumb for all," to borrow a phrase from Robert H. Frank's book *Falling Behind: How Rising Inequality Harms the Middle Class*. It may be smart for an individual, say, who gets wind of a failing bank to tell no one and quietly pull out his or her savings. But when the bank fails—and the economy tanks, along with that person's job—who's smart now? Smart for one, dumb for all. The same applies here. Until there is a stand-down in the education race, no one will want to risk the results of not staying in the game. Parents can control how much they spend on college and—if they have the funds—they have the power to decide whether to invest in private tutoring or private elementary school. What they cannot control is how much other parents spend on their children's education. And so the demands just keep escalating.

The arms race in education is creating a gaping divide between those who are able to keep up and those who aren't, hollowing out the middle. The result is a society of extremes with no average, no middle, and an ever-more-desperate struggle to stay at the top. What was once only a small ding on a windshield is now a crack that is rapidly splitting the country into two tiers—the swimmers and those who are anxiously treading to prevent from sinking. It is here, on this first step into adulthood, where young people's diverging destinies lock in and take hold. The very privileged, or the very lucky, are then most likely to be able to realize the high-achiever dreams. One thing is for sure: Parents today who take a hands-off approach to higher education, letting their children figure things out on their own in the name of independence or because they simply don't have the know-how, are inadvertently putting their children at risk.

Another problem emerges from this arms race—youths' expectations and sense of entitlement have risen like a helium balloon in thin air. As we discuss in the chapter on work, young people increasingly want to work in jobs with high salaries and prestige, but they don't want to make the commitments of time and energy that are required to get the positions they want—a collision course waiting to happen. That same collision course is evident in education. Seldom have so many young people had such high aspirations for college, yet floundered so badly. Nearly seven in ten high school seniors plan to attend some form of college or training after high school. Yet of the three million young people who will show up on campus for their first year, nearly one-half will drop out—without a degree, but often with a big bill—within six years.[1] The odds of dropping out are even more dismal for those who start in community colleges. It is a little-known fact today, but only one-fourth of young adults between ages twenty-five and thirty-four have a bachelor's degree, in a world in which nearly half of all jobs require a degree of some sort.[2]

This alarming disconnect between the very high aspirations of young people and their low graduation rates is one of the key reasons for the longer and more insecure path into adulthood today. Both the demand for more education and the stutter steps that so many young people take while getting that education—and not, as some have claimed, the cost of living or even the burden of debt on young people—delay each milestone along the path to becoming an "adult." With so much hanging on this first step of education, and so many young people struggling to take it, the other milestones in adulthood are quickly delayed. This gulf is also the source of critical early missteps that will have repercussions for the rest of life.

Why is this happening? Why do so many aspire to college only to fail? More important, what does it mean for America when so many young adults are struggling on this first step of adulthood?

Lost Without a Compass

Given the importance of higher education today to earning a living wage with benefits, it is surprising how unprepared many young people are for college and how unformed their plans really are. The news media trumpet stories about this generation's best and the brightest—like Eric Ding, the twenty-five-year-old Harvard cancer researcher who parlayed his interest in breast cancer research into a foundation seeking faster cures, or Jon Favreau, who at age twenty-nine has been helping Barack Obama write his speeches since 2005 and joined the administration as head speechwriter in 2009. This stand-out group has been culti-vated from early on to achieve, and achieve they do.

Or we hear about young people who may not be wunderkinder but are successfully launching professional careers—people like Ben or Lily, whom the Network interviewed. Ben attended an elite undergraduate program on the East Coast and later New York University law school. Today he is working in a top-tier corporate law firm in Chicago, earning a comfortable six-figure salary. Lily graduated from a state university in

California with a degree in math, and at age twenty-five is working on her master's degree while teaching in an inner-city middle school.

The attention given to the top-tier success stories of students with graduate or professional degrees masks a harsher reality. For the bulk of young adults, the story is vastly different. For all the hype, only 5 percent of young adults today earn graduate or professional degrees by age thirty-four.[3] Many more young students are instead like Angelina and Peter.

When Angelina graduated from high school, she had little sense of what she wanted to do with her life. Coming as she did from a traditional family, she assumed that she would get a two-year degree, get married, and have kids. She enrolled in a community college, but when the opportunity arose to spend a few months working at Disney World on the other side of the country, she scraped together enough money for a plane ticket. That experience was a turning point in her life, and when she returned, she enrolled in a four-year university an hour and a half from her hometown.

That path, however, would not be easy for Angelina. Her parents, both farm laborers with minimal education, had never experienced college for themselves and could not help guide her, and her high school had done little to prepare her for the rigors of college courses. Her grades dipped, she switched majors, and she took on too many extracurricular commitments (including a job). Through it all, she rarely visited the counseling and advisement staff for guidance. This led to several spells on academic probation. Today at age twenty-five, she is in her sixth year of college, watching as her more focused and privileged classmates plow their way through a four-year track. She wonders why she wasn't so lucky.

Angelina is following the pattern of many students whose parents are not college graduates. While 61 percent of students whose parents have a professional degree finish college in four years, only 14 percent of the Angelinas of this world do.[4] Angelina often feels out of sync because she is older than her classmates. "Sometimes I'm jealous of them," she says, "because I know that they went to college all straight four years. Now they're graduating and I wish I could have done that. I want my career already. I'm tired of being here, listening to the little freshmen. I just want to graduate and have my life started."

You have to give Angelina credit for hanging in there. The majority of students in her position do not pull themselves off academic probation or dig themselves out of "rookie mistakes," like getting too involved in extracurricular activities or taking the wrong classes. Nor do they get over switching majors, or—even more disruptive—switching institutions. It is at times like these that parents' advice clearly separates the swimmers from the treaders. Not only are first-generation college students like Angelina more likely to attend the least selective institutions (even when they are more than capable of attending selective schools), they are also more likely to take unwarranted detours along the way. Sociologist Elizabeth Armstrong, in her recent study of undergraduates at Indiana University, noticed a distinct trend. "Parents with a college education," she says, "tell their kids, 'No way, don't take Psych 101 again.' Whereas the kids whose parents don't have a clue, they're at the mercy of the advising system. As universities are set up, the more talented kids always get the better advice and better classes."

At least Angelina is nearing graduation. Peter was an average student in his Queens high school. His parents wanted him to go to college, but he was unsure of what exactly he wanted to do. He played in a band at church and loved music, but he didn't know how to parlay that interest into a career. He also considered computer engineering, but his math skills were weak. So he did what many of his peers do—enrolled at the local community college. Yet without guidance, he had no idea what courses to take or how to go about earning an associate's degree. "When I went to register, the classes were filled up, so what was open were classes I never even wanted to take: accounting, which I'm not good at; French—I'd never taken French." He failed both classes, along with a math class, and was put on academic probation.

Peter decided to strike out for Georgia, where an aunt and uncle lived, to attend another community college. "Almost the same thing happened," he says. "For me to be eligible to transfer to a four-year school, I had to take like a liberal arts program, so I was taking sociology, math, English, and gym." He again failed most of his courses. "Everyone says you should go to college, but college doesn't help everybody. I know I should go to college, but I think for some people, college is not for them."

Peter has a point. Yet education or training after high school is a must. Without some form of training, young people face a future of patching together strings of low-wage jobs, forever teetering on the brink of hardship in an unforgiving economy that rewards brains over brawn. Today virtually all jobs paying a decent wage require a degree or certificate. The gap in earnings between those with and without higher education is big and getting bigger. So what do the Peters of this world do when college is not for them?

Their parents didn't have this problem. For the generation coming of age in the 1960s or early 1970s, high school graduates found work in the copper mines of Montana or on the assembly lines of Detroit and made good wages. They could count on steady raises along the way and, more important, they could see a route to advancement if they so chose. There were clear ladders up the ranks of one's job, even for miners and press operators. A miner might advance from running the underground trains to mastering the art of explosion. A laborer could become a master journeyman or leave the rank and file for management. No additional education was needed to climb the ladder; these workers only needed on-the-job training and experience, and their employers were happy to provide the training.

However, in the 1970s and accelerating in the 1980s, these types of jobs gradually began to disappear. The mines closed and Detroit downsized. Low-skilled jobs moved overseas and to other parts of the country where labor was cheaper. Good-paying jobs are now both more highly skilled and in shorter supply, particularly in the wake of the current recession and "jobless" recovery. The competition is fierce—and employers are no longer assuming the responsibility for training workers on the job. That training has now shifted to community colleges and technical schools. Education and training after high school, and throughout one's life, is required to stay afloat. Recognizing the peril of slipping behind in a global world, President Obama in his 2009 State of the Union address called for every working American to commit to getting one additional year of education or training. As president, he announced a $12 billion plan to produce five million more community college graduates by 2020.

Unfortunately, the proposal was pared back to $2 billion for job training in the final bill that passed in March 2010.

This message is not lost on young adults today. In our interviews, young people repeatedly say that college or additional training after high school is necessary to get ahead. This is why 70 percent of high school seniors plan to go to college and why three million students showed up for the first day of college last year. So how is it that Angelina is in her sixth year and Peter has dropped out? Where did these aspirations run into the hard wall of reality?

Going It Alone, and Failing

"Parents [today] want the same thing parents in the past wanted," Melissa Roderick, a professor at the University of Chicago and co-director of the Consortium on Chicago School Research told a *New York Times* reporter. "They want their kids to be middle-class. The problem is that the economy has changed, so doing better now means going to college. And someone has to help them figure out how to do this because the parents don't know themselves."[5]

Indeed, for children in families without college degrees—that is, for approximately 70 percent of Americans—parents often talk very little about college, and when they do, their advice tends to be generic and vague. To these young people, the world of college is the great unknown. This creates what Kim McAlexander, the college adviser at Oregon State University, calls a "bigger fear factor." "Especially if they're the first generation to go to school, they don't know about financial aid forms, what a student's day looks like. They are less likely to seek out help. I can tell fairly soon whether they don't have parental support and they really need extra help navigating."

Since the 1970s, the gap in completing college between students whose parents graduated from college and those whose parents have only a high school degree has grown by 16 percent. A study commissioned by the MacArthur Research Network pinpoints the reasons for this divergence: parenting skills, access to information about educational opportunities, genetics, and the growing inequality in household incomes.[6]

Tyler, a young man from Minnesota, knew he should go to college, but he absorbed that message not from his parents or from high school mentors. He says, "I just thought a four-year degree would be a good thing. I had no idea what I wanted to do, any direction, nothing like that."

Tyler attended an average public high school in the midsized city of St. Paul, Minnesota. Not a star student, he became swallowed up in the middle ranks. His mother was a high school dropout who had spent her life working factory jobs. Tyler saw no connection between what he was learning and his future because no one was making the connections for him. The school's guidance counselors, he told us, were not focused on C students.

"I met my counselor once and that was briefly before I graduated. 'Don't bother going to college' is about what he told me." The overworked counselor, meeting Tyler for the first time, was probably judging his prospects based on his grades, which were average at best. In hindsight, Tyler says, "I think I was kind of ripped off in a way because even just a little advice would have done so much good. I mean, I could have done so many more things if somebody had said, 'Why don't you try this?' or 'This is why maybe you should study.'"

He didn't get that advice because counselors today are overworked and underpaid. In public high schools, counselors have a workload that must leave them exhausted. A typical counselor in a public school attends to 311 students in a school year, on average. Out of necessity, they spend just 23 percent of their time advising students about college. In contrast, counselors in private schools spend more than half their time helping students prepare for college, and their caseload is approximately 234 students. Minnesota, where Tyler went to high school, has the nation's second highest student-to-counselor ratio, at 799 students per counselor.[7] Here again we see the education arms race rear its ugly head. Rather than demanding better services for all students, parents in more elite schools and school districts instead dole out thousands upon thousands of dollars to college consultants to ensure that their children have the strongest possible shot at getting into elite schools.[8] The problem is that many parents, like Tyler's mom, just cannot afford to compete.

Not Ready for College

Tyler is the classic case of a young person lost in the system, not bright enough (on paper, at least) to be noticed by his teachers or bad enough to be noticed by detention officers. Without any guidance from home or at school, and without the internal drive to get noticed, he faded into the background. He went from achieving the 98th percentile on standardized tests in eighth grade to being a C student in high school. "I'm pretty emotional, so I was just full of angst, hating the world or whatever. Certainly how I was treated reflected on how much self-worth I gave myself."

Not surprisingly, Tyler's short college career was a disaster. Unlike many of his peers in more elite schools, he had no clue how to select a college, how to apply, what to expect, or how to fund his education. Rather than the well-planned college search of many of the elite youth, with visits to campuses and multiple applications, Tyler chose to apply to the local university because he drove by one day and saw some students tossing a Frisbee around, having what looked like a fun time. Though his grades were no great shakes, his ACT scores were good enough to get him in (reflecting, no doubt, his natural ability, as was evident in his 98th percentile scores in middle school).

Tyler arrived on campus with little direction, no sense of purpose, and very little high school preparation. The University of Minnesota is a big school, with more than fifty thousand students. It is easy to get lost even with a good map. Tyler had no map. He took a psychology course, a math course, and a smattering of others. He was shuttled into remedial courses in the General College section, the bottom end of the food chain in college. He chose a communications major in an equally haphazard manner without even knowing what communications was. "I think there was a list, basically some choices that the counselor gave, and I think I chose that, I don't remember why exactly." He sank quickly, dropping out after less than a year. "The counselors did as good a job as they could," he says, "but I think what I needed was babysitting, and they just can't do that. And I think I probably just wasn't ready for it."

In today's competitive college game, Tyler was an average student in a system that has little patience for average. This raises another issue. When do we tell students the truth about their capabilities? Is it wrong to dash hopes by telling the truth? Is it worse to mislead students into thinking they can make it when the prognosis is all too clear? Maybe Tyler's high school counselor was right to tell him the harsh truth that he was not college material—or at least not at that moment. It certainly would have saved him money he didn't have. Although he managed to get some financial aid, the complex financial aid system was confusing to him and as a result he didn't use it to his advantage. Instead, he borrowed money and six years later is still paying it off. In the past, Tyler might have found a place in a vocational class that linked him to employers. While these programs still exist today, they often come, as we show later, with a whiff of "loser" and "dumping ground" attached. This lack of a viable alternative without stigma may be one reason that aspirations for college are so high, and misplaced. Expectations are that college is for all, but unlike life in Lake Wobegon, not all children are above average.

"Over the years, the sense that everyone should go to college has escalated to such a level that it's taken as a given now," says McAlexander. "Some students just aren't ready. Now it's sort of an expectation. Even if you're not ready, and even if you don't know where you want to go or what you want to do, you go to college anyway. Most of them flounder and they maybe finish in something they didn't really care about, their GPA is very low, and when they're done, they still don't know what they want to do. They just sort of stick it out and they're unhappy." Unfortunately, for too many—Tyler included—the other viable options are not as clear as the mantra *Go to college*. Feeling like a Little Leaguer trying to play ball in the big leagues, Tyler dropped out.

Benny, who was a better high school student than Tyler, also dropped out of college, but for a different reason. He had the support he needed, but he had no idea what he wanted to do with his life. He was crippled by this lack of direction.

Benny grew up in San Diego in a large Filipino family. He was a B student in high school, and his high school teachers and parents were all enthusiastic about his prospects. Even though he would have preferred to begin at a community college, he enrolled at San Diego State because his mother insisted he go directly to a university. As Benny told us, he still "didn't know what [he] wanted to do."

Benny first considered majoring in biology, but then his sister turned him on to liberal arts, which he figured was flexible and probably less work than biology. As most nineteen-year-olds do, he chose to take the easier route. Either his advisers were absent, or he didn't know enough to use them to their full potential. His parents were just happy he was in college and left it at that. Benny also couldn't quite give up what he perceived as "good money" working in retail. He decided to work on the side, taking two part-time jobs, the first at the Malibu Grand Prix and another at the Disney Store.

Benny's sister had blazed a trail ahead of him, so college was not a big unknown for him as it was for Angelina and Peter. Benny also had the support of a large social network—he was well liked in high school and was active in several groups. In other words, he had a map to help him find his way in the college world. Yet he had no internal compass. He was adrift, and like 40 percent of his peers, he dropped out. Also like many of his peers, Benny eventually returned, this time to a community college, but he, like too many others, would never complete that second try.

Many young people—probably *most* young people—aren't sure at age eighteen, twenty, or twenty-two what they want to do in life. This seems true of even students in the most selective institutions of higher education; indeed, for these students, the college years are actively designed to help them figure it out. Parents of all stripes can nag, cajole, and cultivate their kids toward an interest, but young people rarely listen. They hear lawyer, doctor, cop, or the ubiquitous, "go into computers," and they think, *Nope, not for me*. How many young people, for example, know that it's possible to parlay their love of writing into working as a speechwriter for a CEO or a communications director for a nonprofit? How many know that an interest in law can lead to a job as a customs official? The list of job possibilities is nearly endless, yet for too many young people, these wider—and less prosaic—options are rarely spelled out. Benny liked biology, but saw no connection to a later job. No one was suggesting some of the possibilities that lay before him when he was making crucial decisions about the direction of his schooling.

Benny is not alone. These are difficult decisions, regardless of how much or little support one is given. Even with parents who have interesting jobs, or who work to expose their children to a variety of options, this time of life is both exciting and confusing. Young people are too old to be given "advice" and too young not to need it. The result: They drift.

Today, as the stigma lifts and norms change about living at home beyond age eighteen, many of these young people end up back at home with their parents. While young people of every decade have drifted, confused and at loose ends, opportunity structures today are less forgiving of trifling mistakes. In part this is a direct result of the arms race we noted earlier. When a sizable number of young people are really excelling, employers have a prime pool from which to choose. Decent students with blemishes on their records from dropping out are bypassed for surer hires. More recently, the recession means that older, more experienced workers are also now part of the pool. Finding a foothold in an interesting job is that much harder with this kind of competition. Even drifting has become an art form in today's competitive playing field. Sean Aiken, a young Canadian striking out on his own but unsure of what he wanted to do, decided he'd try a job a week for a year. Savvy, charming, and with a certain marketing genius, he blogged about his jobs, and in a flash was on *Good Morning America* and had a book contract. Compete with that.

Getting It Right

Vanna came from the same kind of background as Tyler, with parents who weren't equipped to help her navigate college. But she had the aptitude and ability to connect with the right mentors to see her through this difficult time. Her experiences show just how critical adult mentors are in the college game. Vanna drew support to her because she was a good student. Without it, she likely would have floundered as Tyler and Benny did.

Vanna's parents had no idea how to help their very bright daughter secure her future, but she was resourceful, and important people in her life spotted her talents and nurtured them. Now a twenty-eight-year-old graduate student in Minneapolis, Vanna immigrated with her family to the United States as Hmong refugees. Her parents were middle-aged when they left Laos, and they did not adapt easily to the United States.

They struggled with the language, and Vanna would help them in their new country as she tried to keep her eyes on her future.

As in many cultures, Hmong parents do not invest as heavily in their daughters as they do sons. Daughters, after all, leave the family for their husband's family. Vanna was no different. "As a woman," she says, "that's what they teach you to do—how to be a good housewife, how to be able to cook and be someone's daughter-in-law." While her parents did not actively discourage her in school, she was not encouraged to express her opinion, "so I think that made it harder for me to."

While many young people are in situations similar to Vanna's, with parents who cannot directly foster their skills or guide them in school, she was able to tap into a wide network of people who helped her figure it out. "I was lucky enough to have mentors and have parents who loved me and nurtured me so that I could find people and be able to find my own way."

High school came easily for Vanna, and she was surrounded by supportive, high-achieving friends who were also taking AP classes, going to math camps in the summer, and participating in study-abroad programs. Those who influenced her most, however, were two Sunday school teachers. "They spent all kinds of time with a group of us," she says of the pair. "They were college-educated, so they always encouraged us to do this thing called college." Later on, as a very bright student, she received support from several teachers. In her junior year, she visited college campuses with her high school guidance counselor. "I don't know what got her doing this, but [the counselor] met with a group of us girls to explore college and college options, and we visited a couple of colleges. I really remember her because of that. She took time outside of her job to do this with us. That was really important." It was important because it gave Vanna a sense of what college was for and how it connected to her future. College for her made sense, personally. It also made sense because she *was* college material. Although her parents didn't know how to guide her through college, others did.

Vanna applied to four colleges in the Twin Cities, knowing that she should stay close to her parents. She chose an all-girls private school with a small student body. Like many eighteen-year-olds, Vanna had only a vague idea about what she wanted to do with the rest of her life. Because she thrived in English classes during high school, she entered college thinking she would major in English. But encouraged by a professor, she attended a seminar where a physician spoke. The lightbulb went on. She knew she wanted to be a doctor. She changed her major to biology and set her sights on graduate school, where she was when we interviewed her.

Young people today need a cheerleader on their team, whether a parent, a mentor, or a counselor or teacher. The game is competitive, and too many are falling behind. Elite parents hover like helicopters because they know how easy it is to fall—and how expensive. Students themselves recognize the boost that parents and families can give them, and more often than not they welcome the advice and guidance. In 2007, at least three-fourths of students said that their parents gave them the "right amount" of help (versus too little or too much) with decisions about whether and where to go to college, the application process, how to deal with officials at college, and even choosing college courses. Unfortunately, minority students, who are also more often from lower-income backgrounds, are much more likely to say that their parents had not helped enough, particularly once they arrived at college.[9] For some, there are mentors and other supports. But too many simply drift. They drift because the message is "go to college," but the distances among saying it, getting in, and actually graduating require remarkable leaps, and without the kinds of supports that parents or other mentors can provide, the odds of succeeding are low.

Vanna had a sense of her future because adults helped her shape that vision and showed her the steps to get there. Getting there meant going to a four-year college. While Vanna was college material and key adults spotted her potential early, Tyler and Benny went unnoticed because the system as it is set up has no room for them. They were not college material—academically for Tyler and motivationally for Benny. But for them, there were no other options, at least not ones that could be clearly identified. A large share of young people like Tyler and Benny end up by default in another college track—the two-year plan at a community college.

The Revolving Door of Community Colleges

Community colleges are the workhorses of the higher education system. In 2008, according to the American Association of Community Colleges, more than 11.5 million students—46 percent of all undergraduates in the country—were enrolled in community colleges.[10] Jobs requiring at least an associate's degree are projected to grow twice as fast as jobs requiring no college experience. Less glamorous, with smaller budgets and strained faculties, community colleges train students for nursing, firefighting, policing, and a host of other meaningful and practical careers. As the Network finds, community colleges are often the avenue for those high school students who have less-than-stellar records, and who need to catch up before transferring to a four-year college. Indeed, nearly half of community college students require remedial course work to get started.[11] Community colleges are also more often the choice of older, lower-income or working-class students, as well as students of color. The average community college student is twenty-nine.

Community college students are approaching school for different reasons from those who attend four-year colleges. They may be retraining for work, or going back to school after having children. They may not know what they want to do in life, so they start in community college with a smattering of classes while they figure out what interests them. The typical plan is to get some credits under their belt before transferring to a four-year program. That's the idea anyway. However, this is the very group of students that has a less formed sense of their futures and of why they're in school—not exactly the makings of success.

Indeed, this approach trips up many students, according to Robert Ivry, senior vice president of MDRC and a nationally known expert on education and social policy. The Network and MDRC collaborated in developing Opening Doors, a program designed to retain and engage more community college students. "Many students don't take a coherent set of classes. They aren't typically given much mentoring by advisers and other faculty members, and they often first have to take 'development courses,' which were once called remedial courses. They're not sure what they want to major in, and so they take a smorgasbord of liberal arts classes that don't fit together."

Peter can certainly attest to this lack of focus. The graduate of New York City public schools who went on to a community college in his neighborhood in Queens, Peter knew he should go to college, but for what purpose was another question. Directionless, he signed up for a smattering of classes, most of which he failed. In his second attempt in Georgia, he also stumbled badly. After dropping an English class he was failing, he enrolled, like more than half of community college students, in a remedial course to meet minimal levels of competency for required math courses down the road.[12] The class required students to pass all the tests during the term to move on. Peter failed three, "so I just said, 'Forget it.'"

"Forget it" is a common response. "Fewer than half of community college students earn a credential in six years," says Ivry. "Remedial classes are a huge falling-off point for kids. They're just not prepared, even after high school. There're too many 'skills and drills' classes, they're too didactic, for students it's boring and they get discouraged."

Many students are as ambivalent and confused as Peter. Community colleges can become a "why not" choice for those in their early twenties who know they need some kind of education but are uncertain what they want to do in life. As a result, rather than poring over colleges listed in *U.S. News & World Report,* community college students often choose their schools for reasons that are less than lofty. "My friends were all going there," one student told us, or "I needed to get out of the city." "I wanted to stay in the city," another said. Other responses include, "It's what I could afford," "My sister went there," and "It was close to home." One student even said he made his choice because of "parking."

Mirabel chose her community college because her friends were attending "and we would just carpool." Her decision making reflects a deeper ambivalence about school for many students. Mirabel wasn't a bad student in high school, just more of a social butterfly. At a time when college admissions offices pore over a student's extracurricular life, Mirabel had little to show. "Just one time I was in extracurricular stuff. It was like, I forgot the name of it." She hadn't given her future much thought. Instead, she followed her friends to community college. "I wasn't sure what I wanted to do. I wanted to maybe become a nurse, or study business, or accounting. One of those. I just wasn't sure. At that point in my life, I didn't really know. I had no major or anything like that." Instead, she enrolled in the General Studies program.

Mirabel was also working part-time, which made it hard, she said, to fit school in "because at that time I liked going out with my friends. And I would just get lazy. You know, you work, and you have class, and you go out. I had a hard time finding time to study. Actually, I didn't know what I wanted to do.

"I think you have to really be into college," she says. "You have to be driven. I think it's just who you are. You can't really blame [others, saying], 'The high school didn't teach me enough.' I think you have to be dedicated and want to go to college."

Now twenty-five, Mirabel recently broke up with the father of her child, and she's living with her parents and her two-year-old daughter. She works full-time processing loans for a real estate agency. She is happy with her job, and hasn't ruled out returning to school, though the possibility seems further and further away. "Gosh," she says when asked if she would ever consider returning to college, "I would really like to go to school just to have something to back me up. You know, later on."

The odds of Mirabel doing so are slim to none. Although most community college students aspire to a four-year degree, the Network and MDRC find that nearly half of all students who begin at a community college drop out and don't enroll elsewhere.[13] Why? They may get discouraged after taking a string of no-credit remedial courses, or they may decide to give up after learning that their credits might not transfer to a four-year school. Ultimately, some just lose motivation because they cannot see the forest for the trees—a college degree begins to seem like more work than it's worth. Others persevere, but their hold on education is tenuous. An example of this is Tanya. Like so many community college students, Tanya is juggling several balls at once: She is a parent, she works two part-time jobs, and she is struggling to make ends meet. Although older students like Tanya are often more motivated to "do it right" than are younger students like Mirabel, they also face many more real-world obstacles.

Tanya grew up in St. Paul, the daughter of a single mother who was putting herself through college at the University of Minnesota. Her mother stressed the importance of education. "She helped me with all my options," says Tanya. "She helped me apply to several colleges, but at that time I was applying into a radiology class and I don't know why I did it. I thought it was cool at the moment but eventually didn't want to go. I was applying for a lot of things and still didn't know what I wanted to do, and then when the time would come I'd get scared. Now I'm trying to get an AA degree, get started somewhere."

Tanya's path has not been an easy one or a direct one. She fell in with a bad crowd in high school, became pregnant with her oldest daughter, now eleven, and dropped out of high school because her boyfriend "was abusive and I didn't want people to see my face." She returned for a GED after her daughter was born—her "wake-up call," she says.

After two more children and a steady live-in boyfriend, Jackson, Tanya is once again back in school, taking two courses at a time between her full-time day job as a teaching assistant and part-time work as a van driver and assistant in a recreation program ten hours a week in the evenings. Her hope is to eventually transfer her associate's degree to a local university for a degree in educational management. In many ways, Tanya is a typical community college student today. At twenty-nine, she is the average age for a community college student, and she has children at home, and is a member of a minority group. Like the majority of her classmates, Tanya is in school part-time and working full-time, and she ultimately hopes to transfer to a four-year college.[14] She has twenty of the sixty-four needed credits under her belt with a long road ahead. "I can see I'm probably going to be somebody old" when she finishes her degree. She is trying to keep a positive attitude, but the prospect of being in school for another ten years is "depressing. This working [two jobs], it's going to take too long. It makes you not want to go at the rate I'm going."

It is this back and forth—the failures and do-overs, the ambivalence about school—that start many young people on a hopscotch path into adulthood. Failure in school sets them on a course of floundering as the jobs don't materialize or those that do don't pay enough to let them get by. They often realize too late that without the resources that a good job offers or that an education helps ensure, setting up an adult life is hard. They then return to community college to try again on a different path. Life, however, often intervenes again, and they never get that coveted diploma or the pay raise that comes with it. With a bachelor's degree, a young person will earn 54 percent more, on average, than those who attended college but did not finish. Imagine how that adds up over a lifetime. And then think of all the people who never finish.

Education with a Purpose

Still, we find some success stories—hopeful, even inspiring ones—among community college students. For these young people, who are often from disadvantaged backgrounds, community colleges are a critical turning point in life and even a source of salvation. Community colleges can also be perfect solutions for students who know they don't want to ultimately work toward a bachelor's degree but need specialized training or a certificate for a job.

Matt, from Iowa, spent his high school years working for his dad's landscaping business. He put in ten-hour days on the weekends and often four to five hours after school during the week. There was little doubt in his mind that he would continue to work for his dad after high school, with the hope of eventually taking over the business when his dad retired. "I considered other things, but I had done landscaping so long, and I liked it, and I also knew that I'd have a good job doing it, too, and that was the major decision maker—that I knew I'd have a good place to work."

Matt chose nearby Hawkeye Community College, a well-established technical school in central Iowa for welders, nurses, auto mechanics, and truck drivers. He signed up for their twelve-month horticultural program. "I didn't feel like I wanted to go to a four-year school 'cause I didn't know if I wanted to commit that much time to it," he says. He enjoyed the program, particularly because it afforded him additional work experience. "I got to work for another landscaper, [and] it still kind of gave me some different ideas and ways to do things and ways not to do things." Matt's school experience, in other words, gave him just what he needed: insights and skills in a field he already liked. It was the perfect fit.

Matt had moderate aspirations, which in this high-powered world might be perceived as shortchanging himself. Yet perhaps his embrace of the less glamorous road of landscaping was just the ticket to a successful launch into adulthood. Eduardo, too, had a more "pedestrian" set of goals. After "hanging out for a while" after high school, working in customer service for a travel agent and holding other odd jobs, Eduardo decided that it was time to return to school. He chose Mira Costa Community College in San Diego, where he fell in with a group of friends who were taking classes in phlebotomy. Those motivated friends inspired and encouraged Eduardo, and within six months he had a medical assistant certificate and a job in the field. After working for a year and moving up, he decided it was time to become a nurse. He re-enrolled at Mira Costa in the Licensed Vocational Nursing program.

Again, having supportive friends in the field was critical. "My friend Tom's an LVN. My other friend, she's a health educator. I have other friends that are RNs and phlebotomists. It's good money, and it's a good experience." The "gap" year spent working was also important because it exposed him to a built-in support network, which bolstered him when courses were difficult or he felt like calling it quits. The gap year also gave him a clearer sense of what the job entailed and how to get there.

Eduardo was also lucky in another way. He started the program part-time, but when the slow progress became a "roadblock to finishing," he was able to get help from his parents. He accepted his father's offer to pay for college, under the condition that he would quit his job and focus full-time on school. He credits this strong family support for his success. Eduardo says, "What helped me the most was that my parents helped me a lot. Like they supported me financially and with [other kinds of] support. Helping me, you know, with my homework. Or telling me, 'Go here to check this book out.' Or my mom even going to get the books for me because I was too busy. My mom pays for my books, pays for my equipment. They also paid off my car." It comes down to parents once again—their importance cannot be underestimated.

With their help, Eduardo was able to finish the program in just under three years. His parents "were so excited. They were so proud when I walked the line in graduation. They told me that's the payback. Not to worry about any of the money."

Eduardo is proud of himself, too. "People look at me more seriously. 'Did you hear about Eduardo? He graduated, got his LVN degree, and he works as a nurse now.' 'He finished school and everything.' I like that feeling." Eduardo's story is a testament to the fact that, even for individuals without a clear vision up front, exposure to a community college or technical school, coupled with support from parents and friends, can provide routes to better-paying jobs. Among those not bound for four-year colleges, those young adults like Matt, who have a distinct idea of what they want to do before they enter a community college or technical school, or like Eduardo, who find their niche once they enter, find their lives are furthered and even transformed by their educational experiences in these settings.

While Eduardo's parents are rightly proud of him, this story raises an important issue. Parents are often shouldering the entire responsibility for their children in less elite schools, whether community colleges or state universities, by tracking down books while their sons or daughters work or reviewing their schedules to warn them against taking unnecessary classes. This is a testament to the major systemic gaps in support on the part of colleges and technical schools. The high price tags of elite schools like Penn or Smith include the perks and "parenting" they provide; they wrap their students in services and supports to ensure they don't fail. And those students rarely do fail. Elite schools graduate roughly 90 percent or more of their students, while nonselective ones graduate only about one-third. It seems that the more vulnerable students—those from families with fewer resources or know-how—would benefit even more from being cocooned in these types of support. And the costs of their mistakes when they drop out with nothing but a bill are more burdensome for them and for society. It is but one of the catch-22s of the anxious middle class.

Beyond "College for All"

All this pain and expense begs the question: Why do students who are unprepared for college, or who are uncertain about what they want to do in life, enroll? "Because they don't know what else to do," says Kris Winter, director of family outreach at Oregon State University. "They're going to college because they think they're supposed to go to college."

Perhaps more important, they choose college because they have few viable alternatives. Our magnet schools and top-tier suburban high schools have done a wonderful job of preparing the best and the brightest for college. However, for every striver, there are many more who hear the siren call of college, but are simply not *yet* college material. They may not be less intelligent, and they could be pushed to achieve. But at this point in their lives, their hearts aren't in it. They do not see the connection between what they learn on the page and how it plays out in real life. Or they are simply not "books" kind of people. And there is no shame in that. Yet as the current feeder system in high school is designed, young people like Tyler, who don't excel in academics or are in trouble, are shunted to the margins, or into a shop class or a vo-tech track, with the implicit message that they are losers. The vo-tech track is often considered a dumping ground for young people with behavior problems or low ability—often two conditions that are self-fulfilling prophecies when kids are tracked early on. Later, once they graduate from high school (if they graduate), they often slouch into a community college program as the next best alternative and patch together some credits in English or history, with a vague plan to transfer to college "later." Sure, some students may stumble into something that clicks with them. But given that more than half of community college students drop out, it is not a stretch to say that those who click are the exception, not the rule. What many students need instead is a system that embraces their talents and creates a viable bridge to training and later jobs in the real world. The problem is, of course, that there are few alternative paths for non-college-bound youth.

It should go without saying that the hope of pursuing higher education rests on having a *high school* degree. Yet high school dropout rates are alarming. According to the National Center for Education Statistics, the dropout rates among people sixteen through twenty-four years old in 2006 were 9 percent.[15] An alternative calculation puts the number even higher, with as many as three in ten ninth-graders today not graduating four years later, and for Hispanics, blacks, and Native Americans, as many as half. In 2000, the most recent census point, a dramatic 14 percent—3.7 million—of all young adults ages eighteen through twenty-four were neither enrolled in school, employed, or in the military, nor had a high school degree or GED.[16] These proportions have most certainly surged upward with the hard economic times that occurred thereafter. These young people have fallen through the cracks. They are not prepared for higher education, but they do need ways to connect to society and play useful roles. We won't improve higher education, and diversity in higher education, if we don't first grasp these basic facts.

Education is the key to success in life, says criminologist and sociologist D. Wayne Osgood, editor of the Network book *On Your Own Without a Net: The Transition to Adulthood for Vulnerable Populations.* Children from the professional classes may be more strongly school-oriented— they are doing well in school and are committed to it. Yet if working-class children are equally directed, they can also be upwardly mobile. Likewise, money and security do not guarantee academic success, as many parents can attest. Sometimes, no matter how firmly parents guide or how diligently they intercede, kids derail or lose interest in school. And like their peers a few rungs down the economic ladder, children from more privileged families run the risk of floundering if they do not gain a sound education. It is too easy and, as we show in the remainder of the book, too perilous to slip at this first step on the path to adulthood— for everyone.

"I think the big issue is, what about the kids who aren't going to college?" says Osgood. "If they can find a good niche in a trade school in a technical field or even construction management, or a higher-level job in manufacturing, then they'll have some resources. But so many are seriously alienated from high school, or they're sort of just mouthing the *I'm going to college* mantra because everyone does. But they don't have the academic skills, and aren't likely to succeed in that. So the question for society is, how do we prepare more kids to get more education and not become so alienated from school?"

A first step, he says, is acknowledging that the problem exists. "I've always been struck by data showing just how unrealistic kids' expectations for education are. Everyone says they're going to college, even kids who hate school. It's nice to have aspirations, but it's a bad sign we let that many people be out of touch. And we need more alternatives— ways to help people get through school, paths they can take if it's hard for them. As a society we have to address how widespread the disaffection is. There's a whole lot who hate school. And we just kind of turn our heads and let it be their problem."

The results of the Network's study lead us to ask what may seem like a politically incorrect question: Should a four-year college degree really be for everyone?[17] College graduates are clearly vital for a vibrant economy and for the future of our nation—but so are many other positions that do not require degrees from four-year institutions. The goal of higher education isn't only getting a better job. But at the end of the day, that's probably what matters most. "Students are ultimately here to get a better job," says Winter. "I mean, some of them are here to learn. But the bottom line: They know they have to get a degree to get a good job."

For young people who don't have the skills for, or even the interest in, a four-year degree, we can strengthen pathways that align with their talents. In today's world, students must get some education or training after high school, and the schools should make visible real options for students who are not bound for four-year institutions. Students should be taught that there are feasible alternatives to four-year institutions and degrees, and that there is value in them. We must ask ourselves: When did becoming nurse practitioners, police officers, child care workers, or landscapers take on the taint of the "also-ran" in life? Not going to college should not mean failure. No students should hate themselves because they repeatedly try but fail.

For those young people who just don't know what they want to do yet, a gap year might be the solution. Britain offers students the choice of deferring their college acceptance for a year. They can use this time to road-test a profession or head overseas to volunteer or backpack in Europe before jumping into college life. Nearly a quarter of a million British students opt for this gap year annually. For students who are well prepared for college and have clear visions of their futures, in contrast, three years of undergraduate work may be enough. For example, students who have taken college courses or gained many Advanced Placement credits in high school may not need four years to complete an undergraduate degree. Similarly, students in specialized programs, such as pre-law or medicine, may not need four full years of undergraduate work before they begin their professional training. All of these options involve breaking up the lockstep way we think about education with the hope of offering more possibilities for students with different desires and needs, which we take up in the final chapter.

More elite parents, too, have a role to play at this critical juncture. That role is simple: Stand down. There is no need to abandon your children's academic career. There is no need to stop wanting the best for them. But the arms race of higher education cannot continue without threatening to rip the country in two. The recession may have been the outside intervention that forced a long-overdue reassessment. We should consider it a golden opportunity to demand more equality for all kids, including those in the solid, but increasingly anxious, middle class. In the United States, we take the approach that it is, for better or worse, up to individuals and their families to find their way into adulthood. A free and open market may serve the country well and drive innovation and excellence. But the extreme emphasis on self-reliance can also backfire. Those with the means can muster the extra funds for tutoring and volunteering in Guatemala and pre-college counselors without feeling the pinch. For the majority, however, it is a much larger sacrifice. Commutes get longer, parents work longer, tensions snap, health suffers. Smart for one, smart for all—that's what we should demand. That means demanding, for a start, education reform that ensures an equal start for all. It means not pulling children out of the public school system but instead demanding better results from public schools and state universities. When all parents put their weight and voice into improvements, they cannot be ignored. It means demanding that more and better counselors be hired. It means creating a network of well-trained and qualified mentors. It may even mean demanding an end to the need for senseless credentialing when on-the-job training or apprenticeships might be a better option. It means a collective agreement that the reality is truly all-for-one and one-for-all. Without it, we will guarantee one thing: a stark future. In a country that increasingly demands education to get ahead, not getting an education locks in disadvantage for generations. In 2009, the largest group of high school seniors in the nation's history, 3.2 million students, graduated. There is no time to lose.

2

Financing a Future

After two decades on Easy Street, young adults awoke in 2009 to a new nickname: Generation R, for "recession." All too suddenly, the party was over and only the hangover lay ahead. While not the creators of the current mess, they will certainly be shaped by it. A recent study shows that people who enter adulthood during recessions more often develop an enduring belief that success in life depends more on luck than on effort. Other studies have found that those who are laid off during recessions earn 20 percent lower wages over their lifetimes than those who are able to hang on to their jobs.[1] This generation's expectations for high starting salaries and fast money were shattered as Wall Street melted down over the course of three months in the fall of 2008. Parents' once-open checkbooks were emptied by falling 401(k)s. The value of the condos they set their children up in tanked. The price of that Ivy League degree floated out of reach for many. Overnight the banks called in the note and far too many people, of all ages, found themselves going under as years of living on borrowed dimes came home to roost.

As the 2008–2009 economic crisis exposed, Americans had been living beyond their means. While debt was once a four-letter word in America, adults—young and old alike—had in recent years become too comfortable with red ink. Savings were at historic lows. Families had fed their spending habits by refinancing their mortgages on the assumption that the value of their homes would continue its amazing climb, only to find themselves underwater when the value of those homes dropped dramatically. Personal bankruptcies crept up, and the number of home foreclosures doubled and even tripled in some areas. Very few people were left unscathed. Debt was fast becoming a universal bond.

The crisis momentarily turned the spotlight away from young adults. Before then, the media had singled out this generation for their spendthrift ways, and others had attributed their "failure to launch" to their crushing student loans and credit card debt. In one of many examples, a lead article in *USA Today* in August 2007 trumpeted: "Students suffocate under tens of thousands in loans," arguing that the "weight of debt is forcing many to put off saving for retirement, getting married, buying homes and putting aside money for their own children's educations." In the less sympathetic version of the story, young people were just spoiled; they expected and needed too much, too soon, in life. They wanted the $1,000 handbag, the plasma-screen TV, and the high-end condo. They gallivanted about the town using Daddy's credit card, enjoyed bottle service at the clubs and designer clothes in their closets, and lived rent-free in expensive condos their parents paid for. After all, they *deserved* it—they've been told so all their lives. They were, according to these accounts, overindulged and coddled.

The media sensationalism over this "strapped" generation may sell newspapers, but it does little to uncover the real story. As we'll show here, certain young people are indeed in very fragile circumstances, often just one step away from financial disaster. But they are in this position not because of college debt or lavish spending. One of the key reasons they skate so precariously close to financial ruin seems almost heresy in this age of contraction: They are afraid to take on debt. That is, they are unwilling, and in some cases unable, to take on the kind of debt that helps to secure a more stable future: debt from a college degree. Given the headlines about the young people who are starting out in life saddled with $60,000, $70,000, or even higher amounts of college loan debt, this proposition seems preposterous. But as we will show, these news stories are often overblown. College costs have definitely risen, but the headlines that claim that kids are suffocating under college debt, burdened by it for decades, are selective at best and damaging at worst.

Much of the debt that young people carry today is *not* college debt. It is the high cost of not investing in college. Indeed, it is usually those who have minimal education or training who become caught in a vicious cycle of debt. Their problems begin when they don't invest in college and, ironically, when they embrace the responsibilities of adulthood too soon. Without solid earnings, they cannot save. Without savings, the simplest setback—a fender bender, a burst pipe, or an unexpected doctor's visit—can force them to pull out a credit card, the bill for which is added to the growing pile at month's end. Making a minimum payment barely makes a dent because the interest on the outstanding balance tacks on about the same amount the minimum payment took off. Add in a late fee or a steep overdraft charge, and it quickly becomes a deep hole of debt. These young people find themselves sinking into the money pit as the bills pile up and their incomes slide. The job market that once supported those with minimal education in relatively well-paid and secure jobs with benefits no longer does so. Most of these jobs have disappeared; to get ahead today, education is no longer a luxury but a necessity.

While this group of young people has underinvested in their futures, there is another group that may have done just the opposite. They may have actually overinvested in their degrees. This is the group that we most often hear about in the headlines. Often from middle-class families, these young people have succumbed to the pressure to buy the best education possible, even when they cannot afford it. Their parents have worked relentlessly to ensure the good life for their children and want those children to do even better than they did. To do that, they've been told, means getting their child into elite private schools, the all-but-guaranteed road to success—no matter how great the cost. And the consequences are only now being reckoned with. The money parents spent on gold-plated degrees may have been more easily absorbed when jobs were plentiful, housing values were on the rise, and stock portfolios were expanding. But today, the story is suddenly different.

For the Cost of a Car Loan

To read the headlines today, you would think every college graduate was saddled with $60,000 or more in debt. Robyn's complaint on the website of the Project on Student Debt in 2008 is typical. Living in Syracuse and working as an art teacher, she is feeling the pinch of college debt:

> My point of view is that colleges/universities and lenders are out to get as much money from students as possible. My personal experience has been one of struggle and frustration...Every penny of my 6 years of school came from federal and private loans, including a semester abroad. Naive and uninformed, my parents and I took out loan after loan. Now I am an educator with $70,000 in debt. I work at a private school, and my income barely covers my meager cost of living.

Hundreds more of these stories appear on this website and others. Of course, these websites are designed for the Robyns of the world. Very few happy graduates without debt, or with manageable debt, write in to sites such as the Project on Student Debt. In the bigger picture, Robyn is in fact the exception and not the rule.

There is no doubt that the cost of going to college has risen. The class of 1968 could expect to pay roughly $1,500 in tuition and fees for a bachelor's degree at Arkansas State, a typical state school, or about $8,800 in today's dollars. At Harvard or Princeton, they could expect to pay approximately $8,000, which translates into $47,000 in today's dollars. Graduates today may swoon over these figures. The price tag for tuition and fees in 2008 at Arkansas State was approximately $20,212 for a bachelor's degree. A degree from Harvard topped out at $130,000 in 2008. None of these figures includes room and board, books, and other expenses. Indeed, the average price tag for tuition, room, and board at a public four-year college rose 67 percent between 1987 and 2008.

With the rising costs, though, came new ways to pay for them. In the late 1960s and early 1970s, college-goers had fewer options to subsidize tuition and fees. There were no education tax breaks, which account for 6 percent of financial aid today. Federal subsidized loans were available, but the eligibility criteria were frequently left up to universities themselves. Today, federal loans constitute nearly half of the financial aid pie. State grants were in their infancy back in the 1960s, as were Pell Grants, which help low-income students foot the bill, although Pell Grants have in no way kept pace with inflation. As a result of the rapid rise in college costs and available financial aid, both public and private, college students are now more likely to rely on loans. MacArthur Research Network member Cecilia Rouse and her colleague at Princeton, Jesse Rothstein, find that two-thirds of full-time students held a student loan in 2004, up from just over one-half a decade earlier.[2] Some of this increase stems from supply—there are more loan options available. Some of it is also spurred by demand—there are both more students and higher costs.

The media stories are right in pointing to the rapidly rising costs of college, and we should be worried about these costs for certain groups, such as low-income families and students of color, as we'll show later. But one point that's overlooked in these sensationalized accounts is that while college does cost more and more students have loans today, that debt is rarely debilitating. Sure, students perceive it as an albatross around their neck—no one likes a monthly bill stretched out over ten or fifteen years, regardless of what it is for—but for the most part, it is still manageable.

Today, the typical college graduate with debt from a public university leaves school owing $20,000. For a loan this size, monthly payments are approximately $250—the equivalent of a car loan. Few complain about a loan for a car, which, unlike a college degree, loses value the minute it is driven off the lot. Due to the higher earning potential of college graduates, the Network finds, the average student has paid back all but $7,000 of his or her debt just three years out of college. An even more surprising statistic is that only three in ten young adult households ages twenty-five through thirty-four have student debt.[3]

Grousing aside, relatively few graduates experience financial straits because of their student debt. The rule of thumb is that graduates should not devote more than 10 percent of their salaries to paying off their student loans. The typical student in 2000 was devoting about 6 percent of his or her salary to student loans one year after graduating.[4] This debt burden has likely risen since then because interest rates on loans have gone up slightly and the job market has tightened. When the 2000 study on debt burden was done, the job market was robust, unemployment was at record lows, and interest rates on student debt were in the 3 percent neighborhood. All of these factors affect the debt burden, which is based on salary, loan repayment terms, and total debt. Nevertheless, it is still likely manageable for the average college graduate.

The key, however, is to graduate. Those who drop out of college with student debt are not reaping the full payoff from a college degree, and yet they still have a college tuition bill to pay. Also, students whose parents are in financial straits themselves, and who cannot help cover the costs if their child runs into trouble, are more likely to feel the pain of burdensome debt, as are students whose academic success is questionable or whose choice of career does not match the cost of their degree. The job market is where the return pays off and if a graduate cannot land a job or has a gold-plated teaching, social work, or creative writing degree, the pain of debt will be felt more acutely. That is why, as we show later, being strategic about college choices is imperative, and even more so as unemployment hovers at 10 percent and the competition for jobs is stiff.

Viewing College as an Investment, Not an Expense

So why all the hoopla over college costs, such as these recent headlines: "Going Broke by Degree," "Rising College Costs Saddle Generation Debt," "Parents of Preschoolers Confront Future College Costs"? College costs have certainly risen, but David Shulenburger, vice president for academic affairs of the Association of Public and Land-Grant Universities, sees it from another angle. For one thing, he says, "We view college as a consumer expenditure rather than an investment." Many conversations about affordability hinge on a family's current income. Is college affordable when it costs 7 percent of a family's annual income to put their kid through school? Ten percent? Yet this question focuses on the immediate year's income rather than on long-term earnings. "If you look at college as an investment," says Shulenburger, "then you're thinking less about the amount and whether you can afford it within your current income versus your earnings stream." When viewed that way, college debt represents just over 1 percent of lifetime earnings for the typical college graduate.[5] It also offers a return on investment of between 6 and 8 percent, which is better than the stock market these days. The same shortsighted view is true of paying back the debt for college students themselves. They tend to look at the payment this month, but not how their degree will affect their earnings down the road. The difference in perspective is one of immediate gratification versus later payoff, or investment.

What Robyn and many like her do not realize is this: Her master's degree will more than double her lifetime earnings over those of a woman who does not go to college. Network economist Sheldon Danziger finds that a woman in 2002 with some master's training (assuming Robyn didn't finish her degree) earned $44,000 on average, while a woman with only a high school degree averaged $20,000. Even if Robyn had only earned a bachelor's degree, she would have earned approximately $300,000 more in her lifetime relative to a high school friend who did not go to college—even after subtracting the original cost of college, the earnings she missed while she was going to school, and other "sunk" costs. The earnings gains from even a two-year degree, Danziger finds, are about $3,000 a year. Earning $23,000 a year versus $20,000 might not seem like much, but that extra $250 a month can mean the difference between living in a dangerous neighborhood and a decent one. Furthermore, this "return" to college—the doors that it opens and the pay premium that it leads to—has *doubled* since 1975, as the job market has demanded higher-skilled workers and as the wages of the lowest-skilled workers have plummeted.[6]

Network economist Cecilia Rouse, who has recently joined the Obama administration's Council on Economic Advisers, agrees: "We as a society really like to consume our income today. When you think about the level of consumption, it's very high. I think a lot of parents aren't thinking intergenerationally when they think about college costs. But after all, that is what they're doing: investing in this generation's future." In an era of consumption, when we spend everything we earn immediately, that long-term perspective is a difficult shift. But it is, we argue, a necessary one. Not sinking $20,000 to ensure your future is shortsighted.

Charlie figured that out quickly. He was set to go to Ball State University after high school to major in theater. However, his world turned momentarily upside down the night of his senior play in high school. Shortly after his big moment on stage, a member of the audience passed out. It turned out to be his mother. She would die of an aneurysm later that evening in the hospital. Although he continued on to Ball State, his heart wasn't in theater. "I hit a spot where I didn't know what I wanted to do and I was almost broke. I just thought it was time to leave. I've never been one to take out loans. I just don't like owing people money. I wasn't ready to grow up, and had no idea of what direction to go in and be happy with."

Charlie dropped out of Ball State the second semester of his second year. He moved in with some friends in a house not far from campus and took a job dealing poker in a small casino for $25 an hour. Not a bad gig for a twenty-year-old. "I was paying bills, being a true bona fide adult," he says. After six months, unfortunately, Charlie's job dried up when Indiana outlawed poker clubs. He tried telemarketing but, he says, "You cannot possess a soul and do this job. I worked it for a week and the money was good, the people were great; the job was horrific."

He knew he always had a job waiting for him at the country club where he'd worked throughout high school, and he didn't want to be "broke-ass when I have a girl [I'm] getting serious with. It was time to go home." He moved in with his dad and started back at the country club as a line chef for $10.50 an hour.

Although the money in his pocket and lack of college debt momentarily felt good, his $600 a month quickly disappeared to bills, car loans, car repair, gas, and a credit card. Having "$450 a month in bills when you're making $600 tops a month at work just doesn't cut it," he says. Charlie was learning what many in his situation soon realize. While even $25 an hour at age twenty-two seems like a lot of money, by one's mid twenties it becomes nothing more than quicksand. The raises slow down or stop altogether, the better-paying jobs require more training, and yet the bills and the responsibilities keep climbing. He was also realizing something else: Taking on a little debt for a bigger payoff down the road is smart. When we talked to Charlie in the winter of 2009, he was on his way back to Ball State for the winter term, and he'd taken out a loan. "If I was really living an adult life," he says, "there's no way I'd be making it. The adult world sucks. I'm going to college to grow down."

The Mercedes Versus the Corolla

Although investing in higher education of some kind is the smartest thing a young person can do, the plan must be strategic. Racking up costs at an elite school such as Yale or Princeton, with their hefty price tags, may not be smart if financial aid is limited and family income is tight. The type of degree and its earnings potential down the road should also factor in to any decision. Caitlan, for example, has a master's degree in creative writing at a time when publishers are in dire straits and newspapers are laying off en masse. The degree is from the School of the Art Institute in Chicago, an elite school with a price tag of roughly $68,000 for the two-and-a-half-year program. The costs did not faze Caitlan at the time. "I vaguely remember someone at the school of the Art Institute sitting me down and saying, 'This is what you'll be paying every month on your loan when you're done. Are you sure you can afford this? Do you want to do this?'" She still owed the University of Texas $25,000, a federal subsidized loan that was growing at 3 percent interest. Caitlan was right in line with the national averages on debt for public colleges when she completed her undergraduate program. Add to it another bill from the master's degree at an elite school, however, and the debt suddenly leaps from manageable to unmanageable.

Today, Caitlan is struggling to manage that debt in a profession that does not pay well by any stretch of the imagination. A career in journalism and publishing, which her degree in creative writing pointed her toward, does not easily support a price tag from the Art Institute. Caitlan has learned the hard way a buried truth in this overly credentialed world: Going to a top-tier university does not significantly improve one's life chances over a school just a little farther down the ladder. The HARVARD or DUKE bumper sticker is not in itself the magic bullet that will propel that young person to the head of the class in life. Those who get into the elite schools will likely do well wherever they go.[7] Those abilities and habits of success (not to mention their parents' connections) that made them shine in high school and got them into the elite college will more than likely follow them in the job force. Sure, it helps to have Harvard on a résumé, but high ability and skill levels, coupled with positive personal traits and habits of success, will more often than not bring equally positive outcomes no matter where someone ends up going to college. After controlling for family background, SAT scores, or family income, studies show that lifetime earnings rarely reflect where students go to college. What they do reflect is whether or not they have the degree. That's the single most critical factor.

"Since I've been here in my position," says David Shulenburger, "our clipping service, particularly in last year, has produced all these tales of woe that little Johnny or Susie are going to have to go to some poor old public university. The point is that we don't know that students learn more and we don't have any evidence to suggest that their earnings or career are any different in an elite school. Given that, the rational consumer, certainly the one who doesn't have the money, ought to look at less expensive schools."

Jamil's parents, immigrants from India, understood that early on when they encouraged their son to choose the local University of California–Riverside over Northwestern University in Chicago for his undergraduate work in pre-med. "We all wanted to go to the school that would give us that decal we can put on our car," says Jamil. "You know, Northwestern or Harvard." But to his parents, he said, the school was not important; the education was what mattered. "Looking back, they're right. I didn't really sacrifice anything by taking the route that I did. You know, maybe life in Chicago would have been different than life in Riverside, but I don't know if that justifies spending my parents' money that they could be using, say, for their retirement, or paying off their house."

He does, however, notice a difference in the perspective of some of his American classmates. "A lot of my classmates, they have a desire to go there [to the elite schools] and their parents also have that same desire to see them there. They're willing to take out the loans and do what was necessary to put them through those schools." The choice of college is much like anything else in life. You can pay the price for a Mercedes if it fits your budget, but a Corolla is just as effective in getting you where you need to go. Jamil for one is happy with his Corolla—and particularly about graduating from medical school relatively debt-free. UC Riverside offered him a full-ride scholarship for his first four years, which cinched the deal for him, and his parents have been able to manage the final years of medical school with minimal loans.

Another example of a student who made a strategic choice in colleges is Lily. A second-generation Mexican American living in San Diego, Lily knew from the start that she wanted to be a teacher. Hers is in many respects a modern story of America—child of hardworking immigrant parents makes good in the world, gets a college degree, chooses a degree that "gives back," and returns to a less fortunate school to teach. Lily's hard work in high school paid off in scholarships that covered much of her undergraduate expense. She feels the luxury of those earlier circumstances now. She's returned to school to get a master's degree, and though she has paid for this one out of pocket, she says she's "got it made." She is enjoying life after a straight shot through college and into the workforce. She is traveling more, spending time with friends, and saving for a home. "I manage to save a lot of my money, so I do pretty well," she says. At age twenty-five, she has a career and very little debt. "I feel like I'm pretty successful. I know I could do more to increase that success, but for now, I think I've done pretty well."

Lily decided early on that she would take on some debt to get her bachelor's and master's degrees. She was strategic, however, in her choice of schools, and she knew that if she taught in a low-income school she would be eligible for a loan forgiveness program. Along the way, Lily no doubt used her credit cards to pave the way through some tight times. She knew that she would eventually earn enough to pay off those loans and debt when she started working as a teacher with a master's degree.

Debt Is Not Always a Four-Letter Word

Another result of this race for the Mercedes over the Corolla is less obvious, but may be even more detrimental. Not only has the race raised the expectations of young people for that brand-name degree, but the focus in the media and elsewhere on the debts of those who were less strategic

may be scaring some kids off from what may be the single most important investment in their lives.

In fact, some young adults may not be spending *enough* on themselves. They may be too "risk-averse" when faced with the prospect of
taking on debt.[8] Debt, in other words, has become an oversized fear
among those who should be investing the most. This fear is, in part, a
hangover from our puritanical upbringing. To be in debt in America
was a curse worse than death. Debt was a sign of weakness, a stain on
one's character. Like a fat man giving in to the éclair, a man in debt
lacked the willpower to control his baser urges. *Defective, delinquent,*
and *dependent* were words of scorn in eighteenth- and nineteenth-
century America, and debtors were all three. Thrift, on the other hand,
was a virtue. Benjamin Franklin tapped into this vein with his best-
selling *Poor Richard's Almanac,* which gave us a host of thrifty aphorisms
that countless schoolchildren still memorize today: "A penny saved is a
penny earned." "Beware of little expenses; a small leak will sink a great
ship." His twenty-first-century counterpart, Suze Orman, tries in vain
still to set people straight with the same message. Although credit cards
and other devices would burst onto the scene in the 1980s, at once
widening access to credit and making it easier, and more private, to
spend more than one's paycheck covered, the fear and shame of debt
would linger in the national consciousness. Witness the personal shame
so many feel today at the loss of their homes, even when it was predatory
lenders who brought them down.

It is, in part, this lingering sense of shame about debt that has made a
select group of young people afraid to take it on, even if it will pay off in
the end. Granted, the country is currently reeling from its spending
spree, so this might seem like a rather fanciful argument. But an old
adage fits here: "You have to throw money out the window to have it
come back in the door." In the current economy, the government must
incur debt to jump-start jobs and earnings—and the same applies to
young people who are just starting out in life. When spent strategically,
as on a college degree, taking on thousands of dollars in loans early in life
is not always cause for alarm. According to the late Nobel laureate
Milton Friedman, people should borrow the most early on when their
earnings are the smallest, save a lot when they are in their highest-

earning years in midlife, and then start spending all those savings after they retire. That theory of investment makes sense—except few do it. People drastically underconsume in their twenties and early thirties by failing to borrow against those assured future earnings for things that will lead to a secure life—homes, education, even taking a chance on a small business. That is not to suggest they should run out and buy the latest iPhone, but young adults should not be gun-shy when it comes to sinking some costs early in life, particularly college costs.

Sam, for example, might do well to rack up the right kind of debt. At age twenty-four, he is living with his parents, his four-year-old son, his eighteen-year-old brother, and his twenty-one-year-old sister in a house his parents recently bought in a modest neighborhood in San Diego. With sole custody of his son, Sam feels the responsibility of being both a father and the eldest son in an immigrant family. His story, like Lily's, is another common first-generation immigrant tale. Sam keenly appreciates the value of a dollar since he watches his father work six, sometimes seven, days a week to keep the family barely afloat. He lives in dread of a similar uphill climb in sand, and so has vowed to "to pay off [his] debt before continuing anything." Very responsible, we nod. Yet for Sam, in his early twenties, his fear of debt may be exactly what is holding him back. He is unwilling to return to school until he has money saved up, and even then he is hesitant to return full-time without also working.

"Realistically, for me," says Sam, "I can't afford to just go to school. I have to work in order to maintain enough money to go to school. My parents wouldn't let me go to school full-time without some sort of income to help support the family, especially with a son now. You know, I definitely need the money. So I might hold off on that bachelor's degree."

Sam is like a lot of young people: trying to be responsible, forced by circumstances to cut corners, work while they attend school, or, in his case, put off going until they can pay out of pocket. These costs, unfortunately, are deterring too many qualified applicants, often from low-income or minority backgrounds, from even applying. A study by the Institute for Higher Education Policy, a Washington-based nonprofit dedicated to access and success in post-secondary education, finds that the primary reason that qualified students do not enroll in college is the perception that it's too expensive.[9] The findings were based on a national survey of students who were qualified for college on the basis of their performance in a college preparatory curriculum and a survey of high school counselors.

Yet this is exactly the time for Sam and others in similar boats to throw caution to the wind and track down financial aid, take out a small loan, and go into debt. His lack of degree keeps him in low-paying jobs. The low pay means he will take longer to save for the tuition. By then life will probably have interceded, which will make returning to school for that increasingly necessary degree or certificate even harder and the resulting life chances even dimmer, the bills more pressing, the credit card more necessary, leaving him constantly treading water against the undertow.

Underwater

Sheila and her husband, Tony, are high school graduates in their late twenties with three kids. A generation or two ago, they might have been able to get by comfortably. But today, their high school degrees don't fare well in a job market where low-skilled but well-paid jobs with benefits have all but vanished—putting them squarely in the growing ranks of the working poor. Tony, the main breadwinner in the family, was recently promoted from a seasonal job as a street sweeper for a subcontractor to a full-time position with the company, making $10 an hour. Sheila makes $360 a month caring for three small children, along with her own three children. This brings their total income to $25,000 a year without benefits. Although to them, Tony's steady job is a step up, they are far behind on some bills, including several credit cards they used in slow times to make ends meet. They are not alone. For the working class, credit cards are often the rescue plan, at 25 percent interest and a slew of fees.

Sheila says, "We got the credit cards because a mortgage company said we needed credit cards to build our credit so we could buy a house. Well, we ended up getting credit cards and screwing up our credit. Then my husband was laid off in the winter because his job was seasonal then. That really put us behind with credit cards, and now we're trying to get back out of debt, but it's so hard. You're getting charged with all these fees every month. They don't understand. We pay them a $50 payment and the next month it's $100 more. How are we supposed to get caught up?" In fact, they rarely do. Young adults like Sheila and Tony (under age thirty-five) who cannot pay off their monthly credit card bills had median credit card balances of about $1,800 in 2008.[10]

Like a lot of Americans of all ages, Sheila and Tony are sinking into the hole, one bill at a time, as their incomes fail to keep pace with the cost of living. Wages for men like Tony have steadily lost ground since the 1970s, to the point that today their paycheck buys them $350 less each month than it did in 1975 after adjusting for inflation.[11] Men with just a high school degree are earning less, their jobs are less steady, and costs like health care are now theirs to shoulder as employers steadily shift these costs onto workers. Today's recession brings home that message even more. In July 2009, fourteen million people were vying for 2.4 million jobs. Young adults barely stand a fighting chance with these odds. Those with more experience will win out, and those without a college degree are the last in line. Even before the recession, young adults without college degrees were struggling mightily.

This sinkhole of declining income and increasing bills is swallowing many more families today, and it has grown wider since 2000. Most of those families are in straits like Sheila and Tony—working in low-wage jobs, struggling with emergency bills and high credit card fees. One indication of this disparity between lower- and higher-income families is the lopsided share of incomes among working-class and poorer families that go to paying debts such as credit cards, mortgages, and car payments. By 2004, about one in four low-income households of all ages spent 40 percent or more of their income on debts compared with 13.7 percent of middle-income households.[12] These numbers do not count debts to payday and other predatory lenders, to which low-income families frequently turn, and therefore the burden is probably understated. For many, credit cards are the answer to that gap when the money runs out at the end of the month and the roof leaks or the car breaks down again—or when the unexpected happens, as it always does.

Peter, the twenty-two-year-old community college dropout from Queens, has had a string of bad luck that is typical of many in his boat— just starting out, few credentials, and balancing on the edge. While he

was attending his second round of community college in Georgia, someone rear-ended his car. "I had to get that fixed, so I ended up using my
credit cards," he says. While his car was being repaired, however, he
missed work when the friend he was depending on for rides failed to
pick him up. As a result, he lost the job, and from then on "anytime I
really needed something, I just used the credit card." If that wasn't bad
enough, the bus company lost his luggage on one of his trips home, including all of the clothes he owned at the time. "Just a whole bunch of
bad stuff was happening," he says. With his grades suffering, credit card
bills mounting, and no clear direction for himself, he dropped out of
school again and headed home to New York. When we last talked, he
was working for his uncle in a new temporary venture. Unfortunately,
his work history at Sam Goody, the Gap, and Toys "R" Us doesn't promise riches.

Like Sam, Peter refuses to take on more debt until he can pay off his
credit cards. "I have to get money to go back to school, so I have to pay
my bills. I'm in debt already, so, you know, college is on hold." College
on hold—probably not the best decision since the only real way to get
out of debt is to get a better job, and that takes education.

Car repairs, covering expenses after losing jobs, and home repairs are
the most common reasons why young people in middle-to-lower earnings brackets use credit cards. Rent, groceries, and utilities also rank
high on the list. In some respects, these everyday expenditures are
telling. Contrary to the common stereotype of spoiled big spenders,
many young people are using their cards to tide them over through the
end of the month. But for many, this type of credit card use is not the answer. It only digs these young people deeper in debt because they are unable to compensate on the other side of the ledger: income. Their credit
cards are a sign of, not the cause of, their financial straits.

Another major source of credit card debt today is health care. Poor and
working-class families have many more health problems than their
more affluent peers. They are in a catch-22 of bad luck and circum-
stance. Their daily struggles add stress and strain to their lives, and their
low incomes land them in neighborhoods and communities that pose
their own risks, such as higher levels of lead, crime, and fewer super-
markets with healthy food. Yet they are much more likely to go without

health insurance, in part because they more often have part-time, temporary, or low-wage jobs that do not offer it. Too "rich" to qualify for Medicaid, the government's health care plan, they tend to go without.

The lack of health care benefits is not confined to the extreme poor or those with unsteady or part-time jobs. Many working Americans today are going without health insurance, regardless of age or income. The share of workers covered on the job has steadily eroded over the years. In 2008, 17 percent of full-time workers and 25 percent of part-time workers were no longer covered by their employers.[13] The erosion of benefits, however, hits those with only high school degrees the hardest.[14] Even when families are covered, they are paying more for that coverage. The average annual premiums for family coverage in employer-sponsored health insurance plans rose from approximately $1,500 in 1999 to $3,500 in 2009.[15] This may be one reason that only one in five workers with the lowest wages participated in their employer's health insurance plan in 2004. It's simply too expensive for some workers to pay $300 or more a month for health insurance premiums when the deductible can hover around $3,000 a year.

Young adults are the least likely to be insured; one-half of all uninsured people in America are between the ages of eighteen and thirty-four. The Network's analysis of young adults and health insurance finds they lack insurance for similar reasons as working-poor adults—they more often hold jobs that do not offer it. They are also still job-hopping in their early careers and are less financially stable. The instability of work in the early twenties, the Network finds, is a key reason that nearly fourteen million workers under age thirty lack health insurance today.[16] The chances of being uninsured have never been higher. When the late Baby Boomers were age twenty-five, only 23 percent lacked health insurance. Today, fully 35 percent are uninsured. Lack of insurance coverage peaks between ages twenty and twenty-four, when about 36 percent of men and roughly 30 percent of women lack insurance. This drop-off coincides with the mandated end of coverage on their parents' policies while the prospect of a steady job with benefits is still a few years off. (The new health care bill will expand the point at which dependent coverage ends to age twenty-six.)[17]

Tricia, a thirty-year-old woman in Michigan, knows what it is to be mired in health care bills. She and her husband of thirteen years and their three children struggle on his salary from his roofing business. "It's still hard," she says. "It's hard every day." They were living in a motel at the time of our interview, "and it's not a place for my children to be, it's not a place for me to be," says Tricia. "It's not a place for my husband to be. But once you get put in that situation, it's so hard to get out because you're paying $1,200 a month to stay in place."

Tricia's health issues compound their struggles. Her husband, like three and a half million other self-employed workers, has no health insurance.[18] Tricia has reached the point, sadly, that she feels she'd be less of a burden on her family if she disappeared. "I have asthma. I was born with it. And I was born with an underdeveloped lung. I'm going to get past a certain age in my life where I'm gonna need oxygen. I have had cervical cancer twice. I've had a little ovarian cyst. I've had major female problems. And I don't have insurance." Worried that she is a drain on her children's futures, she skimps on her own care, "although my husband says they need a mother. But in the same sense we're talking thousands and thousands of dollars of debt. My sister, myself, my mother, we've looked for something, even if it was an experimental thing to use me [as] a test bunny or whatever. But there's nothing out there."

When Tricia's symptoms become too severe, she checks herself into a hospital and "gets a nice big, huge hospital bill" in return. "I have my mother or my uncle who get inhalers and they pass 'em on to me. My uncle tells his doctor, and his doctor is more than willing to give 'em to me. I know exactly what I take." For many like Tricia, a visit to the doctor or an unexpected hospital bill lands on the credit card. For American families of all ages and incomes, medical bills are a leading cause of bankruptcy.

Tricia and others like her skate precariously close to poverty as the earnings of high school graduates continue to sink relative to those with higher education and training. The bills don't stop coming, though. Debt for families like Tricia and Sheila—and increasingly better-off families as well—is mounting all the time. The Network finds that young adults between twenty-five and thirty-four today hold about 70 percent more debt overall than young adults did in 1983.[19] But for many, particularly those with the stellar credentials, their incomes were also rising alongside their debt, so the pinch was less severe.[20]

For the Sheilas and Tricias of this world, however—people who skipped higher education and formed families quickly—debt went north while income went south. Among this group, the Network finds that one in five have debts that would completely wipe out their savings if they were unemployed for three months.[21] One statistic makes this division between the swimmers and treaders clear: Whereas 18 percent of the Tricias would be wiped out by their debt after three months, only 1 percent of her top-earning peers would face the same predicament.

Another striking distinction between swimmers and treaders is how much more often treaders have credit card debt rather than mortgage debt, the latter of which pays for one of the most important assets most Americans will own. Among those young adults who are working in the service sector or other jobs that pay less than $27,000 a year, 20 percent had mortgage debt and 50 percent owed something on a Visa or Master-Card in 2001, the latest data available when the Network study was commissioned. Contrast this with higher earners, and it quickly becomes clear just how tilted the game is. Among the top earners (those earning $90,000 or more), 86 percent had mortgage debt and 40 percent had credit card debt. The destinies of these two groups have likely diverged further since 2001, when these analyses were conducted. What is clear from this picture of lopsided debt burdens is that the emergencies, doctor visits, travel to and from work, burst pipes, and heating bills take a much larger toll on budgets of those barely hanging on. The credit card is a lifeline, but it is also a noose.

The American Dream of Hearth and Home

In another example of the vicious cycle some young people find themselves in when they underinvest early on, Sheila and Tony, and other treaders like them, have debt that prevents them from investing in what has traditionally been the quickest way to wealth and assets—homeownership. Before they got into credit card debt, the couple had hoped to get a mortgage. Now, Sheila says, "Houses are so expensive.

We were looking into a house six years ago. It's unreal how much in six years the price has gone up. I can't see paying $1,000 on a house payment each month. It's such a huge chunk of money that could go for other things." Those other things are bills and rent. However, if they were able to devote $1,000 a month to a mortgage, they would have a built-in savings account in a few years. It is in this important asset (like college, another form of "good" debt) where we see another striking divide among the middle class and those of lesser means. Renters, for example, are about ten times more likely to be "asset-poor" than homeowners: Their assets (home equity included) couldn't carry them for more than three months if they lost their job.[22] Assets gaps are evident across various groups as well. The racial disparities, for example, are stark—asset poverty rates for blacks and Latinos are more than twice those for whites. Unsurprisingly, education also plays a role—asset poverty in households that are headed by graduates of four-year colleges is about one-fourth that of those who have not graduated from high school. These assets—and housing is a key asset in America—more sharply divide the well off and the poor than even income.

Sheila and Tony's circumstances prevented them from buying when their more financially secure peers—and those whose parents were able to help them with down payments and even help to pay the mortgage each month—were able to invest. Young adults, in fact, were the age group that saw the biggest gains in homeownership during the 1990s and into the first years of the 2000s. Between 1992 and 2008, while homeownership nationally grew 5.8 percent, it grew by 58 percent for those under age twenty-five, and 19 percent for those ages twenty-five through twenty-nine. These were by far the biggest gains in homeownership among any age group.[23] The declines in homeownership among those under age thirty-five in the past three years, however, essentially erased all gains accrued in the 1990s, returning us to the same rates of homeownership as in 1982.

Not to be overlooked, what was also growing at this same time was the amount of mortgage debt young people were taking on. In 1983, a young adult under thirty-five typically owed about $64,000 (in 2007 dollars) on a home or condo. In 2007, the latest data available, that had jumped to $135,000.[24] No wonder Sheila and Tony were priced out.

Are Expectations Too High?

The young people we interviewed rarely resembled the spoiled youth we hear about in newspapers and magazines, such as an article in the *Fort Wayne News-Sentinel,* which trumpets "Coddled Twenty-Somethings Enjoy Luxury on Blue-Collar Salary," and claims that "They find solace in $325 Christian Dior sunglasses, a shot of confidence in a $600 Louis Vuitton handbag. Never mind that they still live with their parents…" In our interviews, we more frequently heard echoes of Ben Franklin and the virtue of thrift than we did about designer purchases.

Austin, a twenty-nine-year-old in Minnesota, is notorious for his penny-pinching. "My friends all say, 'Why don't you buy a new jacket?' I'm like, until my zipper busts, my jacket works. I don't need new this and new that. I think some of my friends, as they become mid to upper twenties, they're like, 'Okay. I get it now.' And I think, slowly, young adults will change their saving philosophies." Living at home to avoid "throwing away" money on rent, Austin is saving for a house. He works full-time for a very nice salary. He has little debt, ample savings, and by any measure is getting ahead. To him, staying at home and saving signals maturity and adulthood. Renting and living paycheck-to-paycheck is immature and foolish.

Likewise, Tom, a twenty-four-year-old Chicagoan, is living at home to build his savings. "I have a full-time job and a part-time job," he wrote on a *Chicago Tribune* message board in response to an article on "boomerangers"—young adults who move back home with their parents. "My parents don't charge me rent or any bills because they want me to pay off my student loans and save up for a house. I've been able to save $10,000 in savings and $10,000 in retirement accounts. I'll probably be at home for another two years before I decide to get my own place."

Many young people like Tom who live at home say they make this choice in order to save money for college, a down payment on a home, and even retirement. Many have heard the warnings from financial gurus like Suze Orman to save, save, save—and they are doing so. The rate of savings has risen for this generation. Ninety percent of young adult households in America in 2007 had some kind of financial savings, either in a savings account, a certificate of deposit, stocks, retirement accounts, life insurance, or a trust fund. Forty percent had a retirement account, with a typical nest egg of $12,000, although that amount has likely declined with the sinking stock market of 2008–2009. Thirteen percent had stocks, with a typical value of $4,800. Another 6 percent had a CD with average amounts of $4,400.[25] A study reported in a recent "Your Money" column in *The New York Times* indicates that, among workers who have the choice to start or stop contributing to retirement accounts, those ages twenty-one through thirty-five were more likely to start saving than any other age group—74 percent began saving, while 26 percent ceased. Another finds that about six in ten twenty-five- and thirty-five-year-olds reported saving, slightly higher than rates among the older groups. The recession seems to have sharpened the focus on savings for people of all ages, but especially for young people.[26]

Not everyone is able to save, however. For the treaders of this world, life is a struggle. Their parents are less equipped to support them in ways big and small. They rarely have the luxury, as Tom does, of moving home—if their parents even have a home themselves after the current housing crisis. Their future prospects begin to sink along with their income and savings, while their debts continue to grow. They find themselves in this position not because of a diet of Dior and Vuitton, but because of underinvestment.

The early-adult years are the prime time to invest in the future, which today means education and training. Ben Franklin's warnings against debt and the elevation of thrift have hit home for many Americans, particularly in this difficult economy. Young adults have heard those messages loud and clear. Yet what they haven't heard often enough is that there is such a thing as "good" debt. Investing wisely early on can pay off handsomely in the long run. Perhaps a more telling maxim for so many of our treaders is: "Penny wise, pound foolish." They have forgone education, rushed out of the home, or assumed family responsibilities without the forethought and investment necessary to maximize their success.

For others, whose parents are increasingly lending more money and support to their adult children, the current recession and financial meltdown may usher in a new era of restraint. When parents, as the Network found, spend one-third of the costs of raising a child to the age of eighteen *again* between eighteen and thirty-four, the burden on the older generation is too high. In a survey of eighteen- through twenty-one-year-olds in 2005 and eighteen- through twenty-four-year-olds in 2007, about seven in ten had received financial help from their parents in the prior year.[27] These amounts were not inconsequential. Among those who received assistance, whether they were living with their parents or independently, the average amount was about $11,000 for the past year. Granted, this is the average, and it is skewed upward by those who received large amounts. But it is also true that about one-half of young adults received at least $5,000 from their parents in the past year. This financial help is most commonly given to cover bills, followed by the costs of higher education. Parents also help their adult kids with car payments and, in some cases, rent or the down payment on a home. Tellingly, these figures are significantly underestimated because they do not include imputed costs of room and board for those who live at home with their parents. Whether parents can continue to afford such considerable support is a decision that each individual family must weigh.

———

What we couldn't capture directly in our research is whether social expectations for what it takes to live independently have also risen. Perhaps rather than the hard costs of housing, transportation, and groceries, something more intangible is keeping young adults with comfortable backgrounds from striking out independently. Perhaps the perception of what it means to live comfortably, what is "needed" in life, has changed for this group, leaving them with expectations that are too high. There is clear evidence that what young people consider luxuries and what they consider necessities have changed. According to a 2007 survey by the Pew Research Center for the People and the Press, a nonpartisan public opinion research organization, growing shares of Americans considered things like cell phones, dishwashers, cable television, and other amenities "necessities." The third-floor walk-up with iffy heating and a diet of ramen noodles is apparently no longer cutting it. With affluence comes a longer list of what people cannot live without, and thus Tom and others live more comfortably at home while saving money for their first home instead of opting for the third-floor walk-up. This, of course, is not true for everyone. But the children of better-off families are more likely to be living at home with their parents than those from poorer families.[28]

Interestingly, the deep recession our country is in has caused people to rethink that list of necessities. Pew redid the survey in 2009 and found sharp declines in the shares of individuals who thought the above items were necessities, reassigning them to the "luxury" category. The numbers of items that the public deems necessities have retreated to levels not seen for a decade or more. We've all had a reality check, it seems, and perhaps that third-story walk-up won't seem so bad in the future.

Young adults are clearly not the spendthrifts they are made out to be. Many are saving, and some are living at home to feather a future nest or get a foot in the working world. Still others have made or are making investments in an almost certain return—a college degree. Another group, however, is struggling precisely because they have not invested in some form of higher education. The problem is not anchored in universities and ever-rising tuition—good-quality, low-cost options for higher education abound. If college costs continue to rise while family incomes stagnate, and if a college degree loses its value in the market, there may come a time when college won't pay. That day is not here. And as a country, we cannot afford to see it arrive. As President Obama recently commented, "The countries that out-educate us today will out-compete us tomorrow." In the final chapter, we will discuss policies and programs that can help put higher education within reach for more young people and shift the current view from one of immediate costs to one of investment in themselves and future generations.

3

Job-Hopping or Job-Shopping in a Do-It-Yourself Economy

Stand back all bosses, screamed a *60 Minutes* episode in November 2007: A new breed of worker is attacking everything you hold sacred.

"Faced with new employees who want to roll into work with their iPods and flip-flops around noon, but still be CEO by Friday," the narrator intoned, "companies are realizing that the era of the button-down exec happy to have a job is as dead as the three-martini lunch."

Working hard, paying your dues, keeping your head down—those old rules have apparently been blasted out of the water. This generation is playing by a new rule book, having absorbed the ethos of a new breed of worker—the entrepreneur, the free agent, the foosball-playing, bring-your-dog-to-work whiz kid. Don't expect them to sign on, shut up, and steadily climb the ladder. This generation wants it all *now*. As the *60 Minutes* segment proclaimed, "Generation Y," the under-twenty-four set, may have climbed Mount Everest and excavated Machu Picchu, but they have never punched a time clock and are used to being praised and rewarded for every act and gesture, even for simply showing up.

Not surprisingly, this depiction raised some hackles with members of this generation, who make up approximately one-third of the U.S. workforce.[1] Moments after the episode aired, young people vented in the way they know best. In two days, more than five hundred people logged their opinions on the *60 Minutes* online comment board. "This is just maddening." "Typical fark!" "What overly generalized blather!!!!" were characteristic comments.

One comment that stood out was written by "Jillian," a twenty-four-year-old from Nevada who is putting herself through college by working as a tutor:

> Why should we work so goddamn hard? ... And with so many stories of retirees getting screwed or loyal employees being laid off after 30 years ... I think our generation knows that we cannot rely on the government or company in the future, so we have to take care of business ourselves; do these qualities breed loyalty? NO. It simply causes people to base their lives on something of more permanence, such as friends and family. I don't see a problem with treating a job as a job and not the center of your universe, especially since employers sure don't feel that way about employees ... I think we all recognize that most organizations only value workers for their effect on the company's bottom line.

With that, Jillian sums up the forces that have so profoundly altered the world of work for her generation. Time after time, the young people we interviewed raised these same concerns about the workplace: the insecurity of jobs, wages, and benefits, the disappearing loyalty of employers, and the ebbing centrality of work in defining one's self and life.

The MacArthur Research Network tracked young adults' changing attitudes toward work since the 1970s and overlaid them with changing economic factors, such as declining job stability and weakening social contracts between employer and employee. Unlike the *60 Minutes* segment, we delve beyond the quick, surface depictions of this generation to uncover a broader set of reasons for the shift in attitudes and outlooks toward work. Where *60 Minutes* sees a self-indulged, entitled generation, we see an adaptive response to a dramatically altered workforce (with a little dose of self-entitlement).

In many respects, Jillian is absolutely right. Why pin one's life on an employer who will not be loyal; and why not instead base one's life "on something of more permanence, such as friends and family"? We find that young adults across the board are questioning the centrality of work in their lives. But they are simultaneously hoping to find jobs with greater prestige and higher pay. These aspirations seem poised to crash headlong into a harsh reality. We look more carefully at this oncoming collision and what it means for the destinies of our swimmers and treaders.

Generation Skeptical

Jillian did not come to her conclusions in a vacuum. Jobs have changed dramatically in a very short time. Today's generation has watched as their parents scramble to stay ahead in a new regime of "free agents," "just in time" production, corporate downsizing, and globalization. The world of work has become increasingly uncertain, and it is an increasingly winner-take-all playing field.

As the economy shifted from one of making things to knowing and designing things, it split, as the economist James K. Galbraith and others have argued, into three tiers. On the top end was the knowledge class, an economy based on brains not brawn. The idea economy designs the world, from technology, medicine, law, and architecture, to arts and culture, to financial markets. It reveres the swashbuckling entrepreneur and the creative innovator.

Richard Florida, in his 2002 bestseller *The Rise of the Creative Class: And How It's Transforming Work, Leisure, Community, and Everyday Life,* homed in on a very visible segment of this group, the engineers, scientists, artists, musicians, fashion designers, and, above all, entrepreneurs who are creative in spirit and innovative in design. By 2000, the creative class accounted for one-third of all American workers, and its earnings accounted for fully one-half of all income. This growing creative class points to a trend in American industry: Brain is replacing brawn.

Members of the creative class are young, hip, diverse, and—with their double majors, advanced degrees, and entrepreneurial outlooks—they are also in demand. These are the young workers who can afford to take risks and have thrived on doing so. They want jobs that reflect their interests and tap into their talents and potential, and they want to work with interesting and creative people who can teach them something new.[2] They want to believe they are being heard and, through their jobs, are contributing to something bigger than themselves. Above all, they want to love their work.

"I will not settle for a career I am not truly passionate about," said Sean Aiken in his own manifesto on work in 2008. Sean, the twenty-six-year-old Canadian who managed to finagle a book deal out of his restlessness, epitomizes the quest for an impassioned job. In his ongoing struggle to figure out what he wanted to be when he grew up, he struck on the idea of trying a job a week for a year. In 2007 and 2008, he traveled the country at the invitation of employers—ranging from fashion designers to park rangers to bakers and dairy farmers. He worked at each job for exactly one week, donating his wages to charity. "One man in search of his passion" was his tagline. He posted this on his blog on March 23, 2007:

I am really excited about my generation entering the professional world as I feel we are realizing how important it is to be in a career that we love doing, one that challenges us, and we are demanding more out of a career than just a pay check. As we enter the work place with this increased awareness, we immediately start questioning everything, seeking a greater meaning in all that we do, something that makes sense. To be in a situation in which we feel like we are contributing to some greater good, some vision that we can buy into. How is what I am doing helping the world, helping those around me, helping my neighbourhood, how can I be more socially responsible, what can I do to make a difference?

Sean will no doubt aim for a job in the knowledge economy, most likely among the creative class. He displays in spades some of the qualities that will make him very attractive to businesses: fantastic self-marketing savvy and great social and organizational skills. While he and his peers create and design the new products of tomorrow, the second tier of workers in the redesigned economy will produce them. The constant threat of automation and outsourcing, however, has chipped away at mid-tier workers' bargaining power, and thus their wages have stagnated and their benefits dried up. The hollowed-out middle, once dominated by well-paid, secure manufacturing jobs, where young adults without a college degree could find a path to the middle class, is now a ghost of its original self. The $20-an-hour jobs with a pension and health care have been replaced with $10-an-hour jobs with few if any benefits.

Jason is one of those workers. He spends his days as an automotive mechanic in an Iowa car dealership for $12 an hour. Jason is no slouch. He knows the meaning of hard work. As a teen, he worked after school and weekends alongside his father in their backyard shop. His father was supplementing the family's farm income with an auto shop to make ends meet, and Jason pitched in when he could. In fact, Jason preferred this work to high school. After high school, he earned a quick training certificate and immediately went to work at the dealership. Now he spends his days racing against "the book." This is the time that the corporate execs decided it should take to replace spark plugs, do a tune-up or an oil change, and the many other car repairs that Jason does each day. His take-home pay is determined by the book time versus the actual time it takes him to do the job. Changing spark plugs becomes a literal race to beat the clock. Take too long and it is unpaid time. That pretty much sums up the sense of frantic desperation in mid-tier jobs today, as does this picture of life in the once-mighty manufacturing sector.

As dire as this picture may seem, life in the middle is not as bad as life in the economy's bottom tier—which has been the fastest-growing segment of the labor market. The bottom tier is the service economy, whose jobs—whether housecleaners, nannies, and busboys or Costco clerks, X-ray technicians, and personal trainers—are more nimble, but also lower paid and less secure.

One thing all workers have in common in the new economy, regardless of what they do, is the unrelenting pressure they are under. For the white-collar worker, that pressure means the leisurely three-martini lunches that *60 Minutes* refers to have been replaced by a BlackBerry and a frequent flier card. The once-packed 5:30 train home to the suburbs is nearly empty as the hours logged at the office mount toward sixty- and seventy-hour workweeks, and work no longer ends at the office elevator. The pressure to produce is enormous. Today's elite workers catch the 7:30 train, zip by the drive-through for dinner, cram in homework time with kids, and, once the kids are in bed, check email and pack in a little more work before collapsing into bed themselves around midnight, lest they be bested by some other hungry employee waiting for a chance. The unending demand for faster technology, the increasingly complex world of high finance, and the incessant pressure to innovate keep white-collar knowledge workers both in and under high demand—well paid, but stretched thin and in positions where they must prove their worth each day in order to stay.

The blue-collar worker feels a different pressure—a pressure derived mainly from insecurity. The company man is fast becoming a museum relic. "What has emerged," says Peter Gosselin in his book *High Wire: The Precarious Financial Lives of American Families,* quoting economists James O'Toole and Edward Lawler, "is a social contract in which employees understand they have jobs for as long as they have the right set of skills and . . . the organization has the resources to pay them." Our own research finds that in 1973, about one-half of men between ages thirty-five and sixty-four had been with their current employer for at least ten years. By 2006, fewer than 40 percent could make that claim. Another take on this scenario: More than three-fourths of those born in the 1970s had a stable job at age twenty-six (defined as having held it for more than forty-eight weeks). Only two-thirds of those born in the 1980s could make that claim.[3]

Work-Life Balance

The impact of these myriad forces on work life is enough to make anyone reconsider where and how work fits into life, as this newest generation so decidedly has. The MacArthur Network's research finds the echoes of these big changes in the shifting attitudes toward work since the 1970s. Young people today are less likely to expect and therefore value job stability than they were in the late 1970s and 1980s, and they are increasingly comfortable with change. While they may not expect to be at the same job for very long, they do want that job to be rewarding, both monetarily and personally. They like jobs with prestige and extrinsic rewards. They also want to be integral to the decision-making process at work. Yet, and here is where *60 Minutes* comes in, they are no longer as keen on putting in overtime or spending time learning new skills. Finally, young people across the board are becoming less likely to see work as central in their lives and in defining who they are as individuals. They also hope to find a better balance between their work and outside lives than their parents have. The willingness to climb a corporate ladder or invest heavily in a career is simply less inviting to today's young adults. Jillian offers a hint at why.

After reading Jillian's post, we contacted her to find out more about her. She grew up in Nevada, the daughter of two middle-class parents trying to achieve the American dream. Her mother worked as an X-ray technician and her father at a variety of jobs, including a lucrative stint in real estate. With their rising incomes, Jillian and her sister were able to enroll in one of the wealthier school districts in the area. However, this idyll would all soon crumble.

During Jillian's teenage years, her older sister, Margaret, began to run with the wrong crowd. At home, she was explosive and moody. The family tiptoed around her wild mood swings, doing everything they could to avoid setting them off. But Margaret grew increasingly unmanageable. As Jillian's mother focused her energies on Margaret, her work performance suffered. After missing work once too often, she was summarily fired. "After fifteen years of being a good employee, they fired her!" says Jillian, still astonished. Jillian's father also let his job suffer. Defeated and now broke after sinking their life savings into Margaret's care, the family lost their home and declared bankruptcy.

"I guess that showed me that you cannot count on a company for everything." Just as the rising divorce rate has made many members of this generation skeptical of the institution of marriage, this shredded bargain between worker and employer has made them skeptical of the institution of work. As our interviews so often revealed, young people are wary of counting on one employer for a steady income, and they shy away from investing their entire identity in their job. Anna, who is working as a script developer at Twentieth Century–Fox, is not interested, for example, in "snaking my way up the corporate ladder" at the expense of her health and sanity. "Work can't be my whole life," she says, "my happiness really does mean a lot to me."

The Network's analysis of an ongoing annual survey of high school seniors confirms Anna's and Jillian's skepticism about work's centrality in life. In 1980, three-fourths of young people saw work as being central to their lives. By 2004, only 60 percent thought work would be a defining aspect of their lives. Supporting our findings is a recent survey by the nonprofit Families and Work Institute that finds about one-half of workers under age thirty-seven put family first compared with 41 percent of Boomers. Furthermore, Baby Boomers, the survey reveals, more often "find themselves" through work. It stands to reason that having children might alter one's views about juggling work and family and the centrality of work, so the researchers also zeroed in on parents. When they compared the priorities of Boomer parents with younger adults with children, young parents today were still less work-centric, suggesting a strong generational shift, and not just a "life cycle" shift, in attitudes toward work.

Chuck Underwood, president of Cincinnati-based management consultancy Generational Imperative, which helps companies manage generational differences in the workforce, finds that the youngest workers today put work–life balance at the forefront. They often view long workdays and overtime as an unacceptable intrusion on this balance. The Network's own analysis also finds this general preference for shorter days and less bleedover into "personal" time. In 1976, 60 percent of young people valued more free time outside of work. This preference rose steadily over time such that by 2004, three-fourths of young people, regardless of their college and career aspirations, wanted more free time. Perhaps these young workers have drawn a lesson from their parents, whose work often threatens to consume them.

The growing preference for some form of work–life balance that these trends point to is also reflected in the declining preferences for taking on more responsibility at work and working longer hours. In 1992, according to the Families and Work Institute study, fully 75 percent of young workers under age thirty-seven wanted to move into jobs with more responsibility. By 2002, that was down to 57 percent.[4] The trend is clear: Less is more. This shift of drawing less personal identity and investment from work may solidify even more after the beating the recent recession has doled out. The sense that employers will disappear or that the ax is hanging over one's head is more pronounced today, and it will likely shape the current generation profoundly. The recession may have just snipped off the last threads of company loyalty. Of course, the opposite is also a possibility—the threat of being usurped by a more willing, more committed worker in a tight job market might put personal fulfillment on the back burner.

Let's be clear about one thing, however: Less is more not solely because this generation has been, as *60 Minutes* implies, spoiled from day one. Although there is no doubt a grain of truth to that, the larger reason for the changing attitudes toward work comes from above—from the big changes in the workforce that have made work less certain, more onerous, and more do-it-yourself. Gone is the company man, and may the fittest survive. It is this larger shift in the role of jobs in one's life that has shaped this generation's view on work.

What is worrisome, however, is that although the majority of young adults prefers careers with less commitment, some are better positioned to negotiate this desire. Others with the very same aspirations but who lack the requisite credentials in a knowledge economy are in no position to bargain, and, as we show later, they are likely set on a collision course.

Doing Well and Doing Good

At the same time as this generation seeks more work–life balance and fewer hours than their overworked parents, they still want their jobs to matter. Skeptical as she may be of employers, Jillian still has a dream. She wants a job that is meaningful. While she is leery of giving her life to an employer, either in spirit or in actual years, she is not without ambition and the willingness to commit—to the right job or employer. Jillian and her well-positioned peers are looking for something more. They want to see an immediate impact from the work they do, as it benefits either themselves or others.

The first person in her family to get a college degree, Jillian is now in graduate school in the field she loves: literature. She hopes to eventually get a PhD and teach in a community college or state university "where kids know what's at stake." She wants to ensure that young people like her—those who start out in a community college and pay their own way—find the same inspiration she did. "I want to give back to my community in a tangible sense," she says, and "educate others for the betterment of our society."

"Doing well and doing good are becoming ever-more intertwined," says Tom Watson, author of *CauseWired: Plugging In, Getting Involved, Changing the World,* a book about this generation's approach to giving and civic values. "It is not universal yet in the corporate world, but a lot of people are thinking about what they're going to do with their lives, and they want to see . . . what they do in jobs as doing some kind of good. This doesn't mean they won't be corporate lawyers and salesmen. It's just that they're very attuned to the idea that they shouldn't do a job just to make money." Of the 28 percent of young adults under age twenty-five who were working full-time when surveyed by a major marketing firm in 2006, nearly eight in ten wanted to work for a company that "cares about how it contributes to society."[5] A whopping 97 percent of respondents to the Harris Interactive Poll of Generation Y said they want jobs that allow them to have an impact on the world.

Our Network interviews repeatedly echo the same ideals. At twenty-nine, Ben, a young Chicago attorney in a large corporate firm, was struggling with the decision of whether to give up his lucrative six-figure salary. He had been working in the same law firm for three years when he came to the realization that becoming a partner was not in the cards for him, the first stumbling block in what had been an otherwise charmed career. Ben had graduated from one of the top five law schools in the country and clerked for a U.S. attorney in New York before landing his current position. Lately, however, he had begun to struggle with existential questions about life, happiness, and the role of work. He started to consider other options for work and he even thought about giving up law altogether and going back to school for journalism. Ultimately, though, pragmatism won out; he is now considering a move to the U.S. Attorney's Office.

"One of the things that is of value to me," Ben says, "is working in a group environment and feeling like I'm part of a larger entity." At the U.S. Attorney's Office, he would be working for Uncle Sam. "I'd know who I was representing. I'd be representing the Smithsonian, the Department of Justice." There, he says, he would feel value in bringing lawsuits on behalf of individuals who were facing discrimination or who had been harmed in some way by corporations or big businesses. "I would feel better about myself doing that than defending a large company, I'd have a passion for what I'm doing." In the meantime, he's taking steps toward greater fulfillment by doing pro bono legal work for low-income families in Uptown, a largely poor neighborhood in Chicago.

Samantha also felt the pull of a more rewarding line of work. "The people that my agency serves are the most rewarding part of my job," she says. After college, Samantha worked in a flower shop and later in a job-placement office, neither of which appealed to her. She wasn't using her psychology degree or the skills she'd acquired in college, and she felt she was just clocking in at her job. Across the street from the job-placement office, however, was a small nonprofit organization that helped people with mental and physical challenges to live independently in the community. She was drawn to this small group of folks who were working hard to better the lives of those in need. Working with them, she could apply what she had learned in college. On her lunch hour one day, she asked if they needed any help. They did, and she was hired. Even with the $7,000 pay cut she took, she immediately felt a connection to both the job and the people she served. "I wouldn't be the person I am today if I hadn't had an opportunity to engage in life with them," she says. She also felt that she was making a more meaningful contribution to the lives of the individuals and families she served.

By the time we interviewed Samantha, at age twenty-nine, she had become executive director of the NGO. She works long hours for little pay and "complains a lot sometimes," but never really considers leaving because the job is meaningful. "To me, I want to know that I made a real honest difference for the folks that we provide services to."

The Quest for Meaning Meets Self-Esteem

Giving back through meaningful work may be a hallmark of this generation. Another hallmark, however, is a mismatch between their aspirations and reality. And this is where the collision course begins that can leave young adults frustrated and drifting.

Like Sean Aiken and others of this generation, Dustin has a strong desire for a job he is passionate about, but this desire is coupled with restlessness and uncertainty. "I've always had two or three things going at once," he says. "I still don't know what I want to do."

Dustin grew up in a tight-knit family on Chicago's North Side. His parents, now retired, were old "hippies," in his words, and "totally supportive." For most of Dustin's twenties, he lived next door to them in a second house they owned. When they sold it, he moved, like many Chicagoans, into the "mother-in-law" garden apartment in his brother's two-flat, paying nominal rent and relying heavily on his parents' support. Dustin has a college degree, but he never saw himself as the college sort or the type to be focused on a career. He's not using his degree to move up a corporate ladder. Instead, he sees himself as an entrepreneur. He has dabbled in many things, all freelance in one form or another. His most serious venture was a bar band he led, with dreams of hitting it big. His parents lent him money for demos and promotion when the venture showed some initial promise, but it ultimately went nowhere. Today, at age thirty, he has landed a job with the city government through family connections, but, according to him, it is by no means permanent.

"Maybe people are fine with the long-term," Dustin says. "I don't know. Those who do know what they want to do are sometimes just stuck, I think. Maybe they're fine with that, I don't know. I leave myself outs. I have two or three things going, maybe two jobs and an idea. It's not that I'm afraid of committing to the job. There's something to be said for a pension and a lifelong job, but at the same time, you really have to like that job. You have to be willing to put up with the crap of that job."

Instead, Dustin would rather make a killing by creating a niche product or innovation, so that he could spend the rest of his life living off the interest. He does not need to live like a king—a middle-class income, he says, is fine. "I don't need $10 million. If I could get a 5 percent return on $1 million, that would enable me to have $40,000 a year forever. I'd be fine with that. I'd have my budget. I'd have it all covered, and then I could work a part-time job and maybe travel or volunteer. I'm still figuring out how to get there. I have a list of things I want to try."

Dustin is floundering as he grapples with his high aspirations and the fact that he lacks what it takes to get his foot in the door in a creative, knowledge economy. Being an average kid is not the ticket it used to be. Plain vanilla doesn't count. As Daniel Pink in his book *A Whole New Mind: Why Right Brainers Will Rule the Future* puts it, it's now all about the extra toppings.

In a world where competition comes not only from home but also from across the globe, young adults today must stand out in a much larger, much more competitive pool. Average just doesn't cut it. Dustin's rambling attempts to find a path for himself provide a peek into what it feels like to be competing in this market. His aimlessness is reflected in many of the other interviews we conducted. We repeatedly heard from young adults who wanted: "a job where I'll be respected," "something where I'll grow as a person," "a career where I'll continue learning," "something where I'll engage myself in a lot of different ways." When jobs do not match their lofty aspirations, they often simply move on, like Allen did.

Allen's first job out of college, as a consultant in a government position, lasted less than a year. A graduate of University of California–Berkeley, with a double major in history and ethnic studies, Allen was excited to be earning a salary for the first time in his life. Six months into the job, however, he began to hate it. "I didn't think that my compensation reflected my contribution, so that made me upset, and then the project I was placed on was just dreadful. The people I had to report to, they were definitely 'federal workers,' middle-aged. They were just there to make their paycheck—and I had to work for them! And I was twenty-two, twenty-three, and you get beaten down, you definitely lose interest. It felt like a waste of talent."

Allen's friend hooked him up with a job in San Francisco at a technology start-up, and he thought, "Yeah, work for two years and hit it rich and, you know, go and retire. Go and get my PhD in history." Unfortunately, he clashed with a new supervisor before he could make it rich. The company let him go, citing a lack of integrity. A few months later, however, he was rehired after the supervisor himself was fired. According to Allen, he was rehired because "they were well aware of my capabilities and that was pretty much it." Today, he is working in sales in that company, although he says he and his fellow sales associates are "very disgruntled of late" over the "pay, the lack of direction in the company, and our CEO's an idiot." Allen is looking to make a change as soon as one comes along. "I would definitely make the jump," he says.

Their quest for the perfect job leaves many in this group searching for the right fit. But in reality, only a handful of the best and brightest have the luxury of seeking the perfect job and, in this economy, even many of these young people will have to settle for less. Yet *settling* is often not a part of their vocabulary. The culture that surrounds young people today is one of instant fame and gratification. Glamorous jobs are often not what they seem, and the hard work they entail is sometimes not in this generation's sightlines. This all makes for a rude awakening when the job market does not cooperate, especially for the large middle tier of young people who are not highfliers.

In *The Ambitious Generation: America's Teenagers, Motivated but Directionless,* Barbara Schneider and David Stevenson, a sociologist and education expert, found that 70 percent of teens in a large, nationally representative survey in the 1990s expected to obtain a professional job. Meanwhile, very few said that they wanted to be machinists, secretaries, or farmers. While they had high aspirations, more than one-half of the teens and young adults had little sense of the qualifications or education they needed to get there.[6] Nor were they logically pursuing their goals. Instead, many were drifting and directionless, likely among the career nomads we see in the workforce today. Their expectations outshine their qualifications and, based on our interviews, this mismatch continues to be alive and well today.[7]

As we've already seen in the chapter on education, and will see again in the chapter on parent–child relationships, parents have also set their kids up for this collision course. They have raised children to have unbridled expectations that do not match their characteristics, abilities, and resources. Educators and school systems also reinforce these messages.

The clash between aspirations and achievements seems particularly likely to occur as young adults seek higher education and work. Allen, at least, has the credentials to back him up in his quest for the perfect job. Dustin has absorbed the ethos of meaningful and exciting work, but he's negotiating from an entirely different vantage point. His credentials shoehorn him into a job sector with a lot less flexibility or patience for dabbling, and a lot less generosity and "give."

"Work that makes a difference." "Something you can believe in." "Work you can take to heart." "Being able to see your impact." "Giving back." We heard these expectations in nearly every interview. Being socially useful in a job, however, is often a privilege of the well positioned in life. For young adults like Ben and Samantha, with a college degree and a lifetime of solid achievements, the search for fulfilling, meaningful work that does not intrude too heavily into their lives is an indulgence they can often afford. For the rest, having a job that is meaningful and that gives back is more often a luxury than a reality. The rift between those who are positioned to be selective—even amid a recession—and seek that meaningful job that gives back and those who, unbeknownst to them, do not have that luxury of choice is growing ever wider.

Job-Hopping to Nowhere

Everyone has picked up the notion that jobs should be more than just jobs. The high work ambitions of this generation are not confined to those with college degrees. Those without degrees do not want to work in meaningless jobs either. They do not want to spend ten hours a day patching together two part-time jobs. But the odds are they will be forced to do so. In this brutal economy, their fate is more precarious than ever. As Monica's job-hopping suggests, the collision between their ambitions and reality can be sobering.

Monica grew up in a working-class family in St. Paul, Minnesota. She has a ten-year-old son and rents an apartment in the suburbs. Monica originally planned to attend college and focus on musical engineering, but her plans were derailed when she became pregnant as a high school senior. Instead, she took some accounting courses at a local community college, only to find "it wasn't the right time. I wasn't ready to go to school. It was a lot to be raising a little child, working part-time, and going to school...so I dropped out and just worked for a while."

After dropping out, Monica worked in the accounting department of an insurance company, but she hated it and soon quit. Her mother read about promising job prospects for paralegals, so, with her encouragement, Monica went back to school and later landed a job in a police precinct during an employee's maternity leave. Once the employee returned, though, Monica was out of a job. She moved on to a small legal firm for five months, but they did not have enough work to keep her busy. "I can't handle that. I need to be busy. I cannot stand reading the newspaper all day."

Bored with the job, Monica quit and took a position at a temporary employment service, which placed her in a job testing legal software. By now, she was working pretty far afield from her paralegal degree. "It was a temporary job that they thought would possibly turn into a full-time job or permanent job, but it never did," she says. She worked there for four months before leaving. "Any person off the street could have done the searches and run the testing. You didn't need a paralegal degree," she told us. Ultimately, she became frustrated with the mismatch between what she had imagined and what the reality was turning out to be. Life in the service sector is seldom glamorous, interesting, or well paid.

Monica bounced to a collection agency and then to a mortgage foreclosure firm, a job she held for less than a year. She is once again unemployed and looking for that perfect fit. But the constant shifting and searching are taking their toll. "I have my days where I feel a little panicky that I'm not going to find a job," she says. "I'm thinking maybe if I go back and take a proofreading class or an editing class and a refresher English course. I don't know...I want a job I am going to be at for a long time, and I'm afraid that I am not going to find it."

On the one hand, Dustin and Monica and their fellow twenty-somethings have absorbed the credo of high aspirations and the importance of finding ideal, meaningful jobs. On the other hand, they do not have the credentials, connections, or leverage necessary to catapult themselves into this bracket of entrepreneurs, software programmers, engineers, patent lawyers, and other highfliers. While it has always been the case that not everyone is cut out for the professional, white-collar class, what is different today is that the blue-collar jobs are shrinking and are paying less. Those young adults who cannot bear the thought of another day in a classroom after high school have fewer "good" options today than their parents. Their piece of the pie—the assembly lines, the trades, the shipyards and airplane hangars—has shrunk, leaving more of them to fight for the lower-paying service sector or non-union jobs. They are often forced to piece together a string of jobs, with the hope of finally landing one that meets their expectations, or at least pays enough to cover the bills.

The service sector, broadly defined, is by far the largest today. In 1979, 28 percent of the U.S. workforce was in goods-producing jobs, such as construction or manufacturing. By 2005, only 17 percent held such jobs. Meanwhile, the share working in the service industry (including the higher-paid industries of finance and computers) increased from 72 to 83 percent.[8] Not all of these service jobs are low paid and low skilled. The service sector also officially includes high-paid professionals like lawyers, programmers, and movie stars. However, this sector has only a very small middle tier—workers are either highly paid, like financiers, or they are very poorly paid. In discussing the service sector here, we are thinking about this bottom tier of clerical workers, janitors, delivery drivers, teacher's aides, and the like. This tier made up about 50 percent of the service sector in 2005.

For lower-paid work, hours are less stable, jobs more often involve evening and night shifts, and they are more often part-time. Take Sheila, the mother of three who babysits for three children in addition to her own so that she can balance work and family more easily. The pay is paltry—$360 a month—but she needs the work. With just a high school degree, she relies on the service sector to supplement her husband, Tony's, equally meager wages. Since age eighteen, Sheila has held a string of low-wage jobs, including fast food worker, waitress, data entry clerk at a dental clinic, and nursing home aide. She and a friend even started their own housecleaning business a few years back, but they had a falling-out, which ended that option. She tried to go out on her own, but "I sent [out flyers] and nobody called. It was just not time."

Franco, a twenty-seven-year-old married father of two, delivers cigarettes, tobacco, candy, and groceries to small grocery stores and hotels in New Jersey fifty-seven hours a week. The job pays $12.50 an hour with benefits, and he pulls in about $2,000 a month after taxes. For him, "it's enough to live on if you live a conservative life and, you know, you don't buy a Mercedes or something like that." But if he had his choice, "I would like to have an eight-hour job that pays me more, so I don't have to work all them hours. Maybe I could go from eight till four and come back home and have more time with my kids."

Hand in hand with the rise of the service sector and the more "contingent" workforce is the growth in part-time jobs, particularly for young adults. In 2008, 30 percent of young adults ages twenty through twenty-four were working part-time.[9] Along with part-time work is the rise of temporary workers. One-half of the temporary services workforce is under age thirty-five (versus 36 percent of the permanent workforce), and they typically earn $3 an hour less than the median wage. In these jobs, the workers are employed by temporary agencies, not the companies where they are actually working. This saves employers from paying benefits or sometimes even the prevailing wage at the company. Between 1995 and 2004, total private employment in temporary help services grew by 43 percent, while total private employment overall grew 14 percent.[10] Only one-third of temporary workers preferred this arrangement.[11]

Our treaders struggled to find good jobs before the recession. It will be even harder for them now. As of April 2010, amid a stubborn recession, the unemployment rate for those ages twenty through twenty-four stood at 17.2 percent, much higher than the national average. Many in this group lacked college degrees. Job opportunities are very sparse for these young people. Older workers are clinging to their jobs longer because their retirement accounts have dwindled with the plummeting stock market (another ramification of the do-it-yourself employment contract: More workers now rely on 401(k)s for their retirement). And adding to their misery, their peers with college degrees will begin competing for their jobs as well. While the college-educated are more recession-proof than most, in a sign of the times, a growing portion of college grads are holding jobs that do not technically require a college degree, according to Andrew Sum, the director of the Center for Labor Market Studies. The result: The young, the poor, and the poorly educated are out on their ear.

"Where do you want to be in five years?" we asked Peter, the twenty-two-year-old New Yorker who had "some" college before the current downturn. "I have no idea," he says. "A lot of people have jobs just to pay the bills. What I want to do—I want to do something that I like. I don't want to be in a situation where [I'm saying] 'I hate this job.'"

The question is, will Peter have the privilege of choosing the dream job that he loves? Or will his high expectations slam up hard against the reality of his narrow prospects? His job history in low-wage retail offers him little to fall back on. In his current job as an errand runner, he earns around $250 a week, hit or miss—or $12,000 a year with no benefits.

Like so many of the twenty-somethings we interviewed who do not have college degrees, Peter has absorbed the credo of high aspirations and the importance of meaningful work. He continues to seek a job that matches his goals and pays the bills. Young adults in their early twenties change jobs every year, and those in their late twenties and early thirties change jobs every three years.[12] This translates into nine jobs by the time a person reaches thirty-four. However, for treaders, this job-hopping does not always lead, like that of their above-average peers, to a better job. Nor is it always voluntary. Lower-wage workers change jobs more often because of limited opportunity and vanishing on-the-job training, as well as circumstances beyond their control. Tyler, the young Minnesotan who dropped out of college after floundering badly, would start in a company, begin to move up, and then the business would close or he would be laid off. "Maybe it caught some people by surprise, but I kind of saw it coming," he says. "You just come to expect it."

This instability in the twenties is a dress rehearsal for the next decade, and probably the decade after that. These young people are on their own to figure out their work path, and the road signs keep changing. The likely result: lots of job-hopping, and a lifetime of insecurity instead of a lifetime job. This is hard on families and hard on a national economy. Add to this built-in job insecurity the higher expectations for jobs and work, and we have the makings for a disappointed, disillusioned, and increasingly partitioned workforce (and society). Although

America's workforce has always been divided by blue and white collars, the blue-collar worker was offered a trade-off for doing the kind of job that required a shower after work, not before. That trade-off was good pay, solid benefits, and job security. That trade-off has all but disappeared.

A Fast Start to Nowhere

At a small food-processing plant in Blakely, Georgia, workers toiled long hours to make peanut butter. The small warehouse employed hundreds instead of the thousands that the Bethlehem Steel plant in Gary, Indiana, and its ilk once did. To make a profit, the plant imported cheap peanuts from Mexico and South America and paid its non-unionized workers minimum wage. It also relied on temporary workers to save on back-office personnel costs. A shift supervisor at the plant was topping out at $12 an hour, or approximately $22,000 a year, according to a *New York Times* article in February 2009. At age thirty-one, he could not afford health insurance for his two children. The workers had gone several years without a raise. This is all in the past tense, however, because the plant joined the ranks of many manufacturers when it closed its doors in late 2009.

The shift away from a manufacturing base toward a knowledge and service economy is one reason for the sinking fortunes of many of the young people outlined here, and the starkly divided job world. Beginning in the early 2000s, wages in the service and manufacturing sectors began to converge. This was not because, as some had hoped, wages in the service sector grew, but because wages in the manufacturing sector fell.

A key milestone on the road to adulthood is that first "real" job. Yet the wages of these first jobs have been deteriorating steadily for the least educated. Young adults ages twenty-five through thirty-four with just a high school degree could expect entry-level wages of $11 an hour for males and $9 an hour for females in 2005. Their peers with a college degree were making about $20 an hour in their first job. In fact, as Sheldon Danziger and Cecilia Rouse show in their Network book *The Price of Independence: The Economics of Early Adulthood,* high school dropouts haven't seen their wages increase for twenty-five years, and those with just a high school degree were earning only 7 percent more.

These stagnating wages and the shift away from well-paid manufacturing and into fewer unionized and more service sector jobs takes a toll on our country's overall economic security. Danziger and Rouse find that in 1969, only about 10 percent of men in their early thirties were low earners, in this case earning poverty-level wages. By 2004, that share had more than doubled. Women fared a little better over the same time span, but nearly half of all women were still earning poverty-level wages in their midthirties. "The most recent generation of workers is taking much longer to earn enough to support a family," they write in the introduction to their book, "and at every age, young men are now less likely to do so than their counterparts were a quarter-century ago."[13]

This struggle to find a steady, well-paid job is particularly worrisome. Promotions and raises in the early years of work set the stage for the rest of one's work life. Workers experience the most wage growth during the first ten years of work. In fact, three-quarters of men's wage growth occurs in their first ten years of work. This front-end wage growth is also typically what carries the worker through the rest of the career.[14] While the treaders are making their wages in lower-paid, part-time or temporary jobs—errand running, small manufacturing, retail, and others—their more credentialed peers are logging hours in a profession or a job related to their field. All this adds up to growing insecurity, lower wages, a workforce always on the brink, and a longer road to the other markers of adulthood—marriage, kids, house and home.

Down and Disconnected

Most young adults today face a similar struggle, regardless of where they have their sights aimed. Those with the stellar credentials and those with nothing more than a technical degree or a few courses at the community college under their belt are all struggling to find the right match between their ideas about work and the reality before them. Those in the mid- and bottom tiers, however, will likely struggle much longer as their ambitions butt up against an economy that offers nothing remotely resembling what these young workers might have imagined for their lives. Working less for more pay in professional jobs may be what they *think* they can do, but the reality is quite different.

Since young adults with at least some college are struggling to stay afloat, one can imagine how those without any training or even a high school degree are faring. This is a group of young people who, by their early to midtwenties, have already checked out. They are adrift, often not hooked into school, work, or the military. In what is now a popular word in social service circles, they are *disconnected*. "Their life is clearly not going so great at this point," says Network member Wayne Osgood, the author of *On Your Own Without a Net*. "They don't have much going on in the world of work; many are living at home with their parents, and even in some kind of trouble."

The number of young people nationally who are completely disconnected and on the brink of sinking before they even get started is alarming. Osgood estimated that among the twenty-four million twelve- to seventeen-year-olds in 2005, at least a million and a half would completely disconnect along the road to adulthood. They would reach twenty-five without a job, without being in school, and without the ability to live on their own without family or government support. More alarming: These numbers have been growing steadily over time. The actual numbers of disconnected young people are probably higher because these tallies exclude those who are sent to prison. For black men, the numbers are shocking. More than one-half of young black men ages sixteen through twenty-four are neither in school nor working. The reasons for the disparity between black and white young men are many, and include a very different set of advantages and blocked opportunities. While lack of education is a common obstacle for both white and black men who are struggling to get started in life, black men have the added burden of racism, greater social isolation in inner cities, and an all-too-tempting drug and gang trade that quickly fills the void of lost jobs.

At an age when most young adults are beginning in earnest to forge the connections to adulthood, this group of disconnected youth is at risk of not only floundering personally, but facing protracted bouts of unemployment going forward. They will probably become caught in a vicious cycle between spells in prison and time back at home. Women in this group are likely to have a child by age twenty-five, and to rely on what little is left of the public safety net. Most will struggle to stay one step ahead of poverty. This group's plight imposes severe social costs, not to mention the personal costs of lost potential, as well as the intergenerational legacy.

These disconnected youth may be a harbinger of things to come. Many young adults, not just those who are disconnected, will no doubt work diligently to find a job, and another, and another. But without a sense of stability and the possibility for a brighter future, it becomes hard to plan a life, marriage, and kids. Life quickly becomes discouraging, and anger builds. How long before one gives up and drops out? How long before someone or some organization taps into this growing resentment with tea parties and angry community town halls? How long before the resentment boils over?

Americans have historically pulled themselves up by their bootstraps, relying on hard work and perseverance to compensate for disadvantages. Young adults today still believe in the value of hard work. In fact, in an analysis of a national survey commissioned by the Network, young adults said that one of the most important values they hope to instill in their children is a strong work ethic.[15] In our interviews in all quarters of the country, young adults also talk proudly of their work ethic.

But the work game is stacked against too many young people in low-level jobs. No matter how hard they work, without more education their options will be limited and their incomes are unlikely to ever rise beyond $40,000 a year. Without better credentials, they will float in a world of part-time work, temporary work, or roving from one low-paid job to another.

Though treaders hold many of the same ideals as swimmers, swimmers are buffered by their degrees and their family backgrounds. But they are also in no position to cavalierly quit their jobs in pursuit of the dream job. They cannot afford to meander because, in the end, they are more vulnerable than they think. They can no longer take a middle-class life for granted, and they are but one short step from plunging a long way down.

We end at what is by now a familiar picture. Those with more credentials, more education, and a better springboard will likely succeed in this world of work. They may take a longer path to that perfect job, and they may very well collide with the reality of a workforce that tends to squash ideals like work–family balance and jobs that give back. Or this generation may be the one that begins to change that reality. Their idealism is often combined with a self-assurance and set of credentials that might just be the ticket to change. They could be the generation that demands more work–life balance and gets it, the generation that jumps off the rat race of "always on" work schedules and seventy-hour-plus workweeks. They may just be able to turn the tables on the race for more money and more prestige at any cost. More likely, however, are the odds that they will join the race and become the future innovators, entrepreneurs, designers, and programmers who will inch the country forward with new ideas and new products.

But this is a tiny group. A much larger group will face the reality of a very different economy that does not always allow for the luxury of choice. Those with fewer credentials—and they are the majority, not the Jon Favreaus of Obama speechwriting fame and other highfliers—will likely continue to struggle and do less well than their parents did, a first for this country. Their dreams of a fulfilling job will turn sour quickly. There has always been a successful group and a less successful group in the U.S. workforce. But what is different now is the size of the gap between those in the creative culture and those in the service sector. Without some new solutions and some better paths from school to work, some of which we discuss in the concluding chapter, this group of treaders risks lifelong struggle, teetering forever on the brink. The middle will hollow out, and the center will eventually collapse.

4

First Comes Love,
Then Comes...?

No other milestone along the path to adulthood has changed more dramatically in recent decades than marriage and child bearing. Young people are delaying marriage for longer than at any other time in history. The number of singles has never been higher. More couples are living together before marriage and sometimes instead of marriage. Interracial marriages, once taboo, are increasingly common and will no doubt become more so as this generation of young people, more diverse than any other before it, begins to couple up. Gay marriage has been ratified in several states, with more surely to come. For many, these are worrisome cracks in, or outright assaults on, the institution of marriage. For others, these changes represent the loosening of an oppressive and outdated institution. Young adults today experience an even wider range of options than their predecessors, and these shifts are both welcome and enormously confusing.

As is the case with any change that happens quickly, confusion (not to mention fear) reigns. In many respects, young adults are, like their counterparts from the late 1960s and early 1970s, canaries in the coal mine as they carve out new paths that seem better suited to their lives and times. Although earlier generations broke new ground—particularly in the civil rights, counterculture, and women's movements—this is the first generation to fully feel the effects of the actions of those early pioneers. Our interviews revealed that young people feel both a sense of relief that they have more options before them and a sense of uncertainty as they begin to break the mold, no longer fitting the "traditional" image of coupledom.

As men and women turn thirty and are still single, they begin to wonder if they're normal or if somehow they've been left behind. They look to their parents, but only find more confusion. Their parents are often either divorced or nearing their thirty-fifth wedding anniversary, given that in 1975 when their parents were age twenty-three, the majority were married and had often started a family. As Lela, a twenty-seven-year-old in Atlanta we interviewed, put it, "My parents got married when they were twenty-four and had me when they were twenty-nine, which puts me three years behind marriage and two years prior to having kids. No way am I ready for either of those milestones, so what do I do? Where is my road map now?"

Meanwhile, the cultural conversation swirling about is equally confusing. While many people on the left think marriage is meaningless and outmoded, many on the right see it as a sacred covenant—the moral pillar of society. And yet gay couples on the left battle vociferously for the right to marry, and some of the most conservative politicians are caught in sex scandals when they cheat on their spouses. No wonder very few young adults feel ready to marry. It makes sense that they're confused.

Today's dating scene—step one on the road to marriage—reflects the confusion and exhilaration that these seismic changes have wrought. To today's parents, the ways their children "date" are nearly unrecognizable and sometimes shocking. To today's young adults, the old ways of dating and partnering up just don't make sense.

Hooking Up

Twenty-one-year-old Joel Walkowski captures his generation's take on dating in his winning essay in *The New York Times'* Modern Love contest:

A few months ago I liked a girl—a fairly common occurrence. But being slightly ambitious and drunk, I decided to ask her out on a date. This was a weird choice, as I'm not sure I know anyone who has ever had a real date. Most elect to hang out, hook up, or Skype long-distance relations. The idea of a date (asking in advance, spending rent money on dinner and dealing with the initial awkwardness) is far too concrete and unnecessary . . . Riding my bike home later, I realized I didn't even know what a real date was, beyond some vague Hollywood notion.

Clearly, the time-honored tradition of calling a girl to ask her out a week in advance for dinner and a movie has taken a hit. On many high school and college campuses, the formality of dating has given way to casual and convenient hooking up. Surveys now show that nearly 30 percent of high school seniors say they don't "date" anymore, up from just 12 percent in 1980.[1] Joel goes on to describe the (non)dating and relationships of his generation as studies in practiced, feigned nonchalance. Those who try too hard risk looking vulnerable or, worse, naïve. "Casual is sexy. Caring is creepy," he says. "An encounter is best when unsullied by intentions.

"Hardly anyone I know," Joel continues, "aspires to be 'that guy' or 'that girl,' those once-dynamic individuals who 'found someone' and suddenly weren't so cool. On some level, we envy the scope of their feelings, but we certainly don't want to become them."

Instead, young people today hook up for one-night stands and then go back to being just friends. No fuss, no muss, and NSA, no strings attached. They are, as the saying goes, "friends with benefits." Others might call it attention-deficit dating. Whatever the tagline, the significant difference in today's dating world is this: In the past, dating eventually led to sex. Today, sex eventually leads to dating.

The practice of hooking up is not a fantasy perpetrated by young men. Many young women are the ones initiating the hookups and skulking out the next morning.[2] For some young women, who are generally excelling more than young men in college, "hooking up and casual relationships are a way of not locking down options too early," says Indiana University sociologist Elizabeth Armstrong. Armstrong and her colleague Laura Hamilton immersed themselves, like Jane Goodall in the jungles of Gombe, in the dorms of Indiana University in 2005 to study the college lives and relationships of thirty-three young women for five years. "Exclusive, all-consuming relationships in women's eyes," says Armstrong, "are greedy and devouring. They cause you to lower your sights on education and a career. They get in the way of friendships and getting course work done."

Not all women are as upbeat about hooking up. According to Kathleen Bogle, author of *Hooking Up: Sex, Dating and Relationships on Campus,* women are more likely to find these relationships lacking. They are less enamored than men with the casualness of hooking up and more often disappointed in how often hooking up leads to nowhere. And some things never change. Women who hook up too frequently on college campuses are likely to be tagged sluts, whereas promiscuous men are considered (with some pride) to be players.

Bogle also finds that the hookup culture fades after college, and traditional dating reasserts itself somewhat. However, given that for many, dating is a "new" thing, they are not certain how to proceed or what to expect, all of which can lead to serious confusion. Are we hanging out and hooking up or are we on an official date?

It is unclear whether hooking up is here to stay, or whether these trends will shift and fade as the norms about when (or whether) to marry settle into place. Traditionalism has forever butted up against modernism, with a period of upheaval, fear, and finger wagging in between. This tussle does not mean that the old ideas and behaviors are being completely discarded in favor of something new. What instead emerges is a third way, one that incorporates the lessons learned from the past with the demands of the present. To be at the corner of such profound change and without a road map is both scary and exhilarating. We may simply be at that moment in history where the standard-bearers of the "new" family are making their mark.

We examine some of these changes in this chapter and hear from young people who are grappling with and making a new order. Throughout, we noticed a distinct pattern. While the majority of young people are delaying marriage, sometimes well into their thirties, a small group is doing just the opposite: They are following the old script and marrying early. The young people in this group are very often from religious, rural, or disadvantaged backgrounds. And as we have discovered, the costs of marrying early are high—couples who do so are likely to be divorced in ten years. These couples also often have children early, interrupting or cutting off their education, which is so critical to having a secure life today. The paths and choices of these fast-starters are influenced by their circumstances, and they often further exacerbate their already precarious life positions.

We also find that many young people are living together as couples before marriage. Here again, we see some stark divisions. While some young people are test-driving marriage by living with a partner, others are embarking on a string of live-in relationships, often with children in tow. These latter relationships are much different from those of couples who move in together post-college to "give it a try." They are more fragile, more combustible, and indicative once again of the difficult circumstances in which too many young people find themselves.

So how did we get here? The answer to that question could take up an entire book. We won't delve into all of the factors that explain these social changes, but we do want to pause briefly in the middle of the last century—the anchor point for the "model family" in the public's imagination. The road from there to here was partly built by the parents and even grandparents of today's young adults, who challenged traditions and ultimately helped shape the meaning of marriage and family today.

The Slide Away from Marriage

Many of the assumptions underlying the nuclear family were shattered in the 1960s. Betty Friedan's *The Feminine Mystique* blew the cover off women's discontent as suburban housewives. The advent of the birth control pill in 1960 freed couples from the once-ubiquitous shotgun marriages, and *Roe v. Wade* in 1973 granted further insurance against unplanned pregnancies. Before that in the 1950s, in nearly one-half of teen marriages, the woman was pregnant.[3] The counterculture, women's, and gay rights movements, in the wake of the civil rights era, further pushed the boundaries of convention as both men and women reexamined their roles in life. Everything, including marriage and relationships, seemed up for grabs.

Women were also getting more serious about education. In fact, today women outnumber men in both undergraduate and graduate schools and in degree completion. In certain cities, such as New York, Chicago, and Los Angeles, they are outearning men for the first time. Education and larger salaries are two critical factors in the decision of whom to marry and when, and educated women now have more of both.

"College is the best contraception," says Network associate member Maria Kefalas. "Pursuing a goal, a degree, just makes the idea of having kids and settling down seem, at the very least, bad timing and, at the very worst, a catastrophe." The numbers back this up. Those who are not in school or adrift in school are indeed much more likely to have children in their early twenties. College, in other words, expands horizons, offers a safe place to mature, provides necessary credentials, and opens a door to a brighter future, for both men and women. As we saw in the first chapter, a college degree is the ticket to a better job and, on the whole, greater security and affluence. Although money isn't everything, it does make life a little easier.

With more at stake—not to mention the high divorce rates of their parents—marrying and having children too soon seems imprudent to young adults. *Shouldn't I get settled in my job first so I can make sure that my child will be able to go to a good school in a good neighborhood? Why should I marry my high school sweetheart now that I've seen the world, and it turns out that we no longer have that much in common?*

The economic downturn has pushed the wedding date back even farther. Today's economy (even before the recession) demands a mobile workforce, and it makes more sense to forage for work unattached to a new family.

Me Time

All these factors culminate in one of the biggest changes: the rapid increase in the number of young people living alone, as single heads of the household. To get a sense of the magnitude of this change, in 1950, only

5 percent of young women ages twenty through twenty-nine were single heads of the household. By 2000, 35 percent were. Not surprisingly, at the same time, the age at first marriage rose from twenty for women and twenty-two for men in 1960 to twenty-five and twenty-seven, respectively, in 2000. Michael Rosenfeld, a professor of sociology at Stanford, sees a connection between this shift and the rise of new forms of relationships, including the rise of interracial couples (among blacks and whites, quintupling since 1960), gay couples, and living together without marrying.[4] Living on one's own makes it harder for parents and other family members to influence a young adult's choices. Without the supervision of nearby relatives—a supervision that persisted until quite recently—couples living on their own are freer to carve their own paths into marriage and partnering. Rosenfeld finds that moving away from home to another state increases the odds of a nontraditional union.

For women in particular, this "hiatus" of living on their own, as sociologists Frances Goldscheider and Linda Waite have called it, makes them more leery of marriage. They are also likely to have fewer children and to expect less traditional roles for men and women. Some even argue that this stint of independent living has a greater impact on marriage and family plans than college and employment.[5]

As people become accustomed to living on their own, another thing happens. They become set in their ways, and meeting Mr. or Ms. Right gets harder. Shu, a Chinese American living in New York City, didn't originally plan to be single at age thirty. Relationships would come later, she had decided, as she kept her eye on the prize and got her MBA and settled into a career. But as time passed, she found herself getting more selective about the men she dated. "I think having had personal relationships with different types of guys helped shape me. I think whatever experiences I had in a relationship let me know now what works for me, what doesn't work for me, what I'm able to deal with, and what I will tolerate or not accept for me as a person."

With a salary in the six figures as a bank manager, she earns enough even in New York City to buy a condo, which she recently did. "My mom doesn't understand that," she says of her condo. "She doesn't understand: Why would a single woman do the apartment thing if there's no husband? For me, though, it's the right next step."

For Shu's mother, and many traditional mothers like her, the goal is for her daughter to find a good man and settle down. But Shu, who has fully absorbed the American dictum that girls can do anything, has set her sights elsewhere. "My priorities right now are 'me' time," she says as she watches her mother cook the dinner for their large extended family who are living together in Brooklyn. "I don't think my mother has ever had just me time."

Yet Shu also senses the time pressure and feels ready to shift gears. "The next ten years of my life will be definitely more focused on my personal life and possibly having a family. You know, I'm on pace with my work and school expectations. On a personal side, I'd like to develop that more now, so it's really about taking my personal relationships and making them more complete." The next ten years of her life are her thirties. A generation or two ago, Shu would have planned these steps for her twenties.

Shu recently contacted an old friend whom she has known for years as "just friends." They deliberately decided to start dating, and it's been going very well, with one hitch: He's a teacher in Boston. However, the distance suits her on some level. "What is satisfying about the relationship," she says, "is that I don't have to compromise what's important to me. I think I'd be terrified of getting married at this point, because I'm just not ready for marriage. I wouldn't know how to be married. It's something I want to do, absolutely, but I don't necessarily know if it would make our relationship any stronger or any better. At this point, if we could live together, spend more time together, that would be the best thing."

Wary is probably the best word to describe her and most of her peers' feelings toward marriage—wary of compromise, wary of giving up one's individuality, wary of missing out on something better. Although she knows her boyfriend is a good match for her in many ways, and she cannot imagine "finding somebody else that makes me feel as good as I feel now," she is nonetheless leery of making the move to Boston, or of him moving to New York. "Because we are so different makes it interesting and stimulating. But it also makes me wonder, you know, at what point will that become less exciting?"

Shu also echoes many of her peers when she hedges on marriage, saying she's not sure it will improve her relationship. This hesitancy reflects the long chain of cultural shifts that began in the 1960s and 1970s, when people began questioning the purpose and function of marriage as an institution. "It's just a piece of paper," the conversation goes. And yet, marriage is clearly more than that—otherwise it would have faded long ago. Its bulldog persistence signals something important to us. This is part of why Shu says, "I'm just not *ready* for marriage." All of this examination of marriage has done one thing. It has elevated it in the eyes of many young people. Sitting high atop a pedestal, marriage is something nearly unattainable—hardly just a piece of paper.

You Have to Be an Adult to Be Married

The meaning of marriage is being reimagined. Instead of reflex—something you "do" at a certain age—marriage has become a step that is earned. As the path to adulthood stretches out, and along with it the responsibilities and milestones that mark adulthood, marriage today sits at the end, not the beginning, of a long chain of accomplishments and goals. "Back in the 1950s," says Network chair Frank Furstenberg, "people married hardly knowing each other." They married, he said, without a laundry list of qualities they would like in their mate or the need to know every single aspect about his or her life. They married because the time was right and they'd met someone suitable. (Or quite often, they married simply because the girl was pregnant.) "It began with a hope and a pledge," says Furstenberg, "and often very little to back that pledge up. Today, increasingly, people want to see evidence that it's going to work. That doesn't mean that it *will* work, but they're more wary about the pledge and the hope."

Marriage today, Furstenberg continues, is more demanding and exalted because expectations have risen and, with them, one's standards for the perfect match. Marriage, in other words, is daunting. This is evident in the wariness and achievement-focus of the young women in Elizabeth Armstrong's study. Only a handful of these women imagined marriage happening anytime soon. For the majority, the thought of marrying before their late twenties struck them as plain odd. Yet these women were "everywoman" college students: middle class, from the heartland, slightly conservative, very conventional. "If these girls are delaying marriage, pretty much everyone is," says Armstrong. Indeed, Network findings reveal that only 45 percent of men and 60 percent of women are married by age twenty-eight today, compared with 79 percent of men and 84 percent of women in 1960.[6]

The delay is caused both by the daunting reputation of marriage and because young adults today are not ready to get married until they get all their ducks in a row. Where once, as Furstenberg alludes, young people married first and then together set off on a path toward their goals as a couple, today they forge those paths separately, on their own. Only later, after a string of accomplishments—getting the degree, the job, the condo, settling in the city of their choice—do they begin to consider marriage, as Alex's story shows.

Alex is a recent graduate of Rutgers University now living in Astoria, Queens, where he shares an apartment with his grandmother, covering her rent, buying her groceries, and generally keeping an eye out for her. His parents, Puerto Rican and Cuban, moved the family to New Jersey when he was a freshman in high school for a better education. He and his girlfriend, Trina, met in college and have been together for nearly five years. "She's my best friend," says Alex. "We just get along great. In every endeavor that I've ever undertaken, she's been my number one supporter."

Trina graduated a semester before he did and now works as a paralegal in Jersey City. According to Alex, she is everything he wants in a partner. He clearly adores her, and they "know each other inside and out." And yet he also stresses that they both remain independent. "We both still have our own lives," he says, "so it's worked out."

Alex and Trina love each other deeply, and they enjoy spending time with each other. They also know they will marry eventually. But at age twenty-four, a time when their parents and grandparents were most likely already married, the two are in no hurry to tie the knot. Alex enjoys his freedom right now, and his life, while filled with work, friends, and Trina, has a carefree quality to it. After a day at the office, he makes himself some dinner and watches *The Simpsons* before heading to the gym for a workout. He calls Trina, who lives in New Jersey, a few nights a week. On weekends he goes out dancing, or he and Trina go to the movies or to dinner. Twice a month or so he heads to New Jersey to see his parents, talk politics with his Cuban father, and be pampered by his mother, who fills him in on the family gossip.

He and Trina could marry if they wanted. They have all the "essentials" in place. Alex is not hampered by debt or obligations; he graduated debt-free with a bachelor's degree in biotechnology. They decided to live on their own to get a taste of the world and what life is like as an independent adult.

Alex earns a decent salary working for an oil company, yet he's not feeling the connection he needs at work. He has decided to apply to law school, with plans to specialize in patent law. He has a vision for his life, and he knows how to achieve his aims. "I think the only way to do anything about the future is by doing something today," he says. And doing it alone, he might as well have added. For Alex, this future vision includes law school, a good job, his own place, a sense of settled satisfaction with work and life—and only then, marriage and family. Alex—along with the majority of today's twenty-somethings—is getting his ducks in a row and *then* getting married. As Furstenberg has said, "In years past, being married meant you were an adult. Today, you have to be an adult to be married."

Trina, too, is working toward her own goals. She, like Alex, plans to attend law school. "Hopefully [Trina] will also be a lawyer and we'll be able to work together, which would be nice, 'cause that's how I see us spending our time together." Trina has occasionally mentioned the "M word," but Alex balks. "I can tell you, it's absolutely 'talk to law school' 'cause I can't make that commitment until I have a career. One day, maybe, but not right now."

Some may say Alex is a typical guy, scared of commitment and unwilling to leave the party. The male fear of commitment has been fodder for many books and movies, all with the message that guys are absolutely phobic when it comes to settling down. Michael Kimmel, a sociologist at SUNY–Stony Brook, fills his recent book *Guyland: The Perilous World Where Boys Become Men* with examples of men in their twenties who have no interest in settling down, preferring instead to extend the frat party for another decade. Our culture, he argues, allows them to do this, as their own fathers pass the phone to their mothers rather than give their sons good advice on how to be a responsible adult. Unchallenged to fill their traditional roles of provider and protector, young men continue their adolescent fascinations with Game Boys, boobs, and beer.

That may be true of the select set of guys in Kimmel's book, but the fear of commitment that many men express is not a case of arrested development. It is just the opposite, in fact. Many men acutely feel the pressure of family, responsibility, and the high expectations that women often have for marriage. Like Alex, they are struggling to build their résumés and get settled in a career in a work world that is no longer as stable as that their fathers occupied. They know that expectations for "the good life" require a good salary. They grapple with mixed signals from women, who in one breath talk about equality at home and at work, but in the other want men to pick up the dinner tab. They also grapple with the responsibility. "I'm just not ready for a wife," many say—not to mention the possibility of an ex-wife and the heavy financial fallout of a potential divorce. What that really means is that they're not sure they can live up to the expectations, whether their own or those of others. The fear then is not so much of leaving the party as of high expectations for marriage and everything it stands for.

Alex is not the only one delaying marriage. Trina, too, is hesitant. She may hint at marriage, but she is not yet pressuring Alex to marry. She's still getting her own ducks in a row. Yet the questions become: What if there's always another duck to align? Is the laundry list of things to do first a sign of the high pedestal that marriage sits atop? Have the expectations for the perfect mate become so vaulted, the bar so high, that no one can meet them? Indeed, it would appear that with a decade of me time, the list of qualities young adults expect in a mate has grown to dossier proportions.

The Growing Dossier of Qualifications

Shu was living on her own for nearly a decade when she began dating her current boyfriend. Her hesitancy to make a deeper commitment to him and her concerns about their compatibility mark a deeper issue. After spending so much time on their own, young adults are finding that settling down with one person is not so easy. Their growing pickiness is not surprising. After all, one reason the military recruits eighteen- and nineteen-year-olds is because they are "green" and can be shaped more easily. After too much life experience, the sacrifices and demands of army life start to look less enticing. The same goes for the demands of marriage and cohabitation. The longer one is on one's own, the harder it becomes to compromise.

What do singles in their mid- to late twenties want in a mate? One twenty-six-year-old man from San Diego says he wants someone who "is goal-oriented. Someone where education is really important to them. Family, strong family ties. They're warmhearted. I don't like someone that's selfish or narrow-minded. Also, someone that's simple. They don't look at the materialistic side of a person. They can appreciate someone for their inner self." A twenty-eight-year-old we spoke to in San Diego is looking "for honesty, loyalty, commitment, monogamy. Just reciprocity in every way. Someone with ambition, strong personality, confidence, good sense of self, established." Another young adult, a twenty-nine-year-old woman, talks of an equally "centered" partner. She sees her future marriage as a "place that's together and I like who I am in the relationships. I don't need to change anything about myself to be better in this. It should feel really good."

A cynical person would say, *Good luck with all that.* Such cynicism is justified to an extent. Americans have always put marriage on a pedestal. But this practice can all too quickly make the ideal of marriage unattainable. How many people, on their best day, can meet the above list? In *Marry Him: A Case for Mr. Good Enough,* writer and single-mother-by-choice Lori Gottlieb scolds her generation for having unreasonable standards. "Settling," she says, has gotten a dirty name.

Whenever I make the case for settling, people look at me with creased brows of disapproval or frowns of disappointment. . . . It's not only politically incorrect to get behind settling, it's downright un-American. Our culture tells us to keep our eyes on the prize (while our mothers, who know better, tell us not to be so picky), and the theme of holding out for true love . . . permeates our collective mentality.

The prize is a partner for life who has the qualities and talents that will complement the other. As marriage and family expert Andrew Cherlin says of this new meaning of marriage, "Being married is less a required adult role and more an individualized achievement—a symbol of successful self-development."[7] The qualities are not necessarily that he be only a good provider or she a good mother, but that the mate be simpatico emotionally, intellectually, and spiritually as well—the über soul mate. Young adults want a good companion, an equal. They want a spouse who will share life with them, rather than split off into a separate role. They want to do it all together. Today's young adults are on a quest not for a pragmatic business partner, as their grandparents often were, but a best friend to spend their life with.

Austin, a twenty-nine-year-old from St. Paul, Minnesota, and his girlfriend, Janine, have been dating for five years. They are close, and he talks freely about their relationship in ways his father never would have.

"There's nothing I can't say to her," he says. "So, you are truly each other's best friend. You mean the most to each other. And that's what I like the best. I'm not depending on my brother to be my best friend, or my friend from high school to be my best friend. I know that the person I'm with will always be my best friend. And that's, I think, what should mean most in any relationship." He is not alone. Nine in ten singles in the National Marriage Project's annual survey agree that "when you marry, you want your spouse to be your soul mate, first and foremost."

Yet this quest for a best friend or a soul mate often means that the twenties are spent searching and assessing, culling and rejecting, and the march down the aisle slows to a crawl.

In many respects, Shu and Alex and Trina should be commended. They are taking marriage seriously enough to approach it slowly, taking the time to find themselves and find their perfect match while getting their ducks in a row. Their long path to marriage, however, begs the question of whether they will, in fact, marry someday. In a recent poll by the Pew Research Center, nearly four in ten young adults in their twenties said they were not looking for a mate. Surely marriage is not at its end, given that the majority of young people still say they want to get married. But with the rise in the numbers remaining single at all ages, the increasing numbers who say they're not looking for a mate, and the slow deliberate path toward partnering up, the question hangs in the air: Have we exalted marriage beyond its capacity?

From Hooking Up to Shacking Up

With many more young people delaying marriage, the route that leads directly from dating and romance to marriage is fast becoming an eight-track tape in an iTunes world. Yet the expanding span of singledom is neither a cloistered nor celibate period. Young people do still crave companionship, not to mention sex, and they now have more options to pursue both without the yoke of marriage. Living together is one of those options.

Living together no longer incurs the shame it once did. Today, more than one-half of first marriages are preceded by a stint of living together compared with virtually none fifty years ago.[8] Even since 1980, the number of couples living together has quadrupled to five million. The twenties are a prime time for living together. One-fourth of women ages twenty-five through thirty-nine are currently living with someone outside of marriage, and another one-fourth have done so at some point in the past. The trend shows no signs of abating. About one-half of high school seniors say that they plan to live with someone before they marry.[9]

Yet here we see education and options diverge dramatically. While college graduates are reconfiguring their path to the altar, they often live together first with the intention of eventually reaching the altar. Their counterparts who skip college are more often not getting to the altar at all.

Test Run for Marriage . . .

If the trends hold, Shu and her boyfriend will spend a year or so living together, working out the kinks about who does the dishes and who cooks and which kind of Soft Scrub to use on the bathtub. Their lives as single adults will gradually merge into a fused household, although they are likely to keep their checking accounts separate, at least for the time being. As the rush of initial excitement passes, they will grow comfortable with each other and settle into their combined routines.

At some point after their first anniversary of living together, they will begin to hear the insistent drumbeat from their parents to make it official, and many of their friends will begin to pair up as well. Although the majority of young people today think of living together as a normal step on the relationship road, what distinguishes Shu from others are the signals she receives from her friends and family about the ultimate endpoint. This is not the first in a string of live-in relationships, but rather a test run for marriage. She and her boyfriend will move in together with a clear end goal: marriage.

Ethan met his girlfriend, Zoe, when they were both in college at Johns Hopkins, he for pre-med, she for psychology. Ethan grew up in San Diego, a bright student with a bright future. He got into his dream school, Johns Hopkins, and moved east at age eighteen with his eyes set on becoming a doctor. Almost immediately, he met Zoe, who was living in the same dorm. She was everything he wanted in a woman, and they clicked immediately. "I go for ambitious, career-oriented women who I can talk to," he says, and Zoe fit the mold. "I like women who want to make something out of themselves. Women who are capable of balancing a career and balancing family. And women who can complement me."

The two began seeing each other often. Their relationship was solidified when tragedy struck Ethan's family. His father committed suicide. At about the same time, his mother was filing for divorce from Ethan's stepfather, her second divorce in a relatively short period. If not for Zoe, he says, "if I wasn't able to talk to her and tell her everything that was going on in my life, I don't think I would have stayed in school." But finish he did, in four years with a double major.

At the end of their senior year, they both decided to take a year off from school and work. Zoe found a job in Baltimore, Ethan one in Bethesda, "and things just worked out." They moved in together that summer. At that point, he says, they were both considering marriage, but Ethan was hesitant to move ahead. "I didn't want to marry someone unless I lived with them for some time before. My mother's been divorced twice. I don't want to get divorced. So, I think that's a really good way to know if things are meant to be."

They regarded living together as a trial run for marriage. "I mean, if we can't live together when we're not married, how would we be able to live together when we were married? So, yeah, to me it was just as much preparation for marriage as was dating."

Yet instead of marrying at the end of their trial run, they chose to postpone a little longer while they finished up school and settled into their careers. Marriage will happen in due time, though. Ethan is certain of it. "If she can get an internship at Hopkins, I would have no hesitation about getting married at that time. I just don't want us to be married and away from each other. Our relationship is as close to perfect as you can get. I think we complement each other extremely well."

Ethan and Zoe are well matched, coming from similar families and sharing similar outlooks on life—and on their life together. They agree on the importance of their both having careers, she as a psychologist, he as a doctor. They see children on the horizon, and they get along with each other's families. They see in each other the qualities they want in a lifelong partner. For them, living together is designed to work out any kinks that might arise and to test-drive the relationship before taking the plunge.

. . . Versus Serial Cohabitation

One rung down, however, are those who are heading into the navy as a last resort, have a job on a construction site after dropping out of community college, or are adrift without a clear idea of where they want to go or what they want to be. Without solid prospects for steady work at a steady wage, marriage seems out of the question. More often than not, couples in this position will move in together, but—unlike Ethan and Zoe—they are not using cohabitation as a testing ground for marriage. Rather, they are moving in together as a way to combine finances, save some money on rent, or because other living arrangements suddenly evaporated. For this group, moving in together is more often an unplanned slide into coupledom than a conscious decision to see if they might be compatible as a married couple. More often than not, these couples do not marry at all.

Indeed, one of the most striking differences between swimmers and treaders lies in this interim choice: living together. Although living together is increasingly common among all young adults, treaders are more often serial cohabiters and they more often have children. "Affluent college kids don't raise children while living together," says Network associate member Maria Kefalas, "but lower- and working-class kids do. It's much more often a 'shotgun cohabitation.' "[10]

Tanya and her boyfriend, Jackson, have lived together for five years, since the birth of her third child (his first). The two didn't put much thought into their decision to move in together after their five-year-old was born. "It just happened," she says. "Maybe it was the baby."

Tanya likes the stability of their relationship. "I like the support physically and financially. I feel real secure," she says. She works as a teacher's assistant in a public school and holds a part-time job at a parks and recreations program to help make ends meet for her children, ages ten, nine, and five. Jackson, meanwhile, works as a mechanic. Their relationship is no great shakes, but it isn't abusive or a huge strain, either, a bonus in Tanya's eyes. She knows all too well what the alternative is like.

Tanya got pregnant in high school with her oldest daughter, but the relationship was abusive and it ended within two years. Her next boyfriend, the father of her second child, was also "a mistake." "He was into drugs and couldn't do it," she says of that relationship. Tanya's bad luck is fairly common among our treaders. Many of their relationships are fragile and short-term—more like a string of live-in dates.

Today, Tanya and Jackson occasionally talk about getting married, but she says, "I think it's just talk. We can jump the broom and call it marriage. We don't need a legal obligation right now with me trying to go to school and me wanting to get a house." Part of their hesitation is economic. "He truly believes he's supposed to be the breadwinner and I shouldn't work. Work on more cars, then I will," she says with a laugh.

This breadwinner role that Tanya mentions is a key reason why the relationships of treaders less frequently "convert" to marriage. Both Tanya and Jackson badly want to fulfill what they see as the "normal" way to family: Jackson earning enough so that Tanya can stay home with the children. He would be happy to be able to provide for her and the children, to fulfill that simple American dream. But even this modest goal is so hard to accomplish these days. The factory job is gone, and the earnings of men without a college degree continue to fall or at best stagnate. Tanya's job, like most low-skill jobs in retail, health care, and the helping professions, is low paid, part-time, and without benefits.

Men in particular have always broached the idea of marriage only when they feel financially able to support a family. Many studies have found that men who have unsteady or part-time jobs are more likely to live with a partner than to get married. This pattern is most evident when using education as a measure of economic security. The odds of high school dropouts living together are nearly twice as high as those for college grads. The difficulty of providing for a family is a primary reason why marriage rates plummeted in the Depression, and it is one reason why living together has increased today. Without the means, treaders less often convert those relationships into marriage. For this group of young people, a marriage license has in some respects become "just a piece of paper." These couples are not against marriage, nor do they think that marriage is outdated. Rather, the marriage they idealize—the marriage they see in the movies with the steady job, a nice house, two kids and a dog—is always just out of their reach.

If cohabiting relationships were enduring, few would blink an eye at these statistics. But the world of relationships is anything but stable. Michelle is actually right on track, if trends are any indication.

Michelle dropped out of community college at age nineteen and has held a string of jobs, the most recent as an assistant to an accountant, for $11.50 an hour. Her boyfriend, Robbie, works as a security guard at a casino. The two have been together for seven years, with five of those spent living together. They have a daughter, Missy, who just turned two—"the best thing that ever happened to us," says Michelle, although Missy was not planned.

However, Michelle is now having serious reservations about her relationship with Robbie. She has dreams and goals, and she's not sure he's as ambitious and on track as she'd like him to be. "I'm hoping we'll be together for the long run," she says, "but I don't know. I had pretty much almost broken it off with him last year. It was just like to the point where I don't know what he's doing, I don't know where he wants us to go. You know? And I don't think he does, either."

Michelle will likely join the roughly half of all cohabiting couples who split up by year five. In fact, in a recent study of couples who live to-gether, only 10 percent were still living together five years later, and an-other 44 percent had married. The majority of those who had married were college-educated and employed. Before concluding that this col-lege group has higher moral character, however, consider how the con-version rate widens as income declines. Among women living in poverty, only 31 percent had married their partners. For those better off, 42 percent had married. Money clearly matters. It makes life more sta-ble, not to mention more enjoyable. There is nothing worse than bills hanging overhead or a debt collector calling to make tempers snap, and relationships break. Disillusionment on both parts sets in more quickly when the rent is overdue. Even more stress is piled on when the man of the household, traditionally the breadwinner, cannot hold a job or earn what he considers necessary to fulfill his role. Under these circum-stances, the woman in the relationship may end up earning more and supporting him, but she may choose to institute a "pay to stay" rule, in which case he may simply opt to leave.

And Baby Makes . . . Two

The serial nature of the more tenuous relationships of treaders would be of less concern if it weren't for the children. More often than not in these relationships, the woman has a child. Children, in fact, are one of the biggest distinctions in our story of diverging destinies. While well-positioned young people see children as disrupting their plans and forc-ing them to put dreams on hold, those with less optimistic futures approach children and marriage differently. The Shus of this generation, with their hard-earned credentials and enormous potential, are delaying both marriage and children because they have a clear plan for their futures and ample personal resources to get there. It is possible, and some say likely, that these women are getting pregnant as often as those without college degrees, but because of their brighter futures, they more often terminate their pregnancies, which would, in their view, foreclose their futures. In contrast, the Tanyas and Jacksons, whose future choices are more constrained and who are furiously treading against the currents, are delaying marriage but not children. And why not? With futures that hold limited promise in education and work, the prospect of having a child is less disruptive and is, instead, a potential source of meaning to fill holes created by limited opportunities in other realms.

"I don't think many people aspire to be single mothers," says Network chair Frank Furstenberg, who has followed the lives of a group of teen mothers in Baltimore since 1965, most recently chronicled in his book *Destinies of the Disadvantaged: The Politics of Teenage Childbearing.* "They don't set out thinking, *'I'm going to raise a child and I don't want a man around.'* Yet when they do find themselves pregnant, the choice of keeping the baby is an easier one to make. Often those around them have children, their futures are not ascending a fast ladder of success, and they view having a child as a positive turning point.

"You really have to get inside the heads of these women who are making decisions to understand them," Furstenberg goes on. "Often the school, the family background, peer groups, neighborhoods all provide cues to people about what their future prospects are going to be, and those cues influence the decisions they'll make along the way—how vigilant to be about contraception, when to begin sexual relationships, and what to do if they become pregnant. All those decisions are different depending on the social world you're part of."

That social world contributes greatly to the diverging paths leading up to marriage. Those with more education and, in some respects, more to lose delay marriage and children as they get settled and set, using the span spent living together as a chance to work out the kinks. Those with less on the line delay marriage but not children, and their stints at living together are shorter and less frequently lead to marriage. Marriage itself is a dividing line marking the prospects of the swimmers and the treaders. Those more hopeful that life ahead will come with a good job, some sense of stability, and maybe even a lifelong partner are more likely to eventually take the march down the aisle.

Divided Prospects

The exalted pedestal on which many young adults place marriage might be worrisome on some level. But more worrisome are those who act first and think later. Even in marriage, where one might think love makes few distinctions, we found a sharp contrast in both the timing and the success of the marriages of the swimmers and treaders. Like good schools and safe neighborhoods, happy and successful marriages and families are yet another variation of class privilege in American society. Those with a college education are delaying marriage and children, but their marriages are more successful as a result. While many treaders are moving in together without marrying, a small group of them—many of whom have skipped the critical step of college—are marrying quickly. About one in five young adults marry before age twenty-five today. While this may warm the hearts of those who are worried about the demise of marriage, they may want to think twice. These marriages are more likely to struggle and end in divorce.

At twenty-three, Grace looks back and wishes she had done things differently. She and Larry are both from a small town in Iowa. They married at age seventeen, with special permission from a judge and her parents, because they did not want to be apart when Larry left for California and the army. "He only had so much leave time," says Grace, "and we wanted to have a big wedding. We got married Saturday, and left Monday for California."

For young people like Grace and her peers, who hail from more religious, rural, or disadvantaged backgrounds, the cues they receive are clear: Marriage is one of the first steps "adults" take. Views on marriage are frequently shaped by our surroundings. Religious families, for example, more often marry early because they believe deeply in the sanctity of the institution. In rural towns across the country, reasons for marrying early have less to do with the dictates of the church than with the limited options available to young people and the strong signals their families and the community send to them. As one young man from small-town Iowa says of dating, "I mean, you might as well marry her because you guys have been together for so long and it's not gonna make a difference. It's kind of like the concept around here." Marriage is just what you do at a certain point in your life. Rural youth who are not college-bound see no reason to wait. They have often known their girlfriends or boyfriends since elementary school. They have jobs, even if not great ones. What else is there? Indeed, unlike their counterparts in more urban settings, their choices both of mates and of life paths are more restricted and, ironically, more clearly defined.

These fast-starters differ from other groups because their marriages are often a first step, not the last, in a chain of adult decisions and achievements. Like their counterparts at midcentury, they are marrying early on the assumption that marriage is a, if not *the,* key marker of adulthood. They wed and find a job in short order. These fast-starters are also more likely to have children, which rapidly alters the rules of the game. Although no one regrets having their son or daughter, many say that if they had it to do over, they would wait longer, and get their educations out of the way first.

Or as Grace says, "What would I do different? I'll answer that. I would've waited a little longer to have my kids until I was settled, had a little money, knew for sure everything. But like I said, I don't regret my kids at all. I just wished more for them, that I could give them more... There's a perfect plan, but you can't always follow that."

Grace realizes now that she made a rash decision to marry at seventeen. Her marriage was stressful, she says, "money-wise and the kids. You think you got it all planned out. You fall in love with this person and you go out two or three years and you think, *Okay, we're gonna get married and have our perfect little house, be comfortable every day, have kids.* I really never had anything for myself." She had no "me" time.

In the end, Grace, says, "Larry wanted his space. He wanted independence. I begged him to stay, but he said, no, not this time." A week later, "I found out about her." Grace says that if only she and Larry had lived together first and postponed having children, they might have been spared the pain of divorce.

They were too young to be married in this day and age. Sixty percent of those who marry as Grace did before age eighteen will be divorced by age thirty-four. One-half of those who marry by age twenty will not make it to their fifteenth wedding anniversary. This compares with the roughly 35 percent divorce rate of those who postpone marriage until after age twenty-five.[11]

Diverging Destinies at the Altar

"For the non-college-educated population," claims the National Marriage Project's *The State of Our Unions 2007,* "the marriage situation remains gloomy." Divorce rates by social class are much more pronounced than they were in the 1950s.[12] On many levels, delaying marriage is not so bad, especially given the high divorce rates today. Marriages would become sturdier if they were based on more planning and compatibility. Perhaps that is one reason why the marriages of the college-educated are stronger and happier, according to *State of Our Unions,* and why their marriage rates are up. "Their marriages are more egalitarian, well-matched in education and earnings. The share saying their marriages are very happy has held steady while other segments of the population have been declining in marital happiness." These marriages are stronger, we might add, because the more elite young adults have the privilege to concentrate on their futures early in life, and that ultimately concentrates privilege, which creates a different strategy toward marriage.

As one young woman who married early says, "It makes things a lot easier if you do it the 'normal' way. I wish I had done that. I wish I had gone to school first. And then got a job, and then got married, and then had kids. It just makes everything so much easier. You don't have to find babysitters. You don't have to tune out *SpongeBob* while you're doing homework. You can pay things off in order. You start off with no bills making lots of money. That starts you off in a very different place in life."

Not only college secures this foothold on a more delayed strategy. In addition, the norms, neighborhoods, networks, and opportunities that young people cultivate early in life position them on their future courses.

Young adults are striving to develop their own personal satisfaction, independent of others, which is a commendable goal. In a world with seemingly unlimited opportunities and time—as well as uncertainty—planning may be even more necessary. Gaining credentials and maturity early in life, without the distractions of romance and children, may be just the ticket to creating a more solid foundation from which to embrace a lifelong companion.

But delay how long? Sociologist Frances Goldscheider, who studies the changing roles in marriage, worries that marriage is being put off for too long. Time, after all, is ticking. Although women often feel the imperative of their biological clock, men think they are immune. "Men often say that they want three to four kids 'later,'" Goldscheider says. "But what happens to your retirement savings, let alone plans, when you have three kids in college in your late sixties?" The young men in her classroom look at her, puzzled. "It's the first time they've thought about it. They might not have a biological clock, but they have an earnings clock that is not much different." Although delaying marriage allows one to get all of one's ducks in a row and get settled on a solid path, there is a danger of waiting too long. While no one advocates for a return to shotgun marriages or unhappy couples trapped in unhappy marriages, it is worth asking: How late is too late? What will happen to marriage as more young people delay? We return to these questions at the end of the book.

These very different paths through marriage and parenthood risk hardening our growing class and income divisions in society. On the whole, people tend to marry partners who have similar backgrounds. Those who have college degrees tend to marry others with college degrees. Those with money marry others with money. There are, of course, exceptions, but in general, we rarely marry "up" or "down." We also know that marriage confers some important benefits. It is associated with better health, more income, and improved well-being. Given the tendency to choose partners who are similar to us, and the tendency for those with less affluence and education to live together instead of marrying, the question is, will the elite more often find success in, and benefit from, marriage? Will these benefits exacerbate the already growing rift between the swimmers and treaders of this world? As *The State of Our Unions* puts it, "America is becoming a nation divided not only by education and income, but by unequal family structures."

5

The Unlonely Crowd: Friends and Social Networks

Friends: Would anyone choose to live without them? It would be a very empty life, indeed, were it not for friends. As children, friends let us join in, they cushion our fears, they offer community. Seeing friends ensconced in the new fifth-grade classroom makes all the worries about the new teacher and school year disappear. As we age, friends do much the same, but for bigger decisions, bigger challenges. Friends allow us to be ourselves, flaws exposed and guard dropped. They are, as essayist Joseph Epstein writes, "not concerned with what might be made of one another, but only with the enjoyment of one another." To have a friend is to be healthier, happier, and to have a connection to a community, even a community of just two.

The role of friends should not be underestimated. The stronger our ties to friends, the more likely they will help us out in a crisis (and we them), be sounding boards to our major decisions, and smooth life's bumps. The wider our network of friends, the more likely we are to meet or hear about a future employer or another valuable connection, to expand our views or interests, and to encounter new opportunities. In old age, friends often fill the role of a spouse who has died, preventing us from becoming socially isolated and alone, and, in doing so, keeping us healthy and happy longer. Ultimately, these close personal connections increase our trust in our fellow man and encourage us to cooperate on larger efforts that may not only benefit us directly but also contribute to the greater good. Friends, it turns out, can even help us ward off the common cold.

Friendship also has a dark side, however. Friends can shape our tendency to drink or eat too much, to abandon exercise, or to take too many risks or surround ourselves with too many negative influences. Among young women, friendships can be a format for talking ceaselessly about problems, to the point that some women become clinically depressed as a result. More starkly, three-fourths of murders are committed by someone we know. It is this darker side of friendships that has caught the interest of researchers studying social networks and their impact on our lives in ways both big and small.

In the book *Connected: The Surprising Power of Our Social Networks and How They Shape Our Lives,* Harvard sociologist Nicholas Christakis and University of San Diego political scientist James Fowler find that the size of our social network and our position in it matter more in the end than race, class, gender, or education in whether we get ahead or fall behind. Christakis and Fowler call this "positional" inequality, and in a nutshell it means that people with many ties become better connected to jobs, information, healthy behaviors, and income. Not so surprising to anyone who has ever networked to get a job. But what is truly remarkable is the independent role that friends play in shaping our positions in life—beyond standard influences like income, education, or occupational status. Those with fewer friends or friends who are less connected get left farther and farther behind. "Life," as the Chinese philosopher Tehyi Hsieh has said, "is partly what we make it, and partly what is made by the friends whom we choose."

Young adulthood is the prime time for forging these increasingly critical networks. As we age, the core group of people we can call on to discuss important matters shrinks. Making friends and connecting with others during this time of life might just set the stage for a healthier and more contented future life. Of course it could just as easily set the stage for an unhappier, unhealthier, and less contented life. Our friendships help seal our fates.

Communities of Like Minds

As school is extended and marriage and parenting are delayed, friends have become more prominent, and for a longer time, in the lives of young people. Therefore, the role of social networks has gained more importance. In the not-so-distant past, some of life's biggest decisions were made across the dinner table from a spouse. Today, those decisions are more often being made in the company of friends, across the table in a café. To get a handle on this change, consider this. In 1980, about 40 percent of twenty-somethings were married between ages twenty and twenty-four. Today, half as many young adults are married at that age.[1] Likewise, the number of young people living on their own or with roommates, and not with their parents, has skyrocketed. In 1970, only about 16 percent of young adults ages twenty through twenty-nine were never married and living on their own. Today, the figure has just about doubled.[2] As the sitcoms have so aptly recorded with each passing decade, we've moved from *Father Knows Best* to *All in the Family* to *Friends, Sex and the City,* and *Entourage*.

Craig, a twenty-seven-year-old New Yorker working on his master's degree, captures this shift in his description of a perfect weekend. "I'd play sports," he says, "go out to drink some beers, maybe go out to dance, have a fun time. Sunday I get up at eight in the morning and I go to play baseball till like one o'clock. That's basically my free time. Since I got into grad school, I picked up sailing, surfing, golfing. Recently I've been going golfing almost every day." No wife, no children, no obligations other than graduate school. Until the 1980s, there would have been all three. The median age when women have their first child has risen dramatically over the past few decades, and the share of women who are childless at age thirty has risen significantly as well. Among those who turned thirty in 1984, only about 15 to 18 percent of women of all racial and ethnic groups were childless. In 2000, nearly 50 percent of white women and 25 percent of black and Hispanic women were childless at age thirty. Just twenty years ago, a man like Craig would be spending his weekends with his wife and kids. Instead, Craig hangs out with his friends.

Friends take center stage for other reasons as well. Many young adults have also just come out of one of the most intensely social periods of life, especially if they were in college or the military. Dorms, platoons, and foxholes—all these factors contribute to bonding and strong friendships. Young adults are also more mobile. Unencumbered by family and responsibilities, they can pack up and move across country or to new cities for jobs and a new start in life. Once there, they must make an effort to meet new people—and they do.

To Mia, her loose networks of friends work perfectly for her at this time in her life. At twenty-eight, her work as a marine biologist has taken her from Hawaii to Atlanta with several stops in between. She meets new friends wherever she goes, and the casualness of these friendships allows her to pack up and go without serious tugs of regret when a new job demands she relocate. "This may sound callous," she says, "but if I wanted to pick up and move, I would leave these friends behind. We would remain in touch, I'm sure, but I like the ability to make my decisions and not have those decisions uproot someone else." It also helps that in this day of social networking, email, and Twitter, Mia can more easily maintain her friendships.

The casualness of these friendships will be an important characteristic of her expanding network, and in that casualness is an important boost to her life chances. With every move and every new set of friends, Mia is enlarging the circle of people she can call on for advice, job leads, and dates. Her very mobility is what both expands her network and keeps it loose and wide. Although Americans of all ages who remain in their hometowns or neighborhoods are more likely than those who have left to say they have more local friends, those who have left say they have a *broader* social network.[3] As we show later, broader networks are an important factor that distinguishes those who swim and those who tread as they move into adulthood.

As young adults settle into new cities or new neighborhoods in their hometowns, they seek new communities of like minds. Ethan Watters chronicled these new "families" in his recent book *Urban Tribes: A*

Generation Redefines Friendship, Family, and Commitment. Groups of friends band together against the anonymity of new lives in strange cities. They fill in for family during holidays. They host parties and share meals. They twitter, they e-vite, they go on vacation together. Members may come and go with jobs or relocations, expanding or contracting the "tribe," but its existence is constant. Everyone in the tribe has a role: Some lead, others follow, some are needy, some are impatient, some are embarrassing, others are controlling. In short, the tribe is family.

Families of origin remain very important to young adults, especially their relationships with parents. But these family relationships naturally change as children leave home and begin to live independently. In our interviews, we heard continuously from young adults about how important their parents, siblings, and other family members are to them. They regularly seek their advice. They talk to their parents often, even daily, and their sisters and brothers are a constant presence in their lives. If they live in the same town or city as their families, they go home regularly for family dinners or even to do the laundry. In fact, most young adult children are quick to describe their parents as close or even best friends. But there are some topics that are better suited for friends than for family, even if family relationships are close. When we ask young people what they talk about with their parents, for example, they are often quick to say "everything but sex," and to then mention other personal matters that are more likely to be shared in their romantic relationships or with friends.

"When something big is on the line," says Charlie, the twenty-two-year-old who is just starting out in Ball State University in Indiana, "friends will be there for you. There's been many times when I have a problem and I'll call my friends before my dad or family. It's always better to get a view of a peer, and you won't be judged by a friend, unlike my dad. Friends truly are lifesavers in many cases."

"Friends are definitely taking the place of family in major ways," says Anna, who works at Twentieth Century–Fox. She moved to Hollywood as a twenty-two-year-old straight out of college, leaving behind friends and family to strike out on her own. She made friends quickly, as many young people do when they're in a new city. She met some people at her job, her roommate had a set of friends, and before she knew it, she had a close group of a dozen friends she calls on for big and small decisions alike.

"When you work seventy hours a week, they become a huge part of your life," Anna says. Like Watters's tribe, Anna and her friends create a constantly shifting web of support. "Since I'm not near my parents now and not relying on them for smaller things, I do rely on friends more in ways that my family might provide. We pick each other up at the airport—that's totally a spouse thing. When I was sick with a kidney infection, my friend took me to the emergency room. You just do the things when you can. If you have a job, you're not going to cut out early to do something, but you find a person who has a schedule that will allow them to help out. A friend of mine who is writing a book—she took me to the airport at a weird hour."

In many ways, Anna and her friends are creating communities and networks exactly like those that Robert Putnam in *Bowling Alone: The Collapse and Revival of American Community* claims have all but died. Although odds are that Anna doesn't know her immediate neighbor across the street, which Putnam argues is at the crux of community's demise, Anna and her friends are pitching in for their "neighbors" even though those neighbors are halfway across the city and they only recently met one another. They are forming communities based not on proximity, but on like-mindedness. Anna and her friends share the same ideals and goals for life. They are in the creative world of Hollywood, struggling to get recognized in a competitive field. Most of them are from similar backgrounds, with college degrees and parents who were solidly middle class. They probably even share the same political ideals. And the community they've formed isn't limited to just Los Angeles. Today more likely than not, their community stretches far beyond Los Angeles to friends and friends of friends who live in Indiana, New York, and all the way to Hong Kong.

Not all young adults, however, have these close, interdependent friendships. Instead, they continue to rely largely on their immediate families for support and networking. This can be detrimental because tight-knit family ties are not likely to open as many new opportunities as are broad and loose networks of acquaintances.[4]

Indeed, the degree to which individuals rely on their families versus friends and acquaintances for social support has been an enduring distinction between the working class and the middle and upper classes. The working class has traditionally relied more singularly on kin for social support than the middle and upper classes.[5] This does not mean that young adults of greater means are quick to abandon their families. Families continue to offer support for all young adults today, and that support remains important. What it does mean is that swimmers more often combine this family support with other kinds of contacts, ranging from dear friends to mere acquaintances. They have wider networks. This pattern of distinction between working-class and middle- and upper-class individuals holds whether class is defined by occupational prestige or by income or level of education. The reason for the narrower social base of treaders stems from a broad set of complex forces that land individuals in their status. However, as we show, our social networks determine a lot more than what we do on a Saturday night.

Choose Your Friends Wisely

The communities of like minds that Anna and others have forged are at the heart of the social networks that Nicholas Christakis and James Fowler talk about in *Connected*. Anna's core friends have other friends that she may or may not know. Their friends have friends. Those friends of friends have friends. These three degrees of separation will become the sphere of influence in Anna's life. According to Christakis and Fowler, it is the friends of friends of friends who will be more integral in connecting Anna to the job leads and other important connections in life than her immediate, core set of friends. After all, her core set of friends are all in the same boat, but if they each have five additional friends, and those friends have five more friends, then Anna's circle of contacts for potential jobs, advice, and opportunities grows exponentially. Depending on her level of sociability, she may be at the heart of a broad network of friends and acquaintances or she may be at the periphery. If she's at the heart of it, she will personally know more friends of friends because she will straddle wider groups. If she's at the periphery, she may just stick to a core set of friends and never be introduced to those at the far reaches of the network. Her position within the network will impact its eventual reach.

These social networks—and their importance to young adults' prospects—get to the heart of where destinies diverge between swimmers and treaders. If a person's friends are gangbangers and drug dealers, for example, his or her network quickly becomes a liability rather than a support net. Mariela, for example, fell in with a wrong crowd early in life. "I was the black sheep of my high school," she says. "Everybody knew who I was, but it wasn't a good reputation, you know?" Her reputation stemmed from the company she kept, "because I hung out with a bad crowd, like the gangsters and all that." Mariela graduated early from high school and went to work at KFC. She would later enroll in a technical course for training as a medical assistant. But even then, she says, "I just couldn't get away. You only saw people you knew. I fell right back into it." She was having difficulty, in other words, extricating herself from her own, in this case negative, social network. She had no bridges to other, more positive networks.

Mariela was nineteen when her thirty-year-old then-boyfriend proposed to her. A girlfriend at work had introduced the two of them, and they'd dated for about a year. He was living in a halfway house at the time, working for minimum wage. Mariela had a young daughter from a one-night stand and she briefly considered accepting his proposal, because she thought no one else would be willing to love her and her child. However, shortly after he proposed, a member of the crew was shot and killed at age thirty-three after spending much of his adult life in the gang. This was a turning point for Mariela, who suddenly saw her future laid out bare before her. She knew if she didn't leave now, she'd end up in a dead end, either literally or figuratively. She extricated herself by giving her parents temporary custody of her daughter and joining the navy at age twenty. Within a few months she met her future husband, whom she married right after her twenty-first birthday. The navy, for Mariela, became a bridge to a different social network of both adults and peers.

Friendship can be viewed as a personal choice, freely entered into, but it is formed in particular social, economic, and cultural circumstances, and this has a very significant impact on the people we meet. "If people's main support and connection are with peers who do not have positive friends," says Network chair Frank Furstenberg, who as a sociologist has studied the effects of neighborhoods and friends on the life course, "they're likely to miss out on important supports in the form of connections or information about moving into conventional adult roles. So they can't provide the resources that more positive peers can in bridging a move into a conventional social role." These bridging ties are often the less intimate personal relationships. They are the wide network that people cultivate as they move through life—acquaintances, co-workers, referrals. Young adults who are treading water often lack these broader networks, as do their parents.

Law school student Aviva says of some of her elite classmates at Cornell, "Their father calls up an acquaintance and says 'Hey, I'm gonna take you out to dinner. We'll be talking about my son's future job.'" The reach of these parents is integral in expanding the horizons of their children, finding them summer jobs or internships, and exposing them to new ideas and ways of living. The fathers of Aviva's friends probably don't personally know each of these contacts, but they are able to call on them because their social networks give them ready access to others. Stanford sociologist Mark Granovetter, who has studied weak and tight ties, finds that most people land their jobs not through close friends but from people they had talked to only occasionally or even rarely.

Randy, in his late twenties and still single, is slowly realizing the value of a wide network of contacts. He grew up in a middle-class suburban subdivision outside Detroit. As a kid, he was very active in sports. "There must have been thirty or forty kids within three blocks of my house growing up," he says. "All within a six- or seven-year age difference. With a front yard like ours, we'd have full-fledged baseball games, football games, basketball games." He continues to form friendships based around sports, playing softball and soccer in the summers and moving the competition indoors in the winter. Now five years out of college, he is working as a journalist back in his hometown of Detroit and sharing a rented home with several guys.

When Randy was growing up, he did not realize that his subdivision carried a stigma. Families in the wealthier subdivisions looked down on the kids from Randy's neighborhood, and everyone talked about how much trouble they caused. Through sports, he was able to develop critical bridging ties and as a result he avoided being tagged a troublemaker. "I was an athlete," he says, "so a lot of those kids talked to me." That was not the case for his neighborhood pals. The guys from the wealthier subdivision "wouldn't talk to them because they were from the neighborhood," he remembers.

Randy continued to expand his network after college, even as he continued to live in the "trouble" neighborhood. While working as a reporter on the local paper, he covered a community group for young adults. "I thought this might be interesting," he said, "so I called the guy in charge of it. And I started making friends and going every now and then." His connections there would eventually lead him to the comfortable home he is currently renting, with the option to buy.

Despite his early start on the wrong side of town, Randy managed to use sports to broaden his horizons, and he was not afraid to try new things, like writing about the community group. While Aviva's friends had parents who made sure their children were exposed to potential connections, or who deliberately intervened on their behalf to set them up in life, Randy managed to do it for himself through a growing network of friends and acquaintances, first through baseball and soccer, and later through work.

Young adults who are forging ahead with a solid education and a good job are often distinguished by a wide circle of friends. Ben, the Chicago lawyer, for example, stays in touch with a diverse and widespread circle of friends from both college and high school. "My friends are scattered to the four corners of the earth, but I have a good network of people who come to me with their problems and I go to them with my problems. I also have a tight network here at work as well." A friend from high school recently moved to Chicago from New York, and Ben helped him get settled and even provided him with a few job leads. Likewise Edgar, a thirty-four-year-old African American man who went to a historically black college, has an expansive network of fraternity brothers spread around the country. Unhappy in his job and looking to move on, he put out feelers to his friends, who in turn spread the word. He was interviewing for new positions within a month.

On the other hand, Kelly's circle is small and much more confined. At age twenty-nine, she is the single mother of three young children. She is unemployed and is reluctantly living with her mother in St. Paul. Kelly struggles to find work and day care for her children, and because she does not have a broad network of friends and acquaintances, she finds jobs through the want ads. She is at risk of sinking deeper into poverty. While many other factors influence her situation, she is nevertheless orbiting in a small, insular world, and as a result is less aware of opportunities that might help her to find better child care or learn about job-training options or otherwise broaden her horizons.

Kelly's preponderance of tight-knit ties and the lack of loose ties also increase her risk of poverty. Low-income families are more inclined to rely on close kinship ties for support, limiting their network of information and resources to those they know, and to those in similar circumstances.[6] Certain communities or neighborhoods can be too insular as well. Even the quintessential American small town can be hamstrung by its hallmark close ties. Although people in small towns watch out for one another, pitch in after tragedies, and foster a solid sense of "us," the counterpoint to these close ties is that a person's reputation precedes him or her. If a person is born on the "wrong side of the tracks," getting ahead in life becomes difficult precisely because of these intimate, tight connections. One's reputation is everything, and a misstep can lead to being cast out of the "in" crowd and the job leads, offers, and other privileges of status, sometimes for generations.

"More and more poverty scholars are thinking about the ways in which persistent poverty is perpetuated because the poor are isolated," says Cynthia Duncan, director of the Carsey Institute, a research think tank focused on rural policy. "Those who are isolated are trapped in small, homogeneous, often family-based social worlds where they find emotional support but few connections to a larger world of opportunity. Their ideas about who they are, what they can become, and where they fit—their cultural tool kit, as sociologist Ann Swidler has described it— has been shaped by these immediate kin and friends who are in the same disadvantaged circumstances. Opportunity requires connections to a wider world that can expand that tool kit."

As one young Iowan we interviewed says of her childhood, "You've always known from growing up whose parents had money, and...if you were popular or not, or if the teachers would like you, or if you got into swing choir, or if you got into National Honor Society. I mean, you kind of knew."

Which comes first, the poverty or the limited network, is a complicated question, but regardless of the direction of influence, a lack of loose ties is often evident when poverty is present. As in all things in life, a healthy balance is needed between close and loose ties.

The bottom line: Life's choices are not only individual decisions. We're in a web of social connections that spread far beyond the people we see every day, and some of those influences are positive, and some are negative. These networks may be an overlooked avenue for lessening poverty and dead ends for a large group of young adults. Helping young people cultivate broader networks—with the right connections—could become a critical weapon in fighting poverty, crime, and other social problems. Today's "always on" networked world is providing just that bridge.

Can Facebook Help Treaders Swim?

"I already have 900 friends at NYU," incoming freshman Mike Scolnic told *The New Yorker* in 2007. Scolnic was talking about his Facebook friends, all of whom had signed on to NYU's Facebook page for incoming freshmen. They had checked one another out and had speculated about whether their roommate was a good fit based on his or her music, photos, and ramblings online. Students started keeping tabs on one another well in advance of their first Biology 101 class.

That Scolnic maintains nine hundred friends on Facebook is not unusual in today's always-on, networked world. Online communities such as Facebook or MySpace are at once shallow yet oddly intimate—public yet private. With regular postings and updates, friends can follow the quotidian ups and downs of life, post pictures, and join groups. Strung together, all of this information creates an intimacy that, although not the same as the intimacy gained from living together in a dorm or as roommates, is hardly glib or anonymous, either. Twitter, a microblog where people post "tweets" of information in 140 characters or less to anyone who subscribes, answers the age-old question among friends: "What's up?"...and then some. In some respects, the constant stream of tweets from the serial Twitter user is the virtual equivalent of living together.

The Internet and the social networking sites of young people today can be a stand-in for what elite families often provide for their children: exposure and contacts. The Internet is relatively classless today. In the past, wealthier families were much more likely to have an Internet connection in their homes than low-income families. However, this divide has became much less stark. A Pew survey in 2009 found that about 90 percent of those ages twelve through twenty-four were regularly online, and an earlier Pew survey in 2006 found that six in ten African Americans, and about eight in ten whites and English-speaking Hispanics, use the Internet. In fact, S. Craig Watkins, author of *The Young and the Digital: What Migration to Social Network Sites, Games and Anytime, Anywhere Media Means for Our Future,* finds that young African Americans access the Web for gaming, watching videos, and other social activities for 1.5 hours per day—often via mobile phones—compared with 30 minutes per day for white youths. Clearly, the majority of young adults now have online access.

Think of the Internet as one big schmoozer. When young adults are looking for a job or thinking of moving to another city, their first point of action is to log on to their social networking sites and advertise their plans. "I'm moving to Charlotte. Does anyone know someone who lives there?" Or they can post their résumé and let it be known they are looking for work. Before long, advice will come pouring in from all corners, and a few strong leads on jobs, housing, and new friends may pan out. This kind of mass networking can help young adults make a successful launch. The use of this type of networking is not confined to young adults, either. According to a 2007 survey by CareerBuilder.com, 45 percent of employers use search engines and social networking sites to research job candidates. Of course, there is a potential downside to this, too. Employers can use Facebook and other such sites to find out damaging private information about job applicants.

Social networking and digital media are instrumental in exposing young people to new ideas, broadening their horizons. Young adults who are regularly online confront opinions and ideas that are new to them. They actively participate by commenting on articles, blogging, or writing in forums, interacting with others who might have very different points of view. The Internet can open vistas, connecting people to one another with an ease that has never existed before. "Kids who have access to social networks," says *CauseWired* author Tom Watson in an interview, "are more socially conscious—they find out about more." Young people today are learning about the war in Darfur not from textbooks but from social networking causes. They are digging deeply into environmentalism. They are hearing opinions from Palestinians and Iraqis, which might challenge their take on world events. These young people are no longer limited to the confines of their neighborhoods; they have the world literally at their fingertips. This ability to find connections to causes that inspire or challenge worldviews, as well as the more mundane networks that might lead to jobs, can be invaluable to those with the fewest family resources.

Joseph Kahne, of the Civic Engagement Research Group at Mills College, finds that digital media are more readily reaching those who are typically overlooked—those who do not attend college. These youths are using social networking sites to find out about issues as often as college students, and they are having the same discussions online that college students have in their dorms. "We found that the more they participate in digital media," says Kahne, "the more they get that combination of exposure to both those who disagree and those who share core commitments. They get more exposure to a variety of perspectives." The Internet, of course, is not some Pollyana world where everyone gets along. We tend to balkanize online as we do offline, but so far, according to Kahne, there's little evidence to suggest that we segregate more online than off, and—in fact—some studies suggests that the cyberworld is more diverse than the physical world young Americans occupy today.

Not everyone who goes online ends up pitching in to end world hunger, of course. Many are just interested in keeping tabs on their friends and posting videos of cats doing tricks. However, even the most mundane socializing on Facebook or other social networks can widen young people's real-life networks. It can create the connections to friends of friends of friends that are often critical to getting ahead. When these networks are specialized, like the professional networking site LinkedIn, they can create both tight and loose ties—which, as noted earlier, can also foster opportunities for jobs or career advancement.

Online social networks can also help a person overcome common obstacles to making friends, such as shyness or the inability to find a community of like minds where one lives. Second Life, an online virtual world where players interact in social settings that mimic real life, allows people to be who they want to be, and to create new circles of compatible friends from around the globe. As one participant in Second Life puts it, "Me and a few friends [in Second Life] hold little parties for everyone usually shunned by society, like nerds, gay/bi, disabled, and just about anyone else that feels bad about themselves. Without Second Life, some people wouldn't have many friends." Another example of how virtual worlds can help overcome real-life problems is a project initiated by Global Kids, an organization in New York that helps urban youths become global community leaders. The program immersed young men in the juvenile justice system in a virtual world, Teen Second Life. For these teens, who felt marginalized and stigmatized because of their past actions, being a part of this virtual world empowered them to act as mentors. They became dedicated to keeping kids out of trouble in their offline lives. The virtual world helped them to make valuable connections with others, and it allowed them to see beyond the physical limits of their incarceration.

All this interconnectivity has the potential to widen the social networks of those whose physical networks are more confined and proscribed. Young adults in small towns or chronically poor communities or families can gain access to others with relative ease via the Internet. Whether this ability will broaden the web of connections and serve as an antidote to life situations that contribute to poverty and isolation remains to be seen. But it certainly has the potential to do so.

Creating a Wider Web

Friends and the social networks they create have always been an important factor in who people meet, work with, and even marry. What has changed recently is the longer and more prominent role that friends are playing in young adult lives as the amount of time most youths take between leaving their parents and setting up house with a new spouse or partner grows longer. This is also a stage of life in which young adults begin to plant stakes with initial jobs, routines, and patterns (some healthy, some not), dating and coupling up, and other momentous decisions. If social network researchers are right—and they certainly make a convincing argument—friends of friends of friends are central to determining young people's futures, not only because of who they are (their race, ethnicity, income, or education) but because of whom they are connected to many degrees outward.

Yet we also know that education determines the scope of a person's social network. Those with more education have more people to talk to about things that matter to them, and the chances of having wider networks of loose ties grows with every year of education.[7] High school graduates and even those with just some college circulate in very family-dominated social worlds. Indeed, those with college degrees, for example, have social networks that are nearly twice as large as those with only a high school diploma.[8] However, young adults can overcome this narrow vista much more easily than other, more intractable conditions, such as location, income, or even education. They can join community groups, seek out like minds online, get involved by volunteering, and make an effort to network. None of this takes money—just time.

Friendships can clearly provide a social boost to young adults' futures. The communities of like minds that many young adults are forming today—whether physically close or distant—are important forms of social capital they can exchange for more than just companionship. Friendships are also serving another purpose: They are becoming the "communities" of today. Whereas in the not-so-distant past, young adults had largely settled into physical communities by their mid- to late twenties, today those neighborhoods have yet to be. Instead, this generation is creating communities of like minds with their deep and wide networks of friends and acquaintances, online and off. It is in these more ephemeral communities where the barriers of class, race, and income might begin to break down.

6

The Parent–Child Lifeline

"Success in life is that your kids want to spend time with you once they've grown up." That truism, attributed to Paul Orfalea, founder of Kinko's, is number 99 of the "The Way I See It" series printed on the ubiquitous Starbucks cups.

Somewhere between Orfalea's childhood and his children's, the world of parenting tilted. Not so long ago, parenting reinforced a distinct line between the realms of adulthood and childhood. Children were to be seen but not heard. They played together in other rooms while adults socialized. They ran free in the neighborhood, learning life's lessons by the school of hard knocks. Many parents today, in contrast, are highly involved in their children's lives. Children and parents actually seem to like each other. They shop together at the mall, gossip on the phone, hang out watching the game, and share details of their lives that past generations would never fathom sharing. Parents enjoy the emotional support they receive from their children, and the validation that they still matter. Children enjoy, and often expect, the emotional and financial support they receive from their parents. Some, like Diana West in *Death of the Grown-Up,* have condemned this blurring of boundaries, attributing a rise in the "failure to launch" to parents who can't let go or are just too indulgent.

What do the relationships between parents and children look and feel like as the children move through the early adult years? Much is known about relationships between teenagers and their parents, on the early end of life, and between middle-aged "kids" and elderly parents, on the other. But virtually nothing is known about how the relationships between children and their parents are renegotiated as children become adults. We are especially interested in understanding the ramifications of a longer, more complicated passage to adulthood on these relationships, and how different types of parent–child connections affect the success of young people in a competitive, high-stakes world.

The Network's in-depth interviews with young adults provide an intimate window into the relationships they have with their parents. We uncovered three basic types. The first type is the extremely involved parents of most well-positioned young people. This group has carefully nurtured their children's ability to converse easily and with confidence and to interact comfortably with adults. They have enrolled their children in activities and programs designed to expose them to the types of skills and manners they will need in a world that values critical thinking, leadership, and cooperation. The extremists among them, the infamous helicopter parents, are often mocked for their incessant hovering.

The second type of parents takes a more hands-off approach, mirroring how they themselves were raised. This group believes that children, once they are adults, must live in order to learn. Making mistakes is just part of the deal. While certain advantages come with this approach—for one, young people develop a realistic sense of what it means to be on their own—there are also costs.

The third type of parents is neglectful, at best, and may even be abusive. For young people in these families, parents are not a source of support, but are instead a source of great risk and hardship.

Of course, these basic types of relationships have always existed and, in reality, they fluctuate with the changing circumstances and needs of both parents and children. But as we will see, close and connected parent–child relationships are more typical today, representing a fundamental shift in family life. The absence of close ties is a riskier business now than it was in the past, and having neglectful or destructive relationships with parents is even riskier—especially considering how much support kids are getting from their parents when their relationships are good.

The Spotlight Moves to Kids

Parents today play much larger roles in the lives of their young adult children than ever before. One-half of young adults between eighteen and twenty-five say they see their parents daily, and nearly three-quarters say they see their parents at least once a week. Nearly two-thirds live within an hour of their parents. If they do not see one another, they talk on the phone regularly; nearly eight in ten young adults under age twenty-five talk with their parents by phone daily.[1] Thanks to cell phones, talk is cheap, and thanks to other forms of communication—Facebook, instant messaging, text messaging, Skype—staying in touch is also easy. It wasn't always that way. Many readers will recall waiting in line in dormitories to place expensive long-distance phone calls to parents each month, or every other week at best.

Leave, not stay: This is what most American parents in the recent past groomed their children to do. As Meredith Small points out in her cross-cultural look at child rearing, *Our Babies, Ourselves: How Biology and Culture Shape the Way We Parent,* American mothers in particular were socialized to foster autonomy and independence in their children from an early age. They put their children to sleep in cribs in separate rooms rather than bringing them into their own rooms, let alone their own beds. They preferred playpens and strollers to the prospect of nestling their babies to their bosom all day. Everything American parents did had the ultimate goal of preparing their offspring to stand on their own two feet as adults by age eighteen, if not sooner. American photographer Robert Frank inadvertently captured this impatience with childhood in his 1940s photograph of a New Orleans trolley car. In that picture, the children, clad in stiff suits and dresses, are seemingly in dress rehearsal for adulthood while the adults all stare and frown. Back then, adulthood was serious business, and the journey began early.

In the course of the last century, all of that changed. If the twentieth-century family were displayed in an animation flip-book, the image revealed as the pages whiz by would be of a child moving from the margins to the center of the page, worthy of the care, love, and investment of parents. Children are now, as the scholar Ivar Frones says, rendered useless economically but priceless emotionally.[2]

Not only are children in the center of the page, but they are present for many more pages. Several major shifts at the turn of the last century were critical in moving children to a more sheltered status. The first was compulsory education and child labor laws. These laws reflected the shift in society's perception of children. They were no longer considered miniature adults; instead, they were seen as needing nurturing and protection. Children became people in their own right—and "childhood" and "adolescence" emerged as distinct periods of life characterized by unique developmental tasks and needs.

Even more important, the basic terms of life changed dramatically. We can now count on a long and reasonably healthy life span. In the last century, the average American's life span increased by twenty-five and thirty years, respectively, for men and women. Child mortality also all but vanished, and chronic illness and disability are now confined to old age and concentrated in a short period at the very end of life. Because life can be counted on, we come to know all members of our families— parents, grandparents, great-grandparents, and siblings—for much longer than ever before. This means that our positive relationships can be treasured longer. Of course, it also means that fractious ones will plague us for longer. (Or, if we're inclined to be optimistic, that troubled relationships will have enough time to heal.)

The final significant change affecting children and parents was the shrinking size of families. Big, sprawling families are a thing of the past. Women and couples have more control over the number and timing of births, and those births are far fewer, later, and farther apart than ever before. Coupled with longer life, today's families are now taller and narrower in shape because there are more generations alive at once and fewer people in each generation.

These conditions are precisely the reasons why many families can have greater closeness and connectedness today. Parents can invest greater time, resources, and emotions on the few children they have and know will survive to adulthood. Indeed, parents can now safely assume that their children will outlive them, which was not the case even a century ago. Yet because parents have fewer children, they also have more at stake: The hopes and dreams they have for their children are pinned on just a few of them. All of these changes set the stage for new ideas about raising children, leading directly to the intensive parenting and closer relationships we have come to know today.

There Are No Free-Range Children Here

Tensions between holding on and letting go are typical of parent–child relationships in early-adult life—and these tensions are felt on both sides. Parents must walk a fine line between allowing their young adult more freedom and keeping a careful watch over them (though that monitoring must become less intrusive with age). This dicey line gets even harder to walk after age eighteen, which continues to mark the age of autonomy and adulthood in the eyes of the law.

In her second year of law school at an Ivy League school, Aviva is twenty-three and talks with her mother three times a day. "My mom has a handle on everybody," she says. When Aviva's sister was in college, the family visited every weekend. Luckily for Aviva, the number of visits has eased for her. The checkups have not. Her mother wants to know that she is meeting people and getting out, but also that she is studying and not wasting time or getting into trouble. She wants to know if Aviva is sleeping enough, if her grades are good, and if she is dressing appropriately for law school. "She'll buy me something or she'll make sure I have warm stuff, you know, do you have a suit, do you have good shoes? Is your apartment okay?"

While her mother may believe she is helping, Aviva feels that her parents "will always think of [her] as a little child." Ironically, Aviva's mother phones so often that Aviva has taken to turning off her phone because the calls were disrupting her studying—the very thing her mother was trying to ensure she was doing. Aviva works hard to keep clear boundaries with her parents. "I don't tell them too much," she says, especially where boyfriends and friends are concerned. "I'm very close to them, I love them very much, and I would do anything for them. But there's a barrier that's between me and them. Not from them, but from me."

Although Aviva's mother risks pushing her daughter away with this constant surveillance, Aviva knows just how competitive this world is and she appreciates her family's support. Her mother has been a central presence in her daughters' lives from early on, perhaps out of displaced frustration about her own blocked career in their former home of Ukraine and the family's struggles to gain a foothold in the United States. It is easy to see how she might shift all of her energy to her daughters. Yet in many ways, Aviva's mother is little different from the many middle- and upper-class parents who are highly involved in their children's lives from day one. From the Baby Einstein phase to preschool competitions to traveling soccer teams to violin and orchestra lessons, today's parents are diligently, some might say obsessively, trying to ensure that their children will have bright futures. At the behest of child development experts, families have invested heavily in their children, carefully cultivating them for successful adulthoods. We've all heard the stories—or perhaps have lived them—of the harried mother whose daily schedule of shuttling and organizing playdates, team practices, music lessons, and tutoring classes resembles a CEO's. The pace is frantic, but parents don't want to ease up because the risks are too great. One father living in the suburbs of Chicago admits guiltily: "I wish I could get off the treadmill, but I don't want my kid to lose out."

These parents, largely middle and upper class, are building the "capital" of their children through sports, music, art, and other activities, and are preparing them to make their way in a world that requires assertive, outspoken thinkers. Anxious to ensure that their children stay on a positive academic and social course, they will quickly intervene at any sign of risk. Pierre, a twenty-five-year-old from San Diego, with a master's degree in mechanical engineering, remembers how his mother would go into "Supermom" mode to redirect him when needed and work with his teachers to ensure that he got good grades. "She just started being very involved with my schoolwork, and teaching me how to learn. She's always been there. She just came in there and taught me, and I just surged ahead. It was almost funny." Pierre attributes these activities of his mother, along with the support of the rest of his family, as being the factors that ultimately determined his success in life.

The investments of these parents are probably most pronounced when their children are dealing with college applications and admissions and the critical first year in college. Their efforts often set their children apart from the treaders, who struggle to find their way through the college maze, tripping up frequently and making costly mistakes. These involved parents are also quick to tap into their personal social networks in an effort to maximize their children's opportunities once they graduate from college—helping them to get that coveted internship or job or to be accepted at the graduate or professional school of their choice.

These much-maligned helicopter parents may not be as harmful as we're inclined to think, even if they clearly go too far. A recent survey of parents and students in twenty-four colleges found that students whose parents were in frequent contact with them and intervened on their behalf were more engaged in school, more likely to talk with their professors after class, and more satisfied with and doing better in college than students with less involved parents.[3] This research finding is a logical extension of earlier research on teens, which found no deleterious effects of overinvolved parenting, especially where academic performance is concerned. In fact, parental involvement and monitoring are consistently strong predictors of the achievements of adolescents.

That doesn't mean parents should go overboard. What we might call "Extreme Parenting" can come with real costs. Some problems need to be experienced by young people in order for them to grow—even if it's difficult for parents to resist the impulse to step in and make the save. Recognizing when to hold and when to fold is surely one of the most difficult tasks that parents face with children of any age, but it is particularly tricky once children become young adults and are expected to achieve—or to be working toward—autonomy and independence.

Among the hundreds of young people we interviewed, we did not find many cases of the extreme monitoring and intervention symbolized by helicopter parents, at least not as reported by the kids. Being actively involved in children's lives is different from being a Black Hawk. This middle ground between intense hovering and entirely absent characterizes most parent–child relationships today.

MOM as BFF

As children moved to center stage, the boundary between adults' and children's worlds softened. Parents dispensed with the notion that children should be seen and not heard. They wanted their children to be comfortable among adults. This is not to suggest that parents no longer ruled the roost. They did and still do. Rather, it means that young adults today are not cowed by the adult world and that they have very little reason to think of their parents as distant out-of-touch authority figures. This is a direct result of the fact that new kinds of parents parent in new kinds of ways.

The growing ease of relationships between parents and their young adult children is reflected in the shrinking generation gap. A Network-commissioned study shows that, since the 1970s, differences across generations on a wide range of attitudes, values, and behaviors have narrowed.[4] Gaps are even closing for the most controversial topics, including abortion, gender roles, sex, and civil liberties. Today's youths are more likely to find greater agreement with their parents than did their counterparts in the 1970s and 1980s. The shrinking generation gap means that parents and children today have more in common than they did in the past. There is less psychological and social distance between them, which provides a stronger foundation from which to build close relationships. The more liberated views of recent generations of parents has also been a primary factor in bringing about the more involved and expressive parenting we know today.

Young adults today see their parents, and especially their mothers, as a source of not only advice and counsel, but also companionship and comfort. Valentina's case is typical. "My mom and I are best friends. She calls me every day to tell me how her day went, and I do the same." Her mother says of her visits, "It's like sun comes into the window." Valentina laughs, "How much better can it get?" At twenty-two, she lives in Philadelphia, where she coordinates research while applying to Ph.D. programs in clinical psychology. She sees her parents in New York at least once a month. Unlike Aviva, who actively constructs barriers with her parents to offset the intrusions she feels from them, Valentina exudes openness and warmth in describing her relationship with her parents, whom she says were able to shelter her "with love and warmth so I was able to develop, to thrive."

Jerome's mother plays a huge role in his life. In fact, he readily admits he's a mama's boy. "Me knowing that she's there for me gives me extra confidence," he says. "And I live for her. Everything I do in my life is to show how much I appreciate the fact that she's raised me the way I have been raised. So, all my accomplishments, even my degree—as soon as I got my degree, I gave it to her. 'Cause she earned it just as much as I did."

At twenty-five, Jerome lives with his mother and brother in a Queens co-op the family has shared for twenty-two years. His degree was in education, and today he teaches sixth grade in the city. His teacher's salary ensures that "everything stays afloat," while his mother regains her health after a diagnosis of lupus. Jerome clearly adores his mother, and he is also very protective of her. "She's my best friend," he says. Part of Jerome's closeness to his mother stems from her frail health and from the fact that his father left the family early in Jerome's life.

Jerome's mother struck a middle ground between a hands-off, learn-the-hard-way approach and overinvolvement. She wanted Jerome to feel life's lessons firsthand, and she taught him that he was responsible for his actions. "Even when I was a knucklehead in high school getting drunk, she'd let me get drunk"—but she would also let him feel the consequences the next day. While she allowed Jerome to trip up, she also gave him clear advice.

Jerome would like to move out, but he doesn't want to leave until his future plans fall into place. He's thinking about graduate school and wants to find the right program. Then he and his girlfriend of six months will have to find a place to live. "Personally, I think it's about time for me to spread those wings and leave the nest. And Mom's fully aware of it, she has no problems with it, and she supports me in everything I do." His mother, however, will not be left alone. "She'll come stay with us. No nursing homes, nothing like that."

You *Can* Go Home Again

Since the middle of the last century, growing numbers of young adults like Jerome have co-resided with their parents—staying on at home longer or boomeranging back as needed. In 2007, about 38 percent of women and 43 percent of men between the ages of twenty and twenty-four were living with their parents.[5] After the age of twenty-five, however, proportions march downward with age—at the ages of twenty-five, thirty, and thirty-five, the percentages of women who live at home are 21, 10, and 6 percent; for men, they are 26, 12, and 8 percent. Women have always tended to leave earlier than men to cohabit or marry. It is also worth noting that at the turn of the twentieth century, young people stayed at home longer than those who came of age in the 1950s and 1960s. Indeed, mid-century was a low point for living with parents. The numbers would begin to climb steadily after that, picking up steam beginning in the 1980s. In 1960, for example, approximately 8 million young adults lived with their parents between the ages of 18 and 34. That number would more than double by 2007, to approximately 19 million. Of course, the overall population of young adults nearly doubled at the same time so the proportion of young people living at home increased more slowly, from 22 percent in 1960 to 28 percent in 2007. To leave home quickly in the 1950s and 1960s was normal because opportunities were plentiful and the social expectations of the time reinforced the need to do so—to stay would have been humiliating.

Today's young adults want freedom and autonomy—but living under the same roof leaves relationships between parents and grown children rather murky. Yet very few of the young adults in our interviews were "deadbeat" children, living at home out of laziness. They instead divided into two general camps: those who experienced a serious blunder and had to return home to recover, and those who were earning credentials or saving money to ensure more positive futures for themselves.

Sarah is a good representative of both camps.[6] At age twenty-eight, she only recently moved out of her mother's home. Sarah and her mother have a tight-knit relationship; they see each other several times a week and talk most days. The two grew close after Sarah's parents divorced. The two of them moved from the suburbs to the city, sharing a smaller apartment and carving out a new life together. Sarah's idea of a perfect weekend, in fact, would be to spend it with her mom, traveling and shopping. The two of them still do "the family vacation thing" each year.

Sarah has shuttled between living with her mother and living independently several times. She first moved back home during college, when she was unhappy living in the dorms at the local university. She eventually quit school for what she intended would be a semester to gain some clarity about her future and what she wanted from life. Instead, she married and began working full-time. When her marriage hit a rocky patch, Sarah moved home because she did not want to be alone. She left again when she and her husband temporarily reconciled. However, the marriage could not be sustained, and Sarah returned home after the divorce. Her mother was very supportive, and Sarah used the cushion that living at home provided to return to college full-time.

She felt a little embarrassed about living with her mother, but she regarded it as a temporary situation—and felt she had good reasons for moving back again. "Part of why I moved home to go to school full-time was that she let me live there for free. I just had to pay for my car and health insurance, and she paid for the roof over my head, she paid for the groceries I ate, she paid for the TV I watched, all that stuff. She was still providing me with that, and emotionally, obviously, she still supports me in that way." Sarah makes it clear she is not a "deadbeat child." She had a goal while living at home, and her mother was completely supportive of her as she worked toward finishing her degree. Asked whether her mother enjoyed her company, she says, "I'd still be there if it were up to her! She's single right now, so she loves having me around."

Many people assume that the relationships between parents and adult children are seriously strained when children stay at home or move back. They also assume that there's something wrong with the children who do this—that they are either lacking in character or in dire straits. But as Sarah's case shows, parents often permit and even encourage it. When a young adult lives at home with his or her parents, there can surely be downsides. The squabbles that come with living under the same roof, or discomfort—for both the child and the parents—with the situation can test relationships. However, the benefits typically outweigh the costs.

The benefits from the young adults' perspective range from not having to pay rent, make meals, or do laundry—often said with a guilty laugh—to being able to save money or to get back on track after life has thrown a curveball. Young adults with children also often mention the benefits of having help with child care—usually young women getting help from their mothers. It also gives them a reprieve while finding a good fit in the job market, which can take longer in a less stable workforce. No matter what the benefits are, young adults generally do not take their parents' hospitality for granted. They truly seem to appreciate it.

For all of these reasons, when living at home is done strategically, it can ensure more positive outcomes for kids who would likely be treading harder or sinking faster during the early-adult years. This is particularly true in working-class and poorer families; living at home can help young adults emerge with stronger skills and richer resources to get them launched.

In-House Adulthood

We shouldn't assume that parents resent the support they extend to young adult children. It's natural to focus on what kids are getting from parents and lose sight of what kids might also be giving to parents. When parents get emotional and practical support from their children, it leaves them feeling good. In fact, parents suggest that they get more emotional support from young adult children than children admit to, or are aware of, giving.[7] Relationships are a two-way street.

A look at young adult children from immigrant families demonstrates how much they are giving back to their parents and families. Cultural traditions in many immigrant families emphasize responsibility and obligation, such that young adult children may be required to contribute financially to the household, assist family members, and remain at home until (or even after) they are married. In 2008, large percentages of second-generation young adults (that is, children born in the United States to immigrant parents) between the ages of eighteen and twenty-four co-resided with their parents. Some groups have especially high rates of staying at home—between 64 and 74 percent of young adults from Indian, Dominican, Chinese, Filipino, and Salvadoran/Guatamalan backgrounds still lived at home.[8] Many of these young adults remain in their parents' homes out of a sense of family responsibility or obligation.[9]

As the nation becomes increasingly multicultural, norms about when to leave home, when to stay, and who gives and gets in these relationships may change. Immigrant youths in interviews were much more at ease living at home than native families, as doing so is more culturally acceptable; it's even expected. This longer co-dependence is clear in cases like Valentina's. Her family migrated to the United States from Belarus when she was ten, and she helped her parents navigate a new culture and a new set of rules and bureaucracies. Their close bond, forged by their struggles in a new place, is apparent today and they continue to lean on one another. Yet even young people in native-born families can find themselves providing significant levels of emotional or practical support to parents, such as Jerome was doing for his mother. This latter situation is typical for youth from families that are experiencing financial hardship, the breakup of parents, or unexpected illnesses or deaths.

Many countries in Europe have already experienced the lengthening transition to adulthood and are becoming more accustomed to the slower march to independence. In a Network-commissioned study, Katherine Newman and Sofya Aptekar examined the co-residence of young people and parents across Europe. In countries where this phenomenon is fairly new, living with parents is associated with less life satisfaction. However, the more the practice becomes widespread and stigma lessens, the more satisfied the children and parents become. In some countries, general well-being and satisfaction seem to be enhanced by longer stays in the family home, and the family can be a critical, and welcome, buffer in the face of economic instability, tight housing markets, and other limited opportunities.[10] Europe, and perhaps the United States to follow, might be witnessing a new developmental stage, one the authors term "in-house adulthood." This stage is structured less in terms of an authoritative parent and submissive child, and more as co-equals who reside together, enjoy each other's company, and provide mutual support. More than one-half of all Europeans, the authors point out, approve of adult children living longer with parents. Both parents and children feel that the main disadvantage of leaving home is emotional loss, which seems an indication that young adults and their parents share close bonds in other Western nations, too.

Hard to Say Good-Bye

After such intense involvement for the first eighteen years of life, both children and parents have a hard time letting go. A divorced mother from the Bronx writes to Lisa Belkin in *The New York Times* about the empty nest she is facing as her son strikes out on his own:

> My 19-year-old only son is moving into his own apartment this weekend. He's responsible and smart, so I should be happy at his independence. But I'm scared for him and worried that he is not ready. He knows that I moved out on my own at age 18, so I think he partly feels he's keeping up the "tradition." Outwardly, I'm very supportive and positive about his move. Inwardly, I miss him already. With the winter coming, how will I sleep not knowing if he's paid his utility bill? Did he turn the front eye off the stove before going to bed? Will he remember to call me? I've been divorced from his father since he was three; so it's been just the two of us for so long. I'm proud he wants to spread his wings on his own, but I admit I'll be lonely at first.[11]

The experience of Diana, whom we interviewed, reveals just how emotional departures can be for kids and parents alike—especially parents. Diana's father cried when his daughter left. Diana was an only child and a "daddy's girl." "On the one hand," she says, "we were very close—closer than most people are with their fathers. But on the other hand, our personalities were kind of too similar, so we would clash." After college, Diana returned home for two years while she saved money and moved up the job ladder. The best thing about living at home, she says, was that it was free, she never had to cook, and her parents gave her the freedom to do the things she wanted. As nice as that was, Diana was "utterly ecstatic" when, as a Christmas present, her father gave her enough money for six months of rent. When Diana "did the happy dance," her father choked back tears, stung that she was so excited about leaving. When she jokingly said that he must really want her to leave, he burst into tears. It was a horrible Christmas, she remembers.

In the end, her apartment was close to home, and she and her parents continued to see each other regularly. "If they really wanted to check on me, they still could," she says, "so that transition for them, that emptiness thing, was probably easier." Moving out strengthened her relationship with her father because distance limited their arguments and they learned to appreciate each other more. She and her mother have remained close, and they still meet a few times a week on Diana's lunch break and every Saturday for shopping or an outing. "So, it really wasn't any different for her, except that she didn't see me every night. But I still talked to her on the phone every single day, as I still do. It got to the point where I put my phone on forward at work because she was calling *me* a little too much and it was driving me nutty." Diana has since married and started a family, and her mother frequently visits Diana's new home to help with her son. Diana still talks to her father by phone about three times a week, and she visits her parents once a week or so. Her parents have been and remain her "constant source of inspiration," and she knows they will be there to catch her should she ever fall.

Diana's family is not unusual. Many of the young people in our interviews say their parents felt more pain in letting them go than they did in leaving. That is not to say that leaving is easy for kids. But for children, leaving is the moment they've been working toward, even if they're very close to their parents. For many parents, particularly if they're close to their children, it is the moment they've been dreading after all of the time, energy, resources, and attachment they have invested in getting their children this far. However, the majority are happy to know their children are ready to fly the coop. Indeed, we have more reason to be concerned about the number of young people, particularly those from less privileged backgrounds, who are not getting enough guidance from parents—whose parents are taking a hands-off or hard-knocks approach to getting kids launched into adulthood.

It's a Hard-Knocks Life

Working-class and poorer families more often take a sterner approach to parenting, giving children little guidance, or insisting that they must make it on their own and learn from their mistakes. They encourage or even demand that their children leave home early. *Eighteen and you're out* is a frequent rule in these households. Unfortunately, these parents are telling their children to play by old rules that at best no longer apply in today's world, and at worst may be detrimental to them.

This is not to suggest that the relationships in these families are always strained or distant. Rather, this old-style philosophy of parenting entails serious risks and more negative outcomes for young adult children. Many of them end up forgoing or cutting short training beyond high school and instead take the fast track to work and parenting. Many realize in retrospect that their lives could have taken a different, and often more positive, course had they had more guidance and advice, and even the cushion of support in a place to stay.

Henry, for example, looks back and wishes his parents had been more involved. His parents were the hands-off type and were fairly traditional. He recalls, "You know, if you did something wrong, you were either going to get grounded or you were going to get spanked. You were going to pay the consequences." His was a "normal" life, he says, full of summer vacations, family reunions, and Little League. Although far from hostile or troubled, the family did not talk much, and Henry never knew whether his parents wanted anything for him in life. "They didn't really have plans for me," he says, thinking back.

He didn't have any plans for himself, either. He was a jock in high school, and focused on his grades only enough to remain eligible for sports. He and his parents never talked about college, although Henry knew there was not going to be any money for it if he did decide to go. In fact, he and his parents rarely discussed his future at all. After graduation, Henry fell into a job for a food-delivery service and later a fast-food restaurant. After a year, he got a job at a pharmacy and eventually became a manager. He later moved to his current employer, first in a clerical job and now monitoring electronically controlled systems in a factory for just over minimum wage. All the while, he was still living at home.

When Henry was twenty-two, his parents surprised him by announcing they were selling their house and moving to Florida. Henry had been spending more time at his girlfriend's house, and his parents had begun to press him about his future plans. When he said the two were likely moving in together, it was all his parents needed to hear. They put their house up for sale and bought a place in Florida and a smaller summer home a few miles north of Henry's childhood home. "It was kind of weird," says Henry of his parents' departure. "It was like, I guess I really don't have my parents to fall back on right now. I've got to be my own person."

Henry landed on his feet. He eventually married his girlfriend, and they now live in their own condo with a baby on the way. In hindsight, however, he wishes his parents had helped him develop a clearer plan—that they had sat him down, given him guidance, and pushed him in school. He wishes, in particular, that he'd gone to college. "They just left it all in my hands, saying, 'Well, if you're going to pass, you're going to pass. If you're going to fail, you're going to fail.' " The consequences for Henry were a "just get by" approach to his grades in high school, no thoughts of college, and only a vague idea that he would find a job. Like many teens and young adults, the easy route seemed like the best route to him. While Henry's parents should not be faulted for raising children with the belief that life's lessons are learned through the consequences of one's actions, that approach can be risky in this era of the highly competitive arms race among the elite, with their highly structured childhoods and well-orchestrated paths through school. It can also be risky in this bifurcated economy of a low-wage service sector, which Henry landed in by default, and a more secure knowledge sector. As Henry says now, at age thirty, "I would have liked to have been pushed to think about the future, which didn't happen."

Henry's story illustrates that certain mistakes and costly detours can be avoided, mistakes from which young people may have a particularly difficult time recovering. A hands-off, hard-knocks approach can be damaging if young people are left to their own devices in a highly competitive playing field to make mistakes simply for the sake of learning a tough lesson.

The Long Reach of Divorce

Relative to a century ago, divorce, rather than death, is now the great disruptor of family relationships. Many of today's young adults had childhoods that were heavily impacted by the divorce of parents. The legacy is that some divorced parents find it comforting and less lonely to have their adult children at home, or to have close relationships with them. This is particularly true for mothers, as divorce tends to strengthen the relationships between mothers and their children, especially between mothers and daughters. In contrast, it often fractures the relationships between fathers and children.

Sarah knows the strain that divorce can put on father–daughter relationships. When her parents divorced while she was still in elementary school, it was a life-changing event for her. She wishes her parents had stayed together "just for the family dynamic that would have given me," including siblings and an extended family, because "a lot of times it was my mom and I." With the divorce, she and her mother left their comfortable home in the suburbs for an apartment in the city, where Sarah was enrolled in public school, making new friends and starting over. The divorce was hard on everyone, she says, but luckily for her, her parents avoided fighting in front of her, and her father continued to support her financially after the split.

While Sarah and her mother grew close, the distance between Sarah and her father continued to grow, both geographically and emotionally. After the divorce, she saw him on weekends. When he remarried a few years later and moved to the Southwest, she only saw him during the summers. When we last spoke with Sarah, she had not seen him in two years. "I'm not close to him like I am my mom. He didn't get to see me grow up and be a part of my life." With some tending on both their parts, their relationship has recently "blossomed," and they are beginning to communicate more and find common ground. "We're friends," she says.

Parents' continued bitterness toward each other after a divorce can require young people to negotiate between them. Sometimes, these negotiations simply become too much work for the children, who withdraw altogether. Brian grew up in a small Iowa town where everyone knew everyone's business, which made his parents' divorce when he was in high school doubly traumatic for him. He not only dealt with the fallout at home from two angry and alienated parents, but he felt the eyes of the town on him wherever he went. Rumors, he said, were flying. His parents had never had a good relationship, and they had stayed together long after the love between them had died. "My parents had separate bedrooms for years," he says. "I mean it would have almost been better if they had split earlier. My father would come home from work, eat dinner, and leave and go back to work until late at night just to avoid being in the house."

Today, Brian lives with his wife in Florida and works in construction. Although he remains on friendly terms with his parents, he sees them only once or twice a year. (They talk on the phone twice a week, though, particularly now that Brian's wife is pregnant with the first grandchild.) His parents are still hostile toward each other, even fifteen years after their divorce. It makes for a difficult juggling act at times. Brian's relationship with his mother has soured as a result of her continued bitterness toward his father. "She seems to try to find ways to try to manipulate situations to still try to play one against the other." His father, he says, is more easygoing. "He couldn't care less basically, but there is no way that my mother would even be in the same room as my father." The situation is so tense that he and his wife decided not to invite either of them to their recent wedding. Brian says, "I didn't want the hassle."

As parents divorce and remarry, family dynamics become even more complex and ambiguous. Stepparents and stepsiblings introduce new elements to the mix, and the legacy of hurt feelings and feelings of abandonment color future interactions, particularly as children like Sarah, Brian, and so many others who have been touched by divorce become adults in their own right. No one in these families quite knows what their relationships are supposed to look and feel like, or what kinds of responsibilities and expectations come with them. Unlike intact relationships, these relationships bring strain more often than they do support.

Damaged Relationships

Some of the young people we interviewed had tense or volatile relationships with their parents. In many of these cases, the parents abused drugs and alcohol, were physically or emotionally abusive, or had unstable mental health. Some even abandoned their children. When parents have a tempestuous or abusive relationship with each other, it also has a deep impact on their children.

Theresa's father dragged her down. "My father taught me the bad things in my life. He taught me about drugs, violence, and being a womanizer." Her mother was not much help, either. "My mother called me a loser, a quitter, and a dropout." Nicole was regularly whipped by her father. Denise says she purposefully got pregnant as a teenager to spite her mother, who then beat her, hoping to prompt a miscarriage. Denise later learned of her father's cocaine problem, which fueled his abuse of her, and so many of the other problems in their fragile and explosive household.

Tami ran wild in high school, hanging out with gangs and getting into drugs. And no wonder. Her father beat her and her mother, and cheated on her mother. Tami spent much of her young life seeking emotional support from her mom, and returning it as best she could, as the two of them hunkered down against the rages of her father. Tami would later become pregnant, have an abortion, and be arrested on a drug charge for which she performed six months of community service.

After several tumultuous years, she seems to be straightening herself out and is now working full-time as a computer programmer and resuming work toward her bachelor's degree. While she is devoted to her mother, she has only disdain for her father. "My father cheated on my mother," she says. But not only that: Her father married the other woman in the Philippines and had a separate family with children while still being married to Tami's mother. His second family now lives nearby. Her father is also very "violent," "hardheaded," and "controlling." She and her mother have always lived in complete fear of him.

Tami even had an order of protection against her father because he'd beaten her so badly that she'd ended up in the hospital. But that order didn't stay. Her charismatic father, she says, convinced the police that she was the problem. The duplicitous life they led—happy on the outside, crying on the inside—was a heavy burden to carry all those years. Now that she's an adult, he has less control over her. "He has no say over my life. He was *never* there as a father figure. He was *never* there financially. So basically, he has no power. Only that we're scared of him."

Tami adores her mother. "She is my best friend and my role model because of everything she has to deal with." She admires her mother's strength not only in surviving everything her husband inflicted on her, but also for working her way up the corporate ladder. Her mother's salary, not her father's, has always paid the bills. And she recently filed for divorce. Tami hopes to emulate her mother—she wants to get better at managing her own life. She's living at home partly to recover from her problems, partly to save money, and partly to protect her mother. She says, "We lean on each other if she's feeling down or whatever. I'm there for her, to talk to her, to bring her confidence back up, and vice versa." For Tami, the hardships she's endured have in some ways left her mature beyond her years and, in other ways, still seeking the childhood she feels she missed.

Some destructive relationships can, with years of work, be healed—and some are so bad they cannot. Once children reach adulthood, they may suddenly feel more able to liberate themselves from destructive relationships with parents. These young adults feel empowered by the fact that they need not stay and that they can now choose whether and how to engage their parents. For some young people, this may come with the painful resolution that they are better off without them than they are with them. But the scars remain.

Fending for Themselves

Some young adults have more than enduring scars from a difficult family dynamic: They do not have families at all. Approximately twenty thousand youths age out of foster care each year. Children enter foster care when the state intervenes in cases of abuse or neglect and removes them from untenable and dangerous family situations. The primary purpose of this separation is to protect these children from harm by removing them from their caregivers. In doing so, the state assumes the responsibilities associated with their parenting, including preparing them for independence. Although the state works to reunite children with their families, such reunions are not always possible. In the end, the government, acting as a parent, decides when these twenty thousand foster youth are ready to be on their own.

Their fates, unfortunately, are often bleak. Network member Mark Courtney, a national expert in foster care and the child welfare system, finds that the older children in foster care are more likely to be living in the least family-like settings, such as group homes or institutions, than the overall foster care population. Youths in these settings are less likely to form the kind of lasting relationships with responsible adults that will help them move toward independence. In the early 2000s, nearly four in ten foster youths ages seventeen through twenty had no high school degree or GED. They more often suffered from mental health problems, were more often the perpetrators or victims of crime, and were more often homeless. Courtney found, for example, that 18 percent of these youths reported being homeless at least once since leaving care and turning twenty-one. Just over one-half of males and three in ten females had been incarcerated for at least one night between ages eighteen and twenty-one. Perhaps not surprisingly, given these sobering statistics, former foster children are much less likely to be employed than their peers, and are more likely to rely on public assistance. They earn, on average, too little to escape poverty.[12] Although concerted efforts have been made to help these young adults carve a new path in life, the programs are severely strained and underfunded. Only about two-fifths of eligible foster youth receive independent living services.

Good Relationships Gone Better or Bad

Luckily, most young people have caring parents, and the closeness they feel seems to only get stronger with time. Young adults often talk spontaneously about the appreciation they gain for their parents, especially once they are married or have children of their own. They become more aware of all that their parents went through in raising them, and they begin to realize that their parents won't always be around. Those who have experienced the death of a parent talk about the ways in which their relationship with the surviving parent intensifies after the other dies, and how the death of a parent has brought them closer to their siblings and their own children.

Jennifer, a twenty-eight-year-old single woman who grew up in Iowa and now lives near Boston, sums up a common sentiment: "Initially, you just think of them as your parents. Then, in high school, they are kind of the *last* people that you want to be around. I guess I just didn't really think about all they were doing for me. Since I've gotten older, and looked back on things, I have more respect for them, I appreciate them more now, and I feel like we can talk about it; they tell me their problems, whereas before that would never happen."

Yet even good relationships can go bad, and quickly. Parents can do everything "right" in terms of cultivating skills and opportunities and fostering great achievements in early adulthood—but not have great relationships with their kids. Luke's story provides a stark example.

Luke is twenty-five, a recent Ivy League graduate living in Chicago. His parents gave him both practical guidance and autonomy during his childhood in Denver. "Their philosophy was that there were some pretty fast-and-hard limits, but as long as I communicated with them, everything was okay. They basically let me run my life." They were comfortable with this arrangement, he says, because "I was also good at running it." His parents functioned more as "guidance counselors who had purse strings."

His parents were very supportive of his choices, and served as sounding boards to all of his decisions, whether big, like resigning from his position as captain of the cross-country team out of frustration with the coach, or small decisions, like which languages to take in high school. Luke's parents helped him to enhance his long-term prospects, guiding him clearly along the path from high school to Ivy League. By all accounts they were a very close family.

Until he came out. Luke long suspected he was gay, but not until senior year of high school did he finally apply the label to himself. Yet he would spend much of that year hiding his sexuality from his parents because they were "enormously conservative." He worried, too, that coming out would jeopardize his plans for college if they decided to withdraw their financial support. He made the difficult choice of keeping his sexuality a secret from them throughout his undergraduate career.

When he found out he had achieved a perfect score on the LSATs, Luke knew he finally had the independence he needed to live openly. As expected, offers poured in from all the top law schools. He also reached a point where he felt emotionally independent. The geographic independence helped, too: Chicago was a long way from Denver, and Luke was becoming more comfortable with his sexuality in Chicago's gay community. He now realized his relationship with his parents was no longer honest.

After he came out, Luke's relationship with his parents was very strained, especially with his mother. She was "perturbed and active about it." They didn't talk for three months. "My mom refused to understand how her behavior was hurting me, and it wasn't that I wasn't communicating it; she refused to understand." He and his father were on better terms, and it later came out that his father felt blindsided "by the fact that I didn't want to talk anymore. He didn't realize things were that wrong, and my mom wasn't telling him about these conversations she was having with me."

Much to Luke's surprise, his parents have started going to a support group for parents with gay or lesbian children. "They're showing willingness to try and work better on it," says Luke. However, he is still hesitant to reengage. While his parents are no longer actively trying to hurt him as they once did, Luke still has "a lot of internalized homophobia that is an inevitable result of growing up in the circumstances I did. Just hearing their voices stirs it all up."

Luke's situation, along with that of so many of the young people we have profiled, reveals that relationships with parents are not simply carried forward into adulthood as a matter of course. They are being created and re-created as young people and their parents grow older. Healthy relationships involve give and take on both sides, and they rest on mutual love, or at least obligation. There are no scripts for how parents and their young adult children are "supposed" to relate to one another as the children become adults, especially in the blurry space between.

Rules of Engagement

Family relationships today are complex, not only in the wake of divorce and remarriage, but also because of the much greater diversity in how families look and feel. The connectedness and closeness between parents and kids did not suddenly emerge in the last decade; the "new" relationships between parents and children have been in the making for a long time.

Strong relationships with parents are more necessary for a successful launch into adulthood today—at least in the United States. Most, if not all, of the responsibility for raising children rests in the hands of parents. The presence of strong family guidance and support is ultimately the factor that sharply separates those who swim from those who tread or sink in the transition to adulthood. Closeness helps, but closeness alone will not get young people through college and into better-paying and more meaningful jobs or careers.

The longer and more complicated passage to adulthood has brought new ambiguities for relationships between parents and children. Parents are uncertain what to do when the guidebooks end at age eighteen. There are no norms for "big" kids who are adults according to old standards, but who have yet to achieve the major milestones of adulthood. Relationships are being crafted as they go.

Parents cannot go on autopilot and apply the old rules—"when I was a kid..." or "my parents would never have..." These rules of engagement no longer apply. What's more, a hands-off or hard-knocks approach to parenting can be detrimental to a child's long-term future. This is where our story of diverging destinies continues. These types of strategies are more often the default attitudes of working- and lower-class families, and they exacerbate the vulnerabilities of young adults.

We discovered, expectedly, a tone of resentment in our interviews with the young people who are struggling to make it with minimal or no family support, especially when they can see that their more privileged counterparts are getting a lot more help and are experiencing these years so differently. The things these disadvantaged youth are able to achieve are viewed, in contrast to their better-positioned peers, as hard-won badges of honor. They believe that while their peers with greater privileges have had everything handed to them, they instead have had to make their way without any underpinnings to protect them.

And they're right. So much of the media attention and public discussion of twenty-somethings is focused on the well-positioned young people who are sure to swim. As a society, we pay too little attention to the fates of young people whose parents are unable or unwilling to provide the guidance and support that they so desperately need.

7

iDecide: Voting and Volunteering in a Digital World

"**R**iding down the street to cover the election watch party...
I heard screaming and shouts coming from cars. People were
hanging out of their cars and 'change' was chanted. I knew at that very
moment: Barack Obama won the election," wrote de Nishia on the
Rock the Vote blog. She was one of the thousands who descended on
Chicago's Grant Park to catch the wave of the historic moment. "It
is this generation," says Heather Smith, the executive director of
Rock the Vote, "that is making their mark on politics and shaping our
future."

Early on in the year 2008, *Time* magazine deemed it "the year of the
youth vote." While in years past, the youth vote had always disappointed, things were starting to look different. During the 1990s, only
about four in ten young people under age thirty were turning out for
elections, far below the rates of older voters. Many in the country were
hoping the momentum among young people that had been building
ever so slowly since 2004 would turn into a surge of new voters drawn to

Barack Obama. Without that surge, the problem of voter turnout, so important to a truly robust democracy, was in danger of deepening.

Of this we can be sure: Over the last four decades, young adults have retreated from "civic engagement" of every kind, whether reading newspapers, attending club meetings, joining formal groups, working on community projects, voting, joining unions, or joining religious groups.[1] For some of these indicators, the drop has been very steep. The single exception is a small increase in volunteering.[2]

Civic life is part and parcel of adulthood. The very acts of being civic-minded—voting, volunteering, and taking part in community—are the responsibilities of adults in a society. Children are tutored in these re-sponsibilities at school and at home, and they are given opportunities to practice these tasks at every turn, from running for school council to de-bating to raising money for the less fortunate. The responsibilities of car-ing for and tending to communities and neighborhoods (and the country as a whole) are as important as tending to and caring for families as adults. We care deeply about what young people can do for civic life be-cause the fate of democracy rests on it.

Equally important is what civic life can do for young people. Civic engagement offers important opportunities to build the skills and re-sources of young adults—and the extended passage to adulthood gives them the perfect moment to profit from those opportunities. It's a time in life when young people are naturally taking stock of themselves and society. They're firming up their identities, laying a foundation for the future, and figuring out where they fit in the world.

Why then are so many young people disconnected from civic life? The MacArthur Network analyzed data from a large annual survey of high school seniors that tracks changing attitudes toward such issues as materialism, trust in one's fellow man, trust in government, and many other attitudes and beliefs that shape the ultimate decision to become an active, involved citizen. The Network also collaborated with the Center for Information and Research on Civic Learning and Engagement (CIRCLE), a nonpartisan think tank focused on youth civic engagement and education, to pair up the trends in attitudes and beliefs with the trends in voting and volunteering as a way to get inside young people's heads and understand why they do or do not participate.

What we find is two stories in one. Young people in their late twenties and early thirties approach politics very differently from those in their early twenties. The older group is still feeling the hangover from the Reagan and Bush years, with its rapid rise in materialism and individualism and the consequent rapid fall in social trust. This older group tends to believe that government is the problem, not the solution. As a result, they have disengaged from politics and civic life. Their younger siblings have a substantially different outlook. The Millennials rallied strongly for Obama, who masterfully tapped into their collective hope for the future. Relative to their slightly older peers, they are more likely to see government as a solution to social problems, and they are generally more tolerant and trusting of their fellow man. They are also more liberal, and there are clear signs that this is a generational shift, not simply unbridled, youthful idealism. This younger group is embracing a new model of activism, one that is often less visible to older generations and traditional pundits and civic organizers. They are bypassing the old media and creating their own forms of media. "Be the media," they say, and through Twitter, YouTube, Facebook, blogs, and text messages, this generation has taken to the proverbial "streets" with a finesse and speed rarely seen before. They are using online social networking to support causes, get involved, and rally around issues. They are organizing with the click of a mouse.

While the youngest generation's seemingly newfound enthusiasm is heartening, any optimism we might have that they are making serious civic commitments must be tempered. The recession may have long-lasting effects on this new generation's embrace of political action. A recent study finds that those who enter adulthood during a recession are less likely to have confidence in government and its role in society. They also tend to distrust institutions and see them as ineffective. This distrust of government is highest between ages eighteen and twenty-five.[3]

The Youth Vote

Signs that *Time* might be right about its "year of the youth vote" were first evident in January 2008. The primaries were just getting under way but college campuses were already abuzz about the new guy with the

BlackBerry and the hip young staff. Young people came out in force, doubling their presence relative to the 2000 and 2004 primaries. In many states, youth turnout tripled or even quadrupled. The "youth-quake" was overwhelmingly in Obama's favor. He managed to pull off a feat that had not been accomplished in recent history: He not only talked to young adults, but he listened to them and let them get involved in his campaign. Making them a priority clearly paid off. Students rallying behind him, according to *Time*, kept Obama in the race in those early days.

After the heated primaries in 2008, with the country poised to cross a historic threshold, the youth vote remained critical in the face-off between forty-seven-year-old Democrat Barack Obama and seventy-two-year-old Republican John McCain, who, as a white, privileged male, quickly came to represent the Establishment. That Obama was the first black candidate to be so close to the presidency did not hurt. This generation of young people is the most diverse in the country's history—a simple fact that holds tremendous significance for the future of our nation. More important, though, were the media through which Obama spoke to young voters—YouTube, Twitter, text messages, and the social networking site My Barack Obama (which was quickly shortened to the text-message-size "MyBO").

Traditional methods of recruiting young voters aren't nearly as effective for today's youth. They rarely have landline phones, and cell phone numbers are hard to assemble for automated campaign calls. Young people move frequently, either from dorms to student housing to apartments, or across cities for jobs and relationships. Because they vote less frequently, they do not appear on the traditional databases, and they do not subscribe to daily newspapers or even watch the evening news on television.

Obama found them where they hang out most, on social networks online and on their cell phones, whose numbers he gathered via MyBO. His was the first campaign to fully tap into the digital tools to communicate with this generation. And, in the spirit of the blogosphere and social networking, he listened as well as spoke—he joined the conversation.

Jonathan, a graduate of Northwestern University working for a philanthropic organization in Chicago, sums it up for many in his generation: "There's a resurgence of commitment: There's something about his basic age and he's black. It signals a break from the traditional power model. When you see [Chicago] Mayor Daley in his seventh term in office, you think, 'Okay, business as usual,' or you look at the panel who were implicated in the financial bailout and you think, 'Okay, six well-dressed white men over fifty.' We're always bombarded with images of what power is, but Obama is more inclusive of the younger population. It's a bone to us."

In the final 2008 election, 3.4 million more young people voted than in 2004, and they voted overwhelmingly for the candidate they had helped propel into the limelight.[4] Two-thirds of the youth vote went for Obama. A new era in American politics was born.

The Bandwagon Is Half Empty

Although this news is heartening, a closer look at the statistics takes some of the wind out of its sails. In this so-called new golden age of youth politics, voter turnout in 2008 for those under age thirty was still only about 50 percent, just 4 to 5 percentage points over 2004 estimates.[5] Turnout for those over thirty, meanwhile, was far greater at approximately 70 percent.[6] Underscoring this continuing disconnect, a nationally representative survey of eighteen-to-twenty-four-year-olds the month before the election found that the vast majority (upward of 80 percent) had *not* participated in government-, political-, or issue-related organizations. They had never emailed Congress about an issue, contributed to an online discussion or blog related to politics, or attended a political rally or demonstration. They had never donated money or volunteered for a political campaign. Despite the significant amount of time that this generation spends in the digital world, they had not forwarded a political video online or used Facebook or MySpace to promote a political candidate, event, or idea.[7]

In the end, only a small group of young people are hyperinvolved (about 10 percent) and in the limelight.[8] It is telling that the personal pictures and stories accompanying the *Time* article, and so many others like it, were of students on four-year college and university campuses. The hyperinvolved set shares one characteristic: they are more often college students or graduates. Seventy percent of voters under age thirty in the 2008 election had attended at least some college. Only 30 percent had a high school degree or less. The dramatically different participation of those with and without college experience or degrees reflects a wide social-class divide in political participation. And the gap between college graduates and others in voting and other aspects of civic life has been widening over time, the Network finds.

Where then does this strain of disillusionment and apathy come from? At its most basic, it starts with a lack of trust. The bedrock of trust is the privilege of a hopeful outlook, of feeling that one's voice is heard above the din of everyday demands. When this is lacking, as it so often is for young adults with pinched futures, the urge to vote and to volunteer withers. What develops in its place is the not unfounded cynicism that politics only benefits someone else. The faint voices of young people in trailer parks, rural hamlets, or working-class neighborhoods of urban centers are not loud enough or important enough to matter. Young people, like Sherri, frequently do not see any tangible results of their efforts, and therefore they do not bother to vote.

"We're Not a Politic Family"

Sherri's view on politics and voting represents that of many in Generation X, the older half of young adults today. She also represents the large group lacking a college degree. Just out of her twenties, Sherri has a new Ford Explorer parked outside the mobile home she lives in with her husband, Greg. She feels quite content with life. She and Greg can afford to take a vacation to Las Vegas a couple of times a year, and she likes her job. Working as a waitress suits her "bubbly" personality to a T. Greg works nearby as a bartender and jack-of-all trades at a small family-owned restaurant. The two have been happily married for six years. "He puts up with me and that's what matters," she says, laughing. In her spare time, she devours crime novels, and likes her "soaps" and crime shows on television. She never reads a newspaper, and does not vote. "I should do it, but I don't," she says with a shrug. "I've never voted in my life." She cannot identify any particular issue that gets her worked up. "We don't talk politics. We're not a politic family," she says of herself, her husband, and her parents.

Sherri has never contacted a public official, she has never joined a cause, and she is not a member of any political party. This lack of interest is not unusual. Nationally, eight in ten high school seniors in 2004 had never contacted a public official or given money to or worked on a campaign. (This latter factor has likely changed somewhat with the Obama campaign, however.) These seniors were part of the Monitoring the Future survey, which Network member Constance Flanagan and her colleagues plumbed for information on young people's changing political and civic outlooks across thirty years. They found that taking action via these conventional forms of politics was at its lowest point in three decades in 2002.

Sherri has no firm feelings either way about the economy or the state of the world. "I don't really stay in touch with what's going on. I couldn't tell you what's going on right now over in Iraq. To me, I'm going to live today to the fullest, and I can't change anything else that's going on. So, I'm not going to let all that other stuff bring me down because I have no control over it." When asked why she does not vote, she says, "No time. To me, it was like, 'You know what, my vote's not going to matter.'"

Sherri's disconnect from civic life did not happen in a vacuum. She came of age during a time of fundamental shifts in all those elements of society that engage or alienate voters and active citizens. Social trust is a key ingredient in politics. In examining the thoughts and attitudes of high school seniors over the course of thirty years, the Network finds that social trust started to slide in the mid-1980s and bottomed out a decade later. It has been swinging slightly upward since then. However, the recovery has never reached the levels of trust that existed in the mid-1980s.

There's a link between this declining trust and the other developments that were under way as Generation X was coming of age, specifically the Reagan and Bush I eras, with their rising individualism, shrinking government, and disappearing corporate safety nets, which leave workers on their own to fund their pensions, their health care, and their own job training. Globalization and job restructuring have further increased personal feelings of insecurity and uncertainty.

Insecurity breeds mistrust. When things are shaky, people feel pressure to look out for themselves. "If you start to feel anxious about life, if you feel your job is in jeopardy," says Flanagan, "you will worry that your co-worker might take your job or compete for the same promotion." It is but a short step to a watch-out-for-number-one mentality. People who feel that their jobs are at risk look inward and protect their advantages. Without the backbone of social trust among friends, neighbors, and strangers, how can we expect anyone to believe in a politician? The older half of today's young adults still carry this skeptical sentiment with them and so, too, do those who lack college degrees and are facing an insecure future. People of all ages go to the polls when they feel a shared sense that the world offers them opportunities and promise. When their optimism for the future sags because they feel that their fellow citizens and the institutions that steer their country's progress cannot be trusted, they see no reason to vote. The interlocking relationships among optimism, trust, and voting are visible in the changing opinions of high school seniors. Their optimism toward the future has risen and fallen over the past thirty years in near lockstep with their trust in politicians and government.

Social trust is especially low for those who have the least at stake—the unemployed, the poor, minorities, and members of other marginalized groups. It makes sense that people at the periphery have less social trust. Their lives are less predictable, and the issues that concern them are more often overlooked. As Lara, a twenty-four-year-old Puerto Rican medical supervisor in New York City, puts it, "The electors want to make it seem like they care about your issues, so they want to listen to what you have to say around election time. Once they're elected, they really don't come back to your community."

Social trust is also less abundant among those with less education, like Sherri, who only has a high school diploma. "Just going to college increases social trust," Constance Flanagan says. She has followed this clear trend among groups of young people out of high school and beyond. Individuals who scored low on social trust in high school, but then spent a year on a college campus, suddenly scored much higher. This jump in social trust was brought on by the sense of community that college imparts. "You feel like you know other people are contributing to the common good," says Flanagan. Students repeatedly receive the message, "We care about you; we're looking out for you." That makes people feel connected and less anxious. "It boosts social trust tremendously when kids feel others at school are watching out for them," says Flanagan. "It's something we can really improve on in high schools as a way of encouraging more active involvement in civic life."

Sherri also mentions another factor that the Network has found contributes to the apathy of the younger generation: "We are more interested in money, in having nice things—nice homes, nice vehicles, nice clothes, making a statement." The Network and others have tracked trends in trust alongside trends in materialism. Interestingly, during the 1980s, the desires of young people to have a high standard of living went up as the belief that most people are fair and can be trusted went down. Both have remained fairly stable since 1991.[9] However, Sherri's peers— Generation X—entered adulthood with much lower levels of social trust than their parents and grandparents, and those levels have not climbed for them as they've gotten older.

The thing that connects the rise in materialism and the fall in social trust is individualism. The pursuit of material goods is a largely individualistic endeavor. As the importance of material objects, and the chase to obtain them, rises, people not only begin to care less about their fellow man, but they also begin to worry that others will somehow impede their own earnings and consumption. This creates anxiety, particularly when the means to acquire those items shrink or shift as jobs become less secure.

"Even I don't have a lot of faith in my generation because when I was growing up, it was all about 'Me, Me, Me,'" Sherri says, adding that her generation is not accustomed to thinking about other people or having a critical concern for healthy neighborhoods, communities, and nations. Watching out for "number one" might be necessary during a corporate climb, but it undercuts the nature of a civil society.

No Levers to Grab

Another reason that young adults participate less is that they often feel inadequately informed about civic issues and especially how the political system works. Surveys have repeatedly shown that young adults lack even the most basic civic knowledge and are misinformed about politics and current events. There are unequal opportunities to learn about politics and the political process before adulthood sets in. Schools serving minorities and other disadvantaged youth are less likely to offer enriching civic courses and activities for their students. This lack of opportunity makes it difficult for these youths to participate or take action. Indeed, nearly two-thirds of young people admit that they need practical information about politics before they'll get involved, and approximately one-half say their high schools have not prepared them to vote and evaluate candidates.[10]

The presence and quality of civic education in high schools are at historic lows. While in the 1960s, students took as many as three courses in civics, today they are lucky if they take one semester.[11] Where civic education does exist, it often relies on outdated textbooks that reflect few of the contemporary issues that excite young people. The curriculum is often so deathly boring that it's worthy of satire—a la Jon Stewart's book *The Daily Show with Jon Stewart Presents America (The Book) Teacher's Edition: A Citizen's Guide to Democracy Inaction*.

Families have not picked up the slack. Fewer families discuss politics at home today—another source of information and understanding about civic life and the political system. One-third of young people say their parents discuss politics with them at home less than once a year or never. But young people in families that talk politics are more likely to be engaged and to vote, and vice versa.

Joining Networks, Not Marches

The one iconic image of the mid-twentieth century was the protest. From the 1968 debacle in Chicago to the protests spanning from Berkeley to Antioch to Washington, the "flower power" and antiwar generation of the 1960s took to the streets at a scale rarely seen before. In hindsight, these protests were powerful symbols of how that generation approached politics: head-on, take no prisoners, brook no compromise. By contrast, this latest generation has co-opted the old forms and refitted them to suit their world.

"I don't want to go 'rah, rah, rah,' in some robotic way," says Luke, the gay twenty-five-year-old Ivy League graduate. Luke votes, he gives money, and he reads everything he can online about a candidate. He is, in other words, an atypical young adult. Yet he's "not much of the protesting type. I protested for my first time after Proposition 8 [the ballot measure that prevented gay marriage in California]. It reinforced the reason that I'm not the protester type—which is that the people who organize protests are people who support the right answer for the wrong reasons. You had some guy with the microphone comparing George Bush to Hitler. I mean, just wildly inaccurate comparisons and not responsible. And it just doesn't seem to get you very far."

Luke is repulsed by the radical fringe that seems to appear at most protests. Like many in his generation, he leans more toward a willingness to compromise and find coalitions. A hunting lobby, for example, would be the last group that Constance Flanagan's daughter, a vegetarian, would associate with, but because of her passion for saving natural resources, hunters offer a natural ally in advocating for the preservation of forests and other natural lands. They might want the forests and rivers left pristine for different reasons, but they can work together toward their common goal.

W. Lance Bennett, professor of political science and communication, and director of the Center for Communication and Civic Engagement at the University of Washington, sees a clash between the old and new models of citizenship. He argues that traditional forms of civic involvement—such as protesting, contacting elected officials, and taking an interest in news and public affairs—that adults from prior generations identify as the pillars of a strong civic life are "brittle conceptions of proper citizenship."[12] They fail to speak to the interests of youth, and they fail to take into account the more modern forms of involvement.

The old model of the "dutiful citizen" is inching toward irrelevance for this generation, replaced by what Bennett calls the "actualizing citizen." Their parents and grandparents voted or protested because that was what dutiful citizens did. This sense of obligation was fostered in traditional social groups such as churches, the PTA, the Elks Club, and unions, as well as in the classroom. And when jobs were steady and long lasting, they, too, created a sense of loyalty and obligation. Belonging to a group imparted, or imposed, an identity. Group norms developed; subtle peer pressure encouraged members to be good citizens and to carry their groups' interests to the voting booths. In turn, politicians listened to a "constituency" and the group's members felt they were being heard in the process. With a few exceptions, largely among the religious right, strong membership-based identities are becoming a thing of the past.

Looser and broader social networks—often online—have sprung up in their place. Not only is the digital world offering new forms of communication and outreach, but it is also altering our conceptions of what membership and commitment mean. Groups no longer impose interests on their members. Rather, individuals choose their interests in a bottom-up process based on recommendations from trusted peers, often through loose social networking ties, such as Facebook, Twitter, or blogs. An actualizing citizen has a diminished sense of obligation to the government but a higher sense of individual purpose. Voting is often less meaningful than choosing to buy "green" products or opting to volunteer.

Young adults today find authoritative, one-way messages or demands suspicious. They don't like to feel managed, packaged, and manipulated. Years of being bombarded by consumerist culture have left them with a keen sense of smell for contrived messages. Perhaps that is why only one in five high school seniors in the Network's analysis of Monitoring the Future survey said they had or would attend a protest in 2002.[13]

Today, there are broader forms of protest, like using cell phones and social networks to launch "smart mobs" (in which digital networks are used to coordinate and take immediate, and often spontaneous, group action) or using blogs or Facebook pages to report on news that is overlooked or downplayed in the mainstream media. Theirs are more organic efforts, from the bottom up, more egalitarian and less hierarchical. This generation holds fast to the belief that working together in groups can make a difference, but these groups are smaller, personalized, and more diffuse.

John McCain learned the hard way how much young people suspect canned and overly managed messages from the top. Back in 2000, McCain made a foray into the digital world to reach the youth vote. He held a press conference using the fancy tool of videoconferencing and asked young attendees to email him questions, which he would answer. The event was publicized as one of the first live, interactive political events. McCain was set up for success, but he failed to realize one critical factor. Politicians cannot simply use digital tools as some sort of signal to youth that they "get it." They must take the next step. McCain accepted 250 emailed questions, and he answered only 12. He made the further, fatal mistake of sticking to a script and speaking "on message," rather than spontaneously engaging with the crowd. The response was tepid. His audience saw through the spin and manipulation, and checked out.[14]

One reason Obama was so successful in reaching young people was that not only did his message of hope, change, and "we can do it together" resonate with youth, but he also allowed young people to create and pass along their version of his message to their own networks, and in the process become trusted ambassadors of a larger campaign message among their peers. They had a hand in the process, even if the message was tightly controlled by the Obama team.

Cause of the Moment

This new model of involvement is more evident in volunteering. In one of the "good news" stories of the past few decades, young people today are volunteering at rates that are higher than prior generations. Of course, some of this altruism satisfies the service learning requirements that have been added by many high schools, and some of it pads college applications or résumés. Whatever the reason for this surge of volunteerism, though, the end result is the same: More youths are giving back to their communities. As many as four out of five American high school seniors report that they volunteer. In 2008, nearly 40 percent of first-year college students and 60 percent of seniors reported doing community service or volunteer work during college, and 15 percent of seniors said they planned to continue after graduation. Most young people who do community service or volunteer work, however, do so once a month or less.[15] Nevertheless, the fact that they continue to volunteer after the obligation to do so in high school has ended is hopeful. It signals a first step on a lifelong commitment to political and civic life.

In volunteering, the Network has found that young people choose the causes they support to reflect their interests and identities. They also want to be involved in projects and volunteer efforts that have immediate and visible results and that feel authentic and genuine to them. These factors count far more to them than do institutions and group loyalties.[16] In fact, young people aren't likely to be "lifers" in supporting particular groups or organizations. Their support often ends once their work is over, and then they move on to new causes and commitments. Change is part of the game. Still, the experience of volunteering can be a gateway to lifetime involvement.

Consider Jacquie. Jacquie grew up in a tough neighborhood in Chicago. She understands how quickly life on the streets can interrupt dreams, and she wanted to find a way to prevent those costly disruptions for her friends and classmates. As part of her service learning requirement in high school, a counselor suggested she explore the Student Political Action Committee (SPAC). The two issues the SPAC was focusing on at the time were implementing mandatory comprehensive sex education and restricting military recruitment in high schools. Jacquie felt strongly about both issues. She knew how sexually active her classmates were, and she also felt that the military too often recruited young black men to fight wars they had no business fighting. "Recruiters have had so much freedom in high schools," she says, "to come in and talk to students without the permission of their parents and without the permission of the student. I thought it was an infringement of privacy, not to mention that these are minors, and they're not supposed to be taken advantage of like that while they're in high school."

Jacquie and her fellow SPAC members eventually lobbied at the state capital and won their case for creating a mandatory comprehensive sex education program in high schools across the city. Her excitement is still palpable. "I think all of us had something to do with that! The fact that so many students, and so many parents and teachers, were involved: I think that's what made it successful." They also fought to change the practices in Chicago public high schools so that students had to be explicitly informed of their right to sign an "opt-out" letter prevening their personal information from being distributed to military recruiters. Just before she graduated, the district altered its policy to meet the SPAC's requests.

These immediate and visible successes swept Jacquie up into political life. "I don't really know how to explain it. I *have* to be actively involved in any community that I'm part of. I can't just like sit around and watch things happen," she says.

When the candidacy of Barack Obama, a hometown favorite, was just taking off, Jacquie knew she had to become involved. She found a youth activist organization, and she and students from across the Chicago area traveled to Iowa to campaign in the primaries. They also attended workshops about the political process and social change. Jacquie later campaigned in Chicago and worked as an election judge during the primaries. But it was that moment in the ballot box—her very first—when all her volunteer efforts came to fruition. As an African American eighteen-year-old voting for the first black president, Jacquie suddenly understood the profundity of the moment. "I couldn't believe that it had happened, that all the work we had put into the campaign had actually paid off. And it just shows that citizens, when they come together, they can make anything happen."

Sadly, Jacquie is unusual for the type of neighborhood she comes from, which lacks the kind of connectors that hook kids into a political life. Just as inequities limit the opportunities for jobs and positive role models in tough inner-city neighborhoods, kids in these neighborhoods have unequal opportunities to get involved and challenge those inequalities. Communities like Jacquie's are often isolated politically with few ties to mainstream politicians. People are preoccupied with putting food on the table, with little time to volunteer after a commute home from work on three different buses. As a result, the number of vibrant civic associations in these areas has dwindled and disappeared.

Yet despite these odds, a growing groundswell is helping young people like Jacquie make a difference. "More activists are beginning to work with kids in the middle of Detroit or inner-city Philadelphia," says Flanagan, "and help to see that their frustrations are not an individual issue but a collective issue—and something you can act on politically. They show youth who to talk to, help them find out who is in charge, help them express their demands. Often they don't win, but that's okay. They see how it works and that they can have a voice." As Jacquie learned, the act of demanding accountability from one's political representatives, and seeing change as a result, can be empowering.

Political activism is not the only type of involvement for young people. Many volunteer in more traditional ways, such as spending time on a fund-raising drive, reading to the blind, or delivering Meals on Wheels. Austin, who is living with his parents at age twenty-nine in the St. Paul neighborhood where he grew up, volunteers for two community organizations. He works full-time but manages to put in several hours each week at the local community center swimming pool, where he manages a small team of volunteers who run the swim programs. He began the job in high school and has stayed with it ever since. He also volunteers as a committee member on the local Boy Scout troop one night a week. He has been volunteering with the Scouts since he was eighteen.

Austin echoes many others on the rewards of volunteering when he says, "Whether you're volunteering as a tutor at school, or like me, as a Boy Scout leader, it makes people's lives different. It makes *your* life more fulfilling. And that probably makes you a happier person, which probably makes you better to be around. I think volunteering can be frustrating at times, when people don't appreciate what you're doing. But I think it's meaningful. You make their lives, hopefully, one little bit better each week. And it makes your community better." For Austin, the immediacy of his actions is rewarding. He sees results every day. He is not trying to change the world; he simply gains satisfaction from helping the young boys in his neighborhood gain the chance to succeed.

Austin remains involved in his community today for a variety of reasons, but one of them is likely because he became connected early on through volunteering. Many studies have shown that such an early connection opens up young people's vistas, makes them less individualistic, and deepens their ties to their community, which they carry with them down the road. Flanagan finds that among at-risk youth, in particular, volunteering and service learning opportunities help to widen their networks of crucial "loose" ties to the outside world. In her study of a nationally representative group of more than three thousand young people in their twenties, she finds that those who volunteered during high school were twice as likely to say they had at least one adult they could turn to for advice than those who did not. Six in ten who volunteered said that they were exposed to people of different races and income levels. Engaging in service before age eighteen was related to positive civic values and behaviors in the young adult years. Young people who had engaged in service were also more likely to be well integrated into work or school—and in some cases they carry that ethos of "doing good" with them into the workforce. Their experiences as volunteers shape both the kinds of jobs they desire or choose, and the employers for whom they will work.

Clearly, not all young adults are the disconnected, apathetic generation they are made out to be. Many young people have found a connection to larger causes and ideas beyond the tiny, solipsistic orbit of self. Not only does this outward-looking approach signal a commitment to community ideals, but it is also a clear marker of adulthood. Being responsible for part of a larger world is exactly what is meant, after all, with the "oh grow up" demand.

Pick a Cause, Any Cause

Young people like Austin give their time to causes they believe in. From Save Darfur to Go Green, causes reflect the new model for participation that has captured the imagination of this generation. Causes combine two elements of the "actualizing citizen" that Bennett envisions. They are interest-driven groups with a peer-to-peer network, and they tap into the digital tools that young adults use daily. This move to cause-based activism reflects an overriding shift from institutions to individuals, said Tom Watson, author of *CauseWired,* in an interview. When the government or a lumbering organization is viewed as ineffective, young adults bypass it and develop a more direct route to help. Often these efforts take the form of a "flash cause," an instant reaction to an immediate problem, like the massive response to Hurricane Katrina, or the One Million Voices against FARC (the Revolutionary Armed Forces of

Colombia) campaign that quickly became a worldwide movement. As a result of viral marketing—passing news in ever-expanding webs of contact—thousands of protesters took to the streets worldwide to rally against the organization that the Colombian government considers a terrorist group.

The primary tool that brings young citizens together to make something happen is the Internet. Causes abound online today, and with an ease never before realized, small groups of like-minded people can come together in a mass movement.

"If you think about the Internet more broadly," says Jonathan, "it's an amazing tool to bring people together who care passionately about something—even something esoteric like saving crocodiles in South America. That easy ability to find people online who are committed—it sure beats putting up a sign in the library. That's where the power is, in getting people who are very devoted to small causes together, people who would otherwise have trouble finding each other, and to quickly disseminate information to that group."

According to Tom Watson, "Young people today [are] very oriented to causes because of how they've grown up—with constant access to news and information and with their own ideas, at least for the more elite kids. It's a Do-It-Yourself culture. They train themselves, and then they talk about it constantly. Because of the social network, and because of how much they live and work virtually, they're more open about what they're doing."

The immediacy of the result and the ability to find and tailor a cause to one's interests rather than sending money to a largely faceless charity is a huge draw for this generation. With a click on a Facebook "causes" page or an email or a tweet on a Twitter account, young adults can join a cause that rings true to them. Kiva.org is a good example of this individualized approach, employing the immediacy that this generation so loves. Kiva allows individuals to interact directly with the person they are giving money to. The "micro-lending" website combines small donations into a pool, which it then distributes to individuals on the receiving end. The individuals are real people, with pictures and life stories for all to read. Rather than give to a large, anonymous organization, donors get to help living, breathing human beings. The money buys chickens or a piece of equipment—small-scale contributions that make a world of difference. Most important for this generation, it offers an immediacy that feels good; they can see what they have done, and they feel connected to the cause.

Facebook also feeds the cause-oriented urge of this generation. Many causes on Facebook are frivolous or satiric: "Make St. George's Day a Bank Holiday!" Or the "Derek Zoolander Center for Kids Who Can't Read Good and Wanna Learn to Do Other Stuff Good Too." Others are more serious—the top cause by sheer numbers is the "Support the O Campaign for Cancer Prevention," which claims 4.4 million members, while "Save Darfur" has more than one million members.

Despite their popularity, though, these causes rarely raise much money. The Save Darfur campaign on Facebook has raised an average of about two cents for every member—hardly enough funding to support their efforts. Young adults are at an interesting intersection of commerce and cause. Not surprisingly, marketers have caught wind of the huge potential to "speak to" a generation motivated by causes. They have convinced young people to equate consumerism with charity—a nifty trick. Buy a Gap T-shirt and save a child in Africa. Buy a certain shoe and contribute $5 to the environment. "Buycotting" has replaced boycotting, the old stalwart of their parents' generation.

"Today," explains Jonathan, "we shop at stores that give 1 percent of their proceeds to a cause, and that's how we're engaged. We shop at Whole Foods and buy organic eggs not because we love or even know any small farmers, but because we have a general social conscience. Through these efforts, we've slowed the rise of sweatshops. Walmart is buying cage-free eggs. That's a big thing. I prefer to give my business to someone who is going to do something mildly better. It's one of those no-effort things."

No effort—that's the bottom line. It is easy to click. It is easy to buy a Gap T-shirt. But converting those clicks into action is what worries many organizations and activists schooled in the old way of politics by protest.

Luke is frustrated with how superficial so many causes are. When asked whether he's involved in any civic activity online, he laughs. "You know, I'm a member of the group on Facebook called 'I Have More Foreign Policy Experience than Sarah Palin.' Okay, it's funny, but it's a pretty meaningless section of Facebook, right?"

A click can only get you so far. "You can probably feel too good about a click," says Tom Watson. "It doesn't mean that much at this stage." A click doesn't yet embody real change, which requires significant investments of time and resources. A click doesn't require deeper knowledge and understanding, which are necessary for real change. A click allows young people to feel good without the "opportunity cost" of actually acting—a much harder thing. Yet it is a start. It was, after all, the method that allowed Obama to shatter fund-raising records $10 at a time.

With careful thought and planning, social networking and digital media can help elevate causes to more than a mere click. When organizers stay out of the way and let young adults pass the message along, the odds that young people will stand up and be counted is greater. The digital tools and causes that inspire this generation could be the hook that convinces more young people to become active, participating citizens. These tools and this new model of participation also hold promise for drawing in those who often feel left out of the conversation.

Across the Great (College) Divide

Jacquie, Jonathan, and Luke all share one thing in common: They are attending or have graduated from college. They are involved, albeit in different ways from the past. Whether their involvement is "meaningful," from the perspective of old-school protesters, is a question that will continue to be debated. However, they believe in their causes. Too many young people do not, and the majority of those who are not involved are those who, like Sherri, have chosen not to pursue a college degree or education after high school. Young people without college experience are two times less likely to join in, either voting or donating to a campaign, volunteering or participating in a club or community project, attending a public meeting on a community issue, or working with people on a community problem. Only 20 percent of people under age thirty with no college experience had done any of these things in the last year, compared with 40 percent of those with at least some college.[17] So, while the new youth movement is certainly exciting, particularly after decades of disconnection, that excitement is tempered by the cold reality of a continued class divide between who gets involved and who does not. And even for those with at least some college, the levels don't seem high enough to warrant great excitement.

The gap in civic involvement between those with and without college experience reflects different opportunities to learn about politics and citizenship *before* college. The lack of involvement among those with less education is not the result of character flaws, laziness, or selfishness. Rather, the groundwork that must be laid early in life is too often missing for this group, a groundwork that begins at home but also includes the schools and organizations to which these young people are exposed. The Network and other researchers have found that college-bound youth, for example, more often come from home environments that emphasized the importance of citizenship and participation in community organizations. They more often attended high schools where they studied the Constitution, took part in civic role-playing or mock trials, experienced community service, and had a wide menu of options for extracurricular activities.[18]

Once in college, the opportunities for engagement continue. College environments are natural hubs of social interest and action, and the concentration of young people who live on campuses makes it easier to recruit and mobilize students for political and civic activities. Candidates can hold rallies on college campuses, and young adults can find ready-made outlets to get involved in politics if they so desire. The college years are also intended to expand one's mind. This makes college a prime setting in which young people can explore or wrestle with diverse perspectives and issues. College students are figuring out who they are in relation to the broader world. They are beginning to choose the roles that will guide and shape them for the remainder of their lives. They are solidifying notions of personal commitments, a sense of their own capacity and skills, and a sense of connection to others. All of these things contribute to the stark divide created by college.

For Mai, a labor organizer from San Diego, college opened her eyes to the world around her. She also first began to develop a sense of identity as both a Vietnamese woman and an advocate for social welfare. The ethnic studies program at UCLA, she says, was integral to helping her figure out who she was and her place in this world. "That's where my ideas began to develop into a more political consciousness," she says. "I had a lot of different and really enriching experiences." Mai wrote for an Asian American magazine on campus, she joined various issue-related organizations, and she served in student government, "where we were trying to get an ethnic studies requirement as part of the General Education curriculum." She met many people who would serve as mentors, encouraging her to pursue her developing interests. "I was just very exposed to a lot of different ways of thinking," she says, looking back on her experience. "It was a wonderful time. I felt like I really grew. It was where I decided that in the future I wanted to do social justice work." She has made good on that promise. Today, she continues to work in the nonprofit sector as a labor organizer. She is also active in other arenas—voting, writing her representatives, protesting, and pitching in for her larger Asian American community whenever she can.

In terms of civic engagement, what matters most about the college experience is not so much what it "teaches" young people as what it connects them to in the future—the workplaces, schools, and community organizations they end up in. Individuals with college experience are more likely to end up in settings that foster civic discussion and in which they gain civic knowledge. They are also more likely to be actively invited to join organizations or attend community meetings. They feel pressure to participate because others around them are also participating. For all of these reasons, college experience becomes *the* major player in determining how involved people are in early adulthood and beyond.

When students who are not college-bound graduate from high school, they are presented with few opportunities to get involved thereafter. This is partly because there are now few outlets for them. Those without college experience are much less likely to be connected to a wide range of institutions that are the typical sites of recruitment for these types of groups—including voluntary associations, political parties, and especially unions.

For this section of the population, the withering away of unions has taken a tremendous toll on opportunities for engagement and leadership. According to Constance Flanagan, who has extensively studied the organizing potential of unions, the process of representative democracy is embedded in unions. Union leaders run for their positions, they campaign, give speeches, learn about compromise, and listen to constituents. Union members in turn elect their representatives and learn to voice their concerns in a democratic process. Unions also offer formal training in the democratic process. "It's a way of political incorporation," says Flanagan. "Unions make you feel you're included and have a voice. Except for the very wealthy, the rest of us don't have clout unless we join together with someone. For the rank and file, the sense of solidarity matters and makes a difference." The power and presence of unions evaporated with the demise of the manufacturing sector and the rise of the service sector, leaving the young people in these sectors with fewer opportunities to become acculturated into the political process and to feel that their voices have been heard.

That downward trend could be countered by online communities, with their wide reach and low barriers to participation. The online world carries the potential to level the advantages that some have over others, whether it be an outgoing personality or an impressive résumé, thereby reducing certain forms of social inequality. Online is the public square writ large.

All Can Enter Its Portals

Digital media's ability to reach new audiences in new ways holds hope for bridging the divide between young people who vote and volunteer and those who do not. Joseph Kahne recently completed a survey of video gaming and civic participation as part of the MacArthur Digital Media and Learning Initiative, in conjunction with Pew Internet and American Life Project. He finds several indications that digital media can help bridge the gap between the more elite young adults and the working-class and less fortunate young people. His work on video games, for example, finds intriguing evidence that games with civic content—including games that raise ethical questions, those that offer leadership roles, and those that offer gamers the opportunity to help novices—can encourage youths to get involved offline in civic efforts. Young people who played games with civic content were more likely than those who played games without such content to discuss issues and follow elections (the teens in Kahne's study were too young to vote), to volunteer or raise money for charity, and to work on community issues. These games are not the "chocolate-covered broccoli" learning games of the past—the good-for-you games that espouse poorly concealed civic lessons. These are games like Gamestar Mechanic or participating in the virtual world Second Life, which allow people to form and run their own societies, or to tackle issues such as pollution and poverty by organizing and cajoling thousands of other real-life players to cooperate for a greater good. Given that of eleven hundred teens surveyed, only thirty-nine had never played a video game, these games seem like key tools for engaging a wide variety of young people from all walks of life.

Kahne also finds that participating in other forms of digital media, including social networks, blogs, and Second Life, among others, exposes young people to both those who agree and those who disagree with them. The more they are exposed to this wide range of opinions, the more likely they are to become civically engaged. Other studies have found that heavy users of digital media are more aware of a wide variety of information, including ideas and positions that run contrary to their own beliefs, than are lighter users or nonusers.[19] This flies in the face of public concerns that regular or heavy Internet use is too focused on entertainment and consumption, or that it perpetuates special-interest groups and superficial relationships.

"Digital media," says Kahne, "might provide a way to reach the non-college-bound youth, given there is emerging evidence that kids who don't go to college do use digital media to a significant degree. For kids who have a less smooth transition to adulthood, digital media might introduce them to networks that could pull them in. We find that youth who do not go to college were having discussions on websites almost as often as the college group. That tells us it's possible to reach these kids."

Adulthood Delayed, Politics Delayed

The Millennials' excitement over the last presidential election, coupled with the digital world's ability to capture the interests of an ever broader group of young adults, gives us a measure of hope that they might return to the fold of civic life. We also find hope in another fact: as people get older, they tend to become more involved. The lengthening transition to adulthood itself, therefore, might be one reason that young people have delayed their plunge into civic life. If that is the case, ample opportunities exist to create new hooks to draw them into civic life during this extended path to adulthood. We outline a few of these opportunities in the book's final chapter.

Back in Detroit, Sherri readily admits she should vote and get involved, but like many in her generation, she lacks one of the key incentives that drives people to the polls: self-interest. As the passage to adulthood becomes longer, the traditional opportunities for getting involved in civic life—the PTA, union jobs, new homes and the communities that go with them—are also delayed. These adult milestones motivate people to put a stake in the ground, and that stake is often voiced at the ballot box.

Sherri and her husband have not yet felt those pulls. They have chosen to live temporarily in a mobile home park while they save money for an eventual house, and, without a traditional neighborhood, they do not feel a crystallized sense of community. They are both working in the service sector where the unions that encouraged Sherri's father, who spent his entire career on the floor of a General Motors plant, to vote are now ghosts of their once strong selves.

Sherri and Greg do not yet have children, which would immerse them in the school system, an entity that is, in itself, very political. Not only is the choice of school frequently determined by one's political district, but the schools themselves are typically funded by local taxes. There is nothing quite like paying taxes to get people to the polls. "The laws seem like they affect more people with families and children than just single adults," Sherri says, speaking for many in her generation who have not yet achieved the traditional milestones of adulthood. "I think maybe if I had kids maybe I would pay more attention to things."

Sherri is also feeling secure, both at work and at home. Her job is steady, she is happily married, she sees a decent future for her and her husband, and the indignities of crime or poverty or other social ills have not touched her and her family in any significant way. For her and Greg, there is no reason to rock the boat. They see no benefit to voting.

The stretched-out transition to adulthood pushes the once-standard portals into voting and civic involvement back by as much as a decade. Time, experience, growing interests, and a shift from looking inward to looking outward to society all change with age and maturity. This change in perspective is reinforced in the hundreds of interviews the Network conducted. We had much more meaningful discussions about community involvement with those in their late twenties and early thirties. These discussions had a reflective quality about the civic world that is not as apparent in interviews with those in their late teens and early twenties. As Anne, a twenty-nine-year-old married mother, explains it, "the twenties are a pretty self-involved time... not necessarily in a bad way, but when you're just kind of figuring out your own life. Maybe it's just that you're more inward-focused than outward-focused, and you're not quite as aware of the world around you and your role in it." As people get older, they figure that out—especially, she says, "once you have a family and you realize, 'Okay, I need to help shape the world for them.'"

This delay in civic involvement is also evident in voting data. The Network tracked voting rates among first-time voters dating back to the 1960s and found that with age, voting becomes more common. The generation that came of age in 1960 voted at a high rate from the start and had only modest rises in voting over time. They began voting at a rate of 67 percent; over the course of eight presidential elections, their turnout increased to 78 percent. Each successive generation since has had increasingly lower starting points, but each generation has also become substantially more engaged during their twenties and thirties. Although slower to the starting line, perhaps because the traditional markers of adulthood and adult responsibilities have been pushed back, young people eventually increase their voting. Sinking voter turnout is certainly a cause for concern, but all may not be lost—as young people slowly but surely begin to assume the mantle of adulthood, more will begin to cast their vote.

Hope for the Future

The traditional indicators of involvement in politics and community life among young adults do show alarming declines. But our findings reveal that this generation is delaying, not rejecting, those commitments. We suspect that as young people settle into the roles and responsibilities of adulthood, they will be recruited into civic action and will at the same time plant a stronger stake in politics and government.

Few periods of life embody as much possibility for civic engagement, with as much potential payoff, as the early-adult years—especially in light of the longer passage to adulthood today. While increasing the engagement of young people helps secure the future of our democracy, civic engagement fosters the skills and capacities of young adults. For the swimmers, it can be instrumental in helping them find themselves as they begin to carve out their identities as adults. They can wrestle with social issues, explore and express their personal values and beliefs, have growth experiences, and find like-minded others, to name but a few benefits.

But civic engagement holds far greater possibilities for those who are treading and even sinking. For these at-risk youth, civic engagement can provide an important gateway to building skills, experiences, and resources that they would otherwise not have. It gives them the opportunity to learn important lessons about being a leader, working with teams, and effecting change, and allows them to see firsthand the outcomes of social action. And it also increases these young peoples' prospects by building up their résumés and expanding their social networks. The key to tapping into this potential is creating solid opportunities that ring true to young people. Obama and his team took a first step, but there is a long way to go.

The gulf in civic participation between those who go to college and those who do not is alarming. Ethnic minorities and new immigrants, as well as young people from working-class backgrounds, are less likely to complete high school or attend college. As such, it is important that opportunities for civic involvement be created at work, at church, in neighborhoods, and in other places so that these groups might be better incorporated into the body politic. Providing deep and meaningful civic experiences for teens before college can also lead to higher grades and a more involved school career, as was the case with Jacquie. This might just be the ticket to getting more disadvantaged youth into and through college. In the broader perspective, failing to do this is a disservice—not only to our democratic ideals, but to the future of the nation as well.

In the wake of the recent presidential election, many Americans seemed to have a renewed sense of hope in the government and in the political process. That optimism has faded with the financial crisis and deep recession. Politicians and others in the public sphere must continue to engage with young adults in ways that are meaningful to them.

The growing disconnection of young adults from conventional politics signals a crisis. What seemed like a turnaround in the last major election was, indeed, a change in a positive direction, but at levels that were neither high nor necessarily permanent. It was also carried by young adults in college or with college degrees.

The traditional modes of political engagement matter for the survival of democracy, especially voting. But emergent modes of engagement matter, too, especially digital media, for they will become mainstream conventions in the years to come. Many young people are actively engaged—just not in ways older people might immediately recognize. Youth today are tuned in to new forms of social networking and political action. As Jacquie says, it's important for her elders to realize that her generation is not uninvolved, just involved differently. This potential must be actively nurtured if Sherri and her many detached peers are to become involved in their society and have a say in its future. No less than our democracy is at stake.

8

Converging Destinies: Prescriptions for Change

Who Is Responsible for the Welfare of Young People?

The fates of many young people, not just in the United States but also around the world, ultimately hang on the question of who is responsible for their well-being: young people themselves, their families, marketplaces, or governments?

A globalized economy and the increasingly privatized and deregulated marketplace have placed greater responsibility on families for launching young adults—just as the process of becoming an adult has grown longer and more complicated. More than at any time in recent history, parents are being called on to provide assistance to their young adult children. Yet the ability of families to do so varies greatly based on the resources they have or can access through their formal or informal connections to other people, organizations, and social settings.

The different resources of families lock young people's diverging destinies into place. Those from middle-class and elite families receive significant investments of money, time, and other kinds of support from their parents, which help them make it through their twenties. The differences in financial outlays by household income are massive. Parents whose earnings place them in the top 25 percent of earners nationwide gave their adult children (ages twenty-one through twenty-four in 2007) an average of $17,615 in 2006, while parents in the bottom 25 percent were able to give only about $4,500.[1] For middle- and upper-class youths, these investments build upon the prior two decades in which their parents worked to cultivate their skills and capital to increase the likelihood that they would do well in adulthood. The foundations for their less privileged peers are shakier and often seriously cracked. Of course, it has always been true that some youths do well and others do not, regardless of resources. Having resources is no guarantee of success, just as the absence of resources does not mean that a young person is predestined to fail. But the presence of resources surely increases the likelihood of positive outcomes in early adulthood. And it buffers poor judgments and mistakes, which are more perilous today as the safety nets on which post–World War II generations could rely—pensions and health insurance, steady work with benefits, and company loyalty, to name a few—are fraying.

Middle-class families have been hit hard as they try to piece together the support that young adult children need. Many families that once seemed strongly positioned to help their children are now experiencing new vulnerabilities amid the Great Recession that began in 2008. As the middle class shrinks and family incomes vacillate from year to year in an uncertain economy, families cannot afford to offer the same set of resources to their children.[2] Families on the low end of the middle-income bracket seem particularly vulnerable—they have some, but not ample, resources, and their incomes are just enough to render them ineligible for government support. Yet even for solidly middle-class families, all of this support comes with long-term costs, as decisions are set against second mortgages and compromised retirement funds.

Working-class families can offer even less, as their incomes have stagnated since the 1970s and secure jobs have all but disappeared. In addition to having more limited resources, or perhaps because of it, working-class parents more often believe in early independence for their children, leaving them on their own at a time when many of their peers are benefiting from the extended support of their parents. For those young people whose family lives are more fragile or whose families simply cannot afford to help them, the independence comes sometimes even earlier. Young people who have been in the foster care or the juvenile justice system are abruptly cut off from support when they reach the legal age of adulthood, eighteen or in some cases twenty-one. Not only must they fend entirely for themselves, but it is this group of vulnerable youth who is often least equipped to manage.

Although families shoulder the brunt of responsibility in determining how young people in the United States fare as they make their way into adulthood, governments are also powerful forces in this process. Nations provide dramatically different packages of resources to young people. The amount and type of government support depends on the degree to which young people are seen to be at risk, and on the assumptions that governments make about who is responsible for managing those risks and swallowing the costs. Some governments offer strong scaffolding to young people as they make their way through educational institutions and job markets or form families.[3] Others, like the United States, offer very weak scaffolding for young people, placing a high premium on self-reliance and private solutions to personal troubles. The United States takes a "sink or swim" philosophy, leaving it up to individuals and their families to navigate markets for education, jobs, housing, and partners on their own. This results in highly competitive high-wire acts. During these years, young people make decisions and take actions that have significant cumulative effects over the many decades of life ahead. Good decisions are critical to a successful adulthood, and bad ones can be disastrous. As a result, it is not surprising that a higher proportion of young people in the United States seem to "tread water" or "sink" relative to those in other countries.[4]

The challenges of the transition to adulthood extend well beyond the most vulnerable groups, beyond what might be perceived as small segments of the population. These challenges are felt acutely through the ranks of the middle class. The young person who does not need significant help in entering adulthood seems the exception today. Yet there remains a gaping mismatch between the realities of contemporary life and the assumption guiding laws and policies that, at age eighteen or twenty-one, individuals have crossed the threshold of adulthood where "dependence" magically ends and "independence" magically begins. In reality, few young people today, even those closing out their twenties, would be considered "adult" based on traditional markers such as living on one's own, being finished with school or employed full-time, being married, or having children. And few young people today actually *feel* like full-fledged adults. Even in their late twenties and early thirties, most say they feel adult in some ways but not yet in others.[5] The boundary between adolescence and adulthood has become very blurry in terms of both behavior and state of mind.

One wonders whether a more relevant milestone in today's world is not the achievement of independence, which has long been the central defining characteristic of adulthood, but instead the achievement of strong ties to others—what we might instead call interdependence. To compensate for new uncertainties and the weak scaffolding provided by some families and governments, an effective strategy for young people making their way into adulthood is to build wider and stronger webs of relationships with others. A strong social network of personal and professional contacts can foster development and provide a set of supports that can be activated as needed. Interdependence is not about completely relying on others for one's own welfare, but is instead about knowing how to make and maintain positive, healthy, reciprocal relationships that offer a safety net for oneself and contribute to the safety nets of others.

Meaningful relationships with others have significant effects on a wide array of young adult outcomes—bolstering school achievement, success in jobs, emotional maturity, and satisfaction with life, and keeping problem behaviors such as substance or alcohol abuse in check. On a more superficial level, interdependence can also affect outcomes via wide networks of loosely connected acquaintances who provide access to precious opportunities and resources.

In the United States, the costs for managing the extended transition to adulthood are, to a great degree, private ones, carried by whatever social connections or resources young people and their parents have or can create. Yet the transition takes place within multiple institutional contexts, such as higher education, housing markets, the workplace, and communities. How these institutions interact with, guide, and shape the transition to adulthood is based on old models of life that are often out of sync with our lives today. The investments that society makes in the institutions are important. We must rethink many of these core institutions—including marriage and family, schools and work organizations, health insurance, leisure, retirement—and the policies and practices surrounding them.

We offer several suggestions for new directions. We begin with suggestions for parents, given that most of the responsibility for young adults lies with them—a fact that is unlikely to change. We believe, however, that the marketplace and government should play larger roles in this transition period, easing some of the disparities created by the growing inequalities in families' resources. We therefore offer some fledgling ideas and point to some solid programs that are creating opportunities for those from the disappearing middle class, including clearer routes into school, work, and healthy families.

Parents, Be Present . . .

Parents are not "at fault" for creating a longer and more complex transition to adulthood for their children. As we have seen, many social and economic forces are bigger culprits. But it is parents who play a major role in determining how children are positioned when they reach adulthood, what happens to them as they make their way, and how they fare when all is said and done. Strong, healthy relationships between parents and young adults are one of the most significant factors in determining whether young people succeed in early adulthood. Feeling close to parents is an important part of this.

Even more critical is having the active guidance and support of parents. Young adults need to make their own decisions, but they require guidance now more than ever. Throughout the transition to adulthood, parents should help their children sort out options, contemplate pros and cons, unearth opportunities, and understand the expectations of the adult world. This makes a huge difference, and it doesn't require much in terms of resources. The support of adults other than parents is also crucial, especially for young people who come from fragile families or from families where parents don't have the necessary skills or knowledge.

For this reason, being hands-off and even allowing children to learn by the school of hard knocks when they reach early adulthood is often counterproductive to helping them get ahead. Without the guidance of parents, young people can make serious mistakes that could have been avoided and cannot be easily undone. Hands-off parenting has cumulative consequences in that children, after being left to their own devices for so long, reach adulthood with far fewer skills and fewer well-formed ideas about the future than those whose parents have been hands-on. Intervening in a young person's life to avoid harmful outcomes can only be a good thing. True, it is important for young people to be responsible for their decisions and to learn from their mistakes. But it is also unnecessary to let young adult children make mistakes that are certain to be damaging by not intervening.

All parents and children would benefit from one thing: clear, regular communication. The unparalleled closeness between today's parents and children is the very thing that can open new kinds of conversation as children make their way into adulthood. Whether children are heading off to college, finding first apartments and jobs, or staying at home, both parents and children should talk about their expectations during this time of change.

Consider communication itself: How often do you each want to communicate, and through what medium? What topics are off limits? Similarly, it would be helpful for parents and children to talk about expectations about visits and dropping in, any rules parents have for staying at home (think: sleeping arrangements with boyfriends or girlfriends), and any expectations children have about how parents will interact with their friends, supervisors from work, or college faculty and administrators. And when teens head off to college, it is advisable for their parents to talk with them about how often they'll communicate about their grades and other needs or difficulties. (Under the Family Education Rights and Privacy Act, administrators and faculty can communicate very little information to parents directly about their student.) This is also a critical moment for open conversation about sensitive topics, such as alcohol and drugs, dating, sexual health, and money.

Regardless of whether young people are bound for college, they need to understand that failure happens, and that at some point it will happen to them. Many parents today have fostered a sense of invincibility in their children. Young people often do not understand how much time and effort they must invest if they are to get the grades they need or the jobs they want. This lack of understanding was very apparent in our chapter on education. The mentality of young people today is often that they are consumers of higher education, buying their degrees to ensure a certain kind of future. Many even feel entitled to degrees in exchange for expensive tuition. The growing corporate climates of universities also exacerbate the student-as-consumer mentality.

Many members of this generation have been reared to believe that their potential is limitless. If young people are to be successful, they should have plans for education and work that are detailed and realistic. Not everyone can be at the top. High ambitions cannot be met if clear plans and solid skills are absent. Parents must help their children to honestly assess the skills they have, what they need to do to achieve their goals, and whether those goals are realistic.

It is not just parents who must provide better and more realistic guidance to young adults. So must the institutions that serve young people. Consider grade inflation. In high schools and colleges, grade distributions are heavily weighted toward the upper end. Receiving a C is interpreted as a kiss of death for students, and teachers and professors are often afraid to give them, particularly since they know that doing so might lead to uncomfortable confrontations. But the meaning of C is "average," and most students are, by definition, average. As parents and teachers, we're not being frank with our children and students about their performance and their potential, and what they need to accomplish if they are to get on in the world.

Parents can also help prepare young adults by teaching them a set of life skills that extends beyond book learning. High-achieving and elite parents regularly instill these skills in their children, including etiquette, comfort with and respect for adults, time management, strategic thinking, responsibility, and self-management. All families, regardless of income, can impart these valuable skills to their children. In the case of less advantaged families, however, it's hard for parents to coach children if they haven't learned to play the game or kept up with how the rules have changed. These parents can still help their children, though, by encouraging them to make connections outside the home in after-school programs, Boy Scouts and Girl Scouts, church, and other places that foster these critical life skills.

In our interviews, it is clear that closeness to parents is mostly about mothers, not fathers. Many young men and women have detached relationships with their fathers, and destructive relationships are almost always with fathers and almost always in the lives of treaders. In an era when we herald the "new" father, it is both disappointing and painful to hear these stories continue. But they remind us of how important it is to continue the quest to improve fathers' involvement in the lives of their children—and not just when the children are little. The young adult years are the perfect opportunity for fathers to begin building stronger relationships with their children. If relationships between fathers and children are on shaky ground going into the early-adult years, which is true in so many cases, it's hard to create closeness later on. This is a call for fathers who are uninvolved or marginally involved to get more engaged with their children. It is not just children who benefit: many middle-aged and older fathers want closer relationships with their children. It is an enduring theme in the lives of men.

. . . But Recognize When to Step Back

Being an involved parent and helping in these ways is different from doing *everything* for a child. It is in the doing part that lines are easily crossed, and it is precisely here where parents can get themselves into trouble by going too far. Young adults can and should distinguish themselves from their parents by the time they are in their twenties, even if they have not yet managed to completely separate themselves psychologically, socially, or financially. Despite their best intentions, parents can be overly protective, which only sustains the dependence of children on parents. Tending the skills and opportunities of young adult children is different from coddling them or refusing to let them grow up. Some problems need to be experienced and solved by young people in order for them to mature, even if it is difficult for parents to resist the impulse to step in.

Parents feel a sense of happiness and self-satisfaction in seeing their children succeed in adulthood, but our child-centric culture, which prompts such great investments in children, can also create anxiety, guilt, and shame when children do not succeed, especially among middle-class and elite parents. Not only do these parents often feel responsible for their children when they become adults, but they judge their own self-worth and value on the successes or failures of their adult children.

Parents of young adults should also resist the impulse to say or think "When I was a kid ..." because the expectations and conditions that exist now are not the same as when they were making their way into adulthood. These comparisons will only leave children feeling defensive. Parents should be sensitive to the challenges that young adult children are facing, whether in the economy, school, work, social, or romantic life. They should try to imagine what it must feel like to be where their child is in life, and to ask what it feels like and how they might help. Above all, parents should be mindful of the fact that the relationship they have with their young adult child is being reworked from the child's vantage point too.

The closeness and contact between young people and their parents today is unprecedented. So, too, are the many decades of life in which they co-survive. These simple facts mean that the boundaries between parents and children are no longer as rigid as they once were, and that relationships need to be continually revised not only as children are becoming adults, but as they move through adulthood, become middle-aged, and even come to know their parents in old age. But what this also means is that there are no clear scripts for how adult relationships between parents and children are supposed to go as everyone grows older together.

One basic piece of advice is this: Hyperinvolved parents, step back and don't do so much for your young adult children. Underinvolved parents, step in and get more hands-on. What we are advocating is something like what Michael Kimmel, author of *Guyland,* called in a recent interview, "Power-Strip Parenting: You help keep your kid grounded. You help them plug in. Then, if there's an overload, you run interference."[6] Hyperinvolved parents should turn the wattage down, and underinvolved ones should turn it up.

What's Wrong with Living at Home?

One of the biggest changes between today and the recent past are the growing ranks of young people who live at home with their parents well into their twenties, whether because they've never left or because they've boomeranged back. There has been much hand-wringing and moralizing about this trend. Yet living at home needn't carry the stigma it does in the United States. In fact, too firm a push from parents to leave home, or too impulsive a jump from young people themselves, may lead to trouble.

Living at home can help ensure more positive futures—*if* young people are actively engaged in activities that move them forward while they're at home. Time at home can permit young people to pursue an education, and allow them to offset costs for an interim while they get on their feet. It can offer a built-in set of supportive ties of family and friends to bolster progress toward a successful future. It can lend young people some space to gain work experiences and marketable skills and contacts, especially if they're in low-paying or no-paying internships or apprenticeships. And it can provide resources for other growth-expanding experiences, such as pursuing special interests and hobbies or traveling abroad. Again, what is most critical is that the time at home is used to its full advantage in cultivating skills, credentials, contacts, and experiences.

Living at home also allows young people to save for a future down payment on a home or to gather a nest egg for a stronger launch. In an era of retrenched budgets and tight labor markets, it will take more time to find a decent job to get started. Because earnings in the early part of one's career set the course for future gains, staying at home longer may be a particularly good strategy for those who have a shaky foundation. As long as these young people are contributing to the household in some way and are pursuing higher education, training, or actively looking for work, a longer stay can help ensure a better future—even if it inevitably creates some challenges or tensions. Parents and children should talk about expectations related to rent and other household contributions, rules to live by, how long children can stay, and the like.

While living at home makes good sense in many cases, what if young people are not working, not in school, or not engaged in any forward-moving activities? Should parents resort to "tough love" and kick their kids out of the house? In our view, tough love rarely works. And for kids who have little capital to make it on their own—skills, credentials, steady work, maturity—being kicked out can send them spiraling downward. In these cases, what seems best is for parents to clearly communicate their expectations, to set clear and realistic goals *with* (rather than for) the young adult. When progress isn't being made, parents—and young adult children—must face difficult decisions. Parents' responses must be sensitive to the family's unique circumstances. There are no hard-and-fast rules or tried-and-true responses. But what we can say is this: In our interviews, young people who have been in this situation have, especially in retrospect, told us that they needed guidance and appreciated that their parents didn't give up on them or create ultimatums that might have backfired. When children live at home, however, most of that cost is still carried by parents. Not all families can afford to offer this support to their children.

For young people who are not college-bound or whose families cannot afford to provide for them at home, we wonder whether it might be possible to create innovative, alternative living spaces, subsidized by public or private resources or partnerships, that might mirror what is provided to students who live on college and university campuses. Four-year residential colleges function as a replacement for parents—professors, advisers, administrators, and residence hall directors all track and monitor the academic progress and social life of students, and the very organization of student life, even the curriculum, facilitates friendships and peer groups. College campuses are also full-service institutions, one-stop shops for a wide variety of amenities: housing, meals, shopping, counseling, banking, health care centers, fitness centers, student organizations, and social activities. To some degree, the military is similarly designed to nurture the futures of young adults by providing a setting in which they can live, work, and learn.

Why not design something similar for young people who are not bound for four-year colleges or the military, but who are instead working or commuting to community colleges or trade schools? These residential settings could provide one-stop shopping for job advice and networking. Employers could offer weekend seminars on the kinds of jobs in their organization, the skills required for those jobs, and what typical career trajectories look like. Young people could have access to mentors and job coaches who volunteer their time. They could also find other needed services, such as information on college loans, health insurance, or social supports. As Network associate Thomas Brock of MDRC also notes, it is an irony that the most selective institutions of higher education take the most capable students and wrap them in support, while the least selective institutions provide the least support—and barely any support or advice is directed toward those who are not bound for higher education. Finding ways to create similar opportunities for these latter groups is critical to improving their futures.

Don't Underinvest in the Future

Living at home while preparing for the future leads to one of our most critical messages: Young adulthood is a time to invest. But too many young people and their parents are, for a variety of reasons, risk-averse. They fear taking on debt to finance their futures. As we have argued, however, young adulthood is the prime time in life to take these "risks" and invest in oneself and one's future. This inevitably comes with debt, but there is such a thing as good debt.

Young people as a whole drastically underconsume in their twenties and early thirties by failing to borrow against their future earnings. Young adults and their parents should view college and other forms of training after high school as long-term personal investments rather than short-term, high-price-tag expenditures. As access to college has opened and its costs have risen exponentially, many young adults and their parents understandably worry about how to finance it. It is precisely the

families who are not well positioned economically who may see education as being beyond their reach, something that is discretionary rather
than required. This leads us to worry that those whose lives are tenuous—
our treaders—will be the ones to opt out.

More grants and scholarships are needed for those young adults who
are capable and eager to get started in college, but whose families earn
too little to help them invest in their futures. The value of Pell Grants,
the leading source of grants for low-income students, has not kept pace
with inflation or with the rising costs of college, meaning that these
grants now cover a lower share of the burden of paying for college than
they originally did. The 2010 overhaul of the Federal Family Education
Loan program, a bank-based student lending program, redirects $36 bil-
lion over ten years to Pell Grants for low-income students. The bill also
adds automatic increases, tied to inflation, in the maximum Pell Grant
award. However, this translates to a rather paltry $500 increase in the
maximum Pell Grant for a year. The legislation does make the loan
slightly less burdensome for students by enhancing the income-based
payment plans and shortening the point when loans are forgiven outright. In 2014, young adults will not have to devote more than 10 percent
of their incomes to student loan payments, down from 15 percent today.

Despite these slight improvements, families are being called on to
foot larger bills than ever before, and not all families can keep up. The
GI Bill after World War II is often credited with jump-starting the
streak of innovations and economic advances that positioned the United
States as the world leader in science and technology. It would be more
than a shame to lose the talents of bright young people simply because
they perceive that they cannot afford to attend college. While the middle
and upper classes can invest in their children's futures by sacrificing
some of their luxuries today—and therefore are less in need of government subsidies—the working class and lower ranks do not have that
same leeway. They cannot cut back any more than they already have.

For students who have the credentials to get into the nation's finest
institutions of higher education, the difference between going to a top-
tier school and one just below it won't likely make much difference in
terms of life outcomes. These students are certain to go to college, get degrees, and do well, no matter where they go. Any gains or losses from

going one place rather than another will be marginal. For those with more tenuous credentials, what matters is getting a degree. One's life chances and outcomes will be dramatically different for it. And yes, even in today's house-of-cards economy—especially in today's economy—the evidence is clear: a college degree still pays. The costs of college will be recouped and will result in cumulative gains in earnings over a lifetime of work.

This comes with an important caveat: We can say with certainty that college pays off when students finish. If they get there and fail, it's another story. For students who are ill prepared for college or unsure about whether it's right for them, it can be an expensive way to wander. It's also a serious risk for a young adult to take on college debt if the likelihood of failure is high. Without a degree, young people will lack access to the jobs and opportunities that will make it possible to pay off these loans.

While some of the responsibility lies with the students' earlier education in elementary and high schools and with parents, some of the risk of not graduating lies in the incentive structures at universities themselves. Federal funding is tied to enrollment rates, not graduation rates. Flipping the equation and tying funding to graduation rates might spark new innovations and support services for at-risk students. Likewise, other perverse incentives that favor churning freshmen through the system should be reviewed. Prospective students and their parents are often at a loss about graduation rates, as they are rarely published in meaningful forms—at least not as frequently as enrollment rates. Magazines such as *U.S. News & World Report* should include college rankings by graduation rates along with the other criteria that they advertise. They might follow the example of *Washington Monthly,* which has devised a measure of the "social mobility" of a college—the number of at-risk and low-income students the school graduates. The formula predicts a school's likely graduation rate based on its percentage of Pell students and its average SAT score. Schools that outperform their forecasted rate score better than schools that match or miss the mark. Another positive step is that the federal Department of Education now informs financial aid applicants of the graduation rate at the college to which they are applying. More of these efforts should be instigated.

Money is a touchy subject for most families. Yet understanding money and budgeting is perhaps one of the most important lessons families can teach their children. Young adults may make some bad mistakes with credit because they are inexperienced in handling money or because they do not understand the fine print of their credit cards or loan arrangements. A solid dose of financial literacy is as important as learning world history or quadratic equations. High schools and colleges offer little course work on managing spending, taxes, and saving, and few students understand the practical meaning of the debt they are accruing. The assumption is that this is the responsibility of children's families. Yet in many families, parents rarely talk to their children about finances; family finances may even be kept under wraps. Much more should be done in schools and at home to equip young people with the skills they'll need to manage finances in everyday life once they're out there on their own, such as teaching children how to manage checking accounts, how credit cards work, how credit scores are determined, what it means for one's future chances of getting loans for homes and cars, and how to establish a budget. Parents should voice clear expectations for who will pay for what—and young adults should definitely be responsible for some part of the outlay. When parents cover all expenses, they do not foster financial independence.

Beyond College for All

There is another topic we talk little about in this country: the reality that not everyone can or will succeed. There is an enduring myth of self-invention and a level playing field for all. However, the playing field is very different for young people depending on the family, school, and work environments in which they and their families are embedded.

Everyone has heard the mantra: *College is the ticket.* Yet we fool ourselves in believing that a four-year college degree is possible for and desired by everyone. In fact, it seems dangerous to mislead students into thinking they are college material if it is clear they are not. Yet the very ones who need good counseling, clearer direction, and stronger directives are the very young people who don't get these things. It is here that more supports are needed. Guidance counselors in high schools may have helped in the past, but these services have been severely pared down or outright eliminated from fledgling or failing schools. As with parental support, the lack of such services in these under-resourced and challenged schools is all the more debilitating for students when it is measured against the extensive guidance services provided by privileged schools, with their troops of counselors writing letters, making calls, and helping with applications.

Jonathan reminded us of how starkly different the realities were in two different high schools. At his high school in a wealthy suburb of New York, "Something like 95 percent of the kids went to four-year colleges," he says. "And there's a reason for that. There's a whole infrastructure built up to make it happen. There are counselors who are dedicated. English classes are focused on writing essays... All of a sudden, you're aware of how many resources you have."

Contrast this with Tyler, who saw his high school counselor only once and was told not to strive for anything beyond high school. The counselor's advice may have seemed cruel at the time, but he understood something many do not: Not every high school senior is college material, and neither academic counseling nor basic remedial courses in a college environment can compensate for a lifetime of little guidance or skill building. It's also important to recognize that not everyone is truly ready for college at age eighteen. If we are to be frank with kids about their futures and their performance, we must offer realistic and equally valuable alternatives to four-year degrees. Tyler's counselor told him to not bother with college, but he didn't tell Tyler what to do instead. Young adults like Tyler need alternatives to the college path.

Some training beyond high school is necessary today. But "training" should not always be equated with a four-year college degree, at least straight out of high school. For some youths, other, less direct routes may be more fruitful, effective, and profitable. A gap year between high school and college might be just the thing for students who lack direction, giving them time to explore their interests and mature. Service opportunities like the Peace Corps or AmeriCorps can be invaluable in connecting young people with mentors and expanding their horizons. Other teens should be afforded clear paths from high school to work via a stop in some well-directed training program. To make these paths "real" for them we must give them clear ideas about what it means to "go into computers," for example: what jobs are available in "computers," what it takes to get those jobs, and what kinds of training they need.

We certainly should not lose sight of how to equip as many children as possible with the skills they need to be successful in higher education. But with the dropout rates in college as high as they are, and fewer than half of community college students ever making it to a four-year school, it is important to create valuable and productive alternatives. Educators and parents must provide more comprehensive guidance to young people so that they can more easily discover what they're best matched for, what steps they need to take to get there, and find the best options that are out there for them. This is particularly important for our treaders, but also for many of our swimmers, who—despite being highly skilled—are often wandering through college without direction. We outline some of these alternatives below, but there are many possibilities that need to be explored in order for us to secure these young people's futures.

Some young people also simply need more time to find their way. Whether we like to admit it or not, social class has a stronghold on the destinies of young Americans. We have seen its legacy time and time again in our analyses and interviews. We must therefore allow for the possibility that some very capable young people from disadvantaged backgrounds will need a little extra time to catch up. Giving up on them too soon would be tragic. These students need programs that lessen the risks of trying and failing. Promising ideas include "freshman forgiveness" policies that reduce the toll of poor grades in the first year on academic standing or financial assistance, loan forgiveness or reduction to ease the burden of those who try but fail early on in college, or other plans that stagger risks and costs to acknowledge the fact that some students have serious vulnerabilities coming into college.

Most universities are also now offering comprehensive and extended orientation to incoming students to help them make the transition into college. This isn't just about introducing new students to the college; it's about acquainting them with a wide range of support services on campus that are meant to foster their success. It is also about teaching students how to be successful in their courses, how to manage their time, and how to make social connections but also manage social life alongside their academic demands. These things are particularly important for students who are first-generation college-goers, who come from disadvantaged backgrounds, and who have other academic vulnerabilities.

In the end, what is most critical is that all young people be helped to find a direction that matches their interests and skill sets, and that they be provided with a clear sense of the steps that are required to get there. Below we outline ways to help young people forge a successful path to school or work.

Career Academies as a Route from School to Work

One promising option for those who are not bound for four-year colleges is the high school career academy. "This is not the old vo-tech model," says MDRC's Robert Ivry, who has long been involved in evaluating the effectiveness of these programs. Rather than relegating students who are not on the college track to the ugly stepsister role, as is often the case with the vocational track in high schools today, these programs serve a broad cross section of students. "They're neither stigmatized nor elitist," says Ivry of these career academies. "They include students who also take AP classes and those struggling. Career academies make the educational experience come alive by bringing coherence to classroom work. The programs tie all classes together around a career, and in doing so they make school feel more relevant." Currently there are twenty-five hundred of these academies around the country operating as schools within schools and serving approximately thirty to sixty students per grade. Some of the academies are funded through states. Students take classes together as a cohort, mix traditional academics with career-focused studies, and take part in various internships or apprenticeships.

A career academy in California, for example, focuses on the health industry. During students' freshman and sophomore years, the curriculum focuses on work readiness in addition to basic studies. They might learn about the SAT process and receive other preparation for college, but the majority of the focus is on career development. By their junior year, the students are shadowing health care providers on the job, which exposes them to the range of options available in the field. In their senior year, they complete a paid internship in a local hospital. "They are high-quality jobs," says Ivry. "They're working in medical labs in hospitals, or if they're in a computer academy, they're working at Intel, or they're at the launchpad in Coco Beach, Florida, if they're in an aerospace academy." The classes offered in career academies also reflect students' career interests. Students in the health care academy, for example, read about the discovery of penicillin in their science classes. "It's really exciting," says Ivry. "It gives them more of a sense of purpose, more a feel of what it's like to work in the real world."

Students in career academies like the fact that they are better known by their teachers. They also have a greater comfort zone with their teachers. In many high schools, students who are not college-bound often feel that teachers are not as engaged with them as they are with their college-bound peers. In career academies, these students suddenly feel that school is more relevant and they have a greater sense of purpose. The programs also do something else that is invaluable for low-income youth: They provide personal references and experiences for résumés, things that these students' more privileged peers take for granted.

MDRC has rigorously evaluated several of these career academies, and the results are astonishing: Eight years after high school, career academy students were earning significantly more than their peers who were not in the program—in total, $30,000 more over the eight years combined. "That is equivalent to the earnings gains from an associate's degree," says Robert Ivry. "That's not to say kids should skip the degree, but clearly there's a labor market payoff to career academies." Those earnings also allowed young people to make a more successful transition to adulthood. They were more likely to be married, to not be single parents, and to be living independently from their parents than their classmates who did not go through the program.

Improving Community College Experiences

Improving the community college experience is also on the agenda of reformers, including the Bill and Melinda Gates Foundation. The Obama administration has also recognized the important role of community colleges in strengthening the skills and opportunities of those who do not or cannot go on to four-year colleges by proposing $2 billion in additional funding for job-related training. The administration also plans to more tightly link community colleges with employers.

Community colleges are a critical ladder to success for students who cannot afford or are not prepared for four-year schools, those who are returning to school after time in the workforce, or those who have been sidetracked by early family responsibilities. However, a variety of factors—ranging from a lack of financial aid to inadequate student services and poor "remedial" classes—can impede student progress.

Community colleges and their students are also, in some ways, the wave of the future. The traditional model of higher education is rapidly changing, with student demand for more convenient class times (evenings, weekends, or in intensive spurts) and formats (completely online or online mixed with face-to-face instruction); for flexibility in transferring courses across institutions and in moving between full-time and part-time statuses; and for lower-cost options, to name a few. There is no question that the University of 2020 will look dramatically different from the institutions we know today, and the four-year full-time program done in residence will be a much less frequent pathway through higher education.[7]

Several innovative programs are in the works to improve retention and graduation rates at community colleges. One novel program, on which the Network is collaborating with MDRC, is Opening Doors. Opening Doors is designed to test a handful of interventions meant to improve graduation rates and later job success for low-income students. In the sites that focused on an intervention based on "learning communities," for example, small groups of students moved through a common set of classes, which gave them the ability to assist one another, form study groups, and build relationships that carry the potential for support beyond the classroom. Other sites offered interventions in child care, intense career and education counseling, or small performance-based financial incentives. The different elements of these programs are being tested in a range of community colleges across the country, including those that serve nontraditional and low-income students.

These evaluations have been very promising to date, particularly in light of the rigor of the evaluations. MDRC is using a control group and experimental group to test the programs' effectiveness. The study compares the experiences of students who receive the Opening Doors interventions with those of students who simply receive existing services. The study design allows evaluators to conclude with certainty that the program itself is responsible for any resulting differences in the groups' outcomes.

Early results of the performance-based financial incentives, for example, show fairly strong gains among a population of largely low-income single mothers in Louisiana who have returned to college. The financial stipend encouraged more of these students to register for college and to register full-time. Students were more likely to persist in their course of study, being about 30 percent more likely to register for a third semester than students in the control group. The program also increased the number of credits that students earned, and had a positive impact on some social and psychological outcomes, like feeling positive and more able to accomplish long-term goals.

The gains that result for community college students with these kinds of interventions, and the gains that result for non-college-bound high school students in career academies, point to the possibility of real success for at-risk youth when programs are well designed and when they address the true needs of students and the emerging workforce. Too many young adults are entering the world of work sorely unprepared for the types of jobs that will be available to them, or without the types of soft skills—things like showing up on time, dressing appropriately, and taking instruction from superiors—that are necessary to stay employed and to advance.

Often, though, even when a four- or even two-year degree isn't necessary for effective on-the-job performance, it will still be imposed as a job requirement. An emphasis on finding ways to certify that applicants have the specific, requisite skills for a job seems preferable to rigidly clinging to degrees that may have little to do with the job itself or an employee's performance in it. This strategy, too, would open up opportunities for non-college-bound youth to compete for positions for which they are genuinely suited.

On the Job Without a Net

The landscape for jobs will change dramatically in the future. Some argue that the "Great Recession" that began in late 2008 is the nail in the coffin for many industries, and that we are in the midst of a fundamental restructuring of the labor market. Who knows what things will look like five or ten years from now, but one thing seems certain: New industries will emerge from the ashes of this collapse, and those industries will demand higher-skilled workers who are even more flexible and nimble than workers today. General skill sets that are transferable to a variety of jobs may be most beneficial in this rapidly changing economy. Workers of all stripes will likely change jobs over the course of their careers. It seems inevitable that job-shopping will become the new model of work. In this sense, young people will be served well in the future if they learn how to be adaptable and flexible in the labor market. All signs suggest that young people are indeed comfortable with this flux and that they may even prefer it.

If the economy continues to be dominated by service sector jobs, however, we face a split workforce of low-paid and high-paid employees, with a hollowed-out middle, unless protections are carved out for workers at the bottom. Reinvented unions could rally for those protections as they did in the 1940s and 1950s in the manufacturing sector, which contributed to the strong middle class our country enjoyed for decades. The Reagan era, coupled with internal union corruption, signaled the beginning of the end of the old union model. But that does not mean that unions have no place in today's workforce in which workers are responsible for their own safety nets, their own training, and their own retirement.

With or without unions, companies across the board should reinvest in on-the-job training. In 1979, companies spent $20 billion in current dollars on job training. Today, they spend only $6 billion, according to a report by the National Employment Law Project. Training is imperative if workers are to move up the ranks into better-paid and more complex jobs. A system of standardized training and recognized credentials that workers can carry with them from job to job would make sense given the highly mobile workforce today. This training should be aligned with regional workforce demands. To accomplish this, more co-ordination is needed between employers, government leaders, community colleges, and trade schools. A universally recognized set of skills and credentials for jobs would help prepare a workforce for the specific demands and core competencies of a job, and in doing so, better ensure that tuition is money well spent.

Apprenticeships allow new workers to gain a broad perspective on what a field entails and learn the applicable skills in a structured, directed way. For young adults, they are invaluable routes to solid jobs. Job shadowing is another option for those who are uncertain of what they want to do. There are many opportunities to improve the transition into the workforce, but they require cooperation on the part of employers, and strong partnerships between employers and schools, especially high schools, technical schools, and community colleges.[8]

As benefits wither, health care becomes a growing concern for millions of Americans. Young adults are the most likely to be uninsured. The new health care law will expand health insurance coverage for many of these young adults. The new law, for example, allows young people to remain on their parents' health policy through age 26. Several provisions make insurance more affordable as well. For example, uninsured individuals can now receive sliding-scale subsidies to purchase health insurance in state exchanges if their employers do not offer insurance and if their incomes are lower than 400 percent of the poverty line. Public programs such as Medicaid have been expanded slightly as well to cover more low-income families.

The pressure on employers to provide insurance has increased. Larger employers will now be fined $2,000 per full-time employee if they do not offer coverage and if they have at least one employee who receives a premium credit through an exchange. Small businesses have the option of purchasing insurance through an exchange as well, which may lower the cost of providing insurance. However, part-time workers are not covered under the new law. Young adults are often more likely than older workers to be in part-time positions.

These parameters are hardly set in stone. Revisions are on the horizon and a strong opposition in Congress is threatening amendments to the law. However, as of April 2010, the Congressional Budget Office estimates that the legislation will reduce the number of uninsured by 32 million in 2019 at a net cost of $938 billion over ten years, while reducing the deficit by $124 billion during this time period.

The Promise of Civic Participation

Obama's election in 2008 capitalized on the youth vote and on the new forms of social media that define this generation. Doing so is critical for our society and for the future of democracy. Civic experiences in high school and college have been linked not only to later community involvement, voting, and volunteering, but also to academic achievement, college attendance, and college graduation. A curriculum that emphasizes and even requires civic engagement could therefore be an important tool to hook young people into lifelong civil participation. Service learning opportunities in high schools have shown great promise in creating active, involved citizens.[9] Though "service learning" can mean a variety of things, it always involves community service projects that are closely connected to formal instruction and curriculum, and it often involves close partnerships between schools or colleges and communities. The hallmark of service learning experiences is that they are hands-on, involving community service or volunteering, visits to government or community institutions, debates or discussions, mock trials or roleplaying. They encourage actively "doing" democracy by mobilizing students to foster dialogue and make change in their schools and communities around issues that matter to them.

Although a case could be made for investing in many emerging programs, we highlight a handful that we think should top the list. The first group is national service programs, such as the Service and Conservation Corps, which operates in forty-one states and the District of Columbia. Like the earlier Civilian Conservation Corps (CCC) created during the New Deal, the Service and Conservation Corps builds and improves the nation's infrastructure by renovating public housing, conserving its public lands, and restoring its environment by creating and staffing public parks.

AmeriCorps is another excellent example. It combines community service with opportunities to develop life skills and a stipend to help pay for college. Indications from early analysis by the Network are that it effectively incorporates young people into the body politic. Some participants, for example, gained experience by taking charge and leading a team. Those from working-class families (earning under $40,000 a year) reported that they learned new ways of thinking from others. Participants learned to manage time under pressure, and became more realistic about their personal and professional skills.

The new Edward M. Kennedy Serve America Act (PL 111-13) increases the numbers of slots in AmeriCorps programs by adding several new corps and fellowships. In addition, the act increases the education award of these programs, adds flexibility in how young people can both get engaged in service and balance other responsibilities, targets the needs of low-income communities, and prioritizes the inclusion of marginalized youth.[10] It also creates tax incentives for employers who allow employees to take paid leave for full-time service, among other innovations.

Programs such as Youth Build, Youth Corps, and Civic Justice Corps all deserve more attention. A year spent doing national or community service is particularly helpful for young people who are still trying to figure out what they want to do after high school or while they are in college. The same is true after college, as young people are contemplating next steps. And, though they are highly selective, programs such as the Peace Corps and Teach for America offer important opportunities within which to explore one's self and career choices. These programs, along with the suggestions for enhanced work supports and more solid paths from school to work, are also examples of the potential to create an infrastructure that is currently lacking for this extended transition period.

All Ducks Are Not Created Equally

The final capstone in young people's lives today is marriage and family. No longer are most young people setting out on life's path together as a couple, sharing accomplishments and milestones. Today, they are getting their ducks in a row first, and then marrying—if they marry at all.

This decision to delay marriage has distinct advantages, as well as some often overlooked consequences.

Getting one's ducks in a row before settling into marriage and family may lead to stronger relationships. After all, older people know themselves better—they are familiar with their needs and desires, their strengths and limits, what they most need in a partner. Young people who delay marriage until their late twenties or early thirties are also more mature, and are better equipped as spouses or parents to handle life's ups and downs. And they are farther along in education and work, which adds a semblance of security to relationships and eases the strains of skimpy finances. Young adults who delay marriage have also played the field, which conceivably helps them choose a better match for themselves. These are all good things. Experiencing "me-ness" early on seems helpful in so many ways.

It is particularly important for women to get their ducks in a row before marriage. Even in modern relationships, women continue to shoulder the majority of the responsibilities for child care, and their jobs and careers continue to take a hit as they cycle in and out of work in response to family demands. The toll for women is even more considerable since they now have higher educational attainment than men. Perhaps nowhere are their losses more apparent than in the face of divorce, as women struggle to reclaim their financial independence after having been detached from the labor market.

Yet it may not be necessary to have it all figured out before getting married. Creating such a separate life before marriage comes with decided downsides. Couples may have fewer experiences in common. They may be more set in their ways. They may be pickier about possible partners, making it difficult to find someone who meets the long list of qualifications. Although some "me-ness" time up front is good, too much of it for too long can also compromise the possibility of "we-ness" with a committed partner or spouse.

We are not suggesting that everyone rush out of the gates to get married at age twenty-one. To the contrary, the research is clear: Waiting to marry and have children until after college or training is a key to stronger marriages and more promising futures. Nothing cements diverging destinies, and forecloses futures, like early marriages and, especially, early childbirth. The other factors are less critical. Buying a home, being debt-free, finding the perfect job—none is as imperative to accomplish before marriage as education.

One critical consequence of delaying marriage too long is a larger, demographic worry. The longer couples delay marriage, the fewer children they have. The population risks graying as people live longer and the birthrate dips lower. Every generation must replace itself with equal or higher numbers or there will not be enough workers to support retirees. Many European countries are currently facing this dilemma. The United States has managed to largely sidestep the issue until now because our immigration rates are so high. The percentages of people who significantly delay marriage, never marry, or remain intentionally childless are higher now than at any other time in American history. The time is nearing when we must face the ramifications of this important trend.

Of course, there are also very real biological clocks for women's fertility, despite the fact that new reproductive technologies have made later fertility possible. Although most view the biological imperative as the sole domain of women, the clock is ticking for men as well. Men may envision themselves working hard, getting set in a career, and then marrying and starting a family. Long hours are spent at the office early in a career in return for the assurance of earnings and a comfortable retirement down the road. If men wait to have children into their late thirties or early forties, however, their retirement is going to look very different from what they imagined. Having children at age forty means their children will graduate high school at about the same time fathers expect to retire. College bills have a funny way of cutting into retirement savings.

Holding off on marriage, and particularly on having children, until after age twenty-five, is the soundest plan for this day and age. This is not a revolutionary message for college-educated parents who have emphasized the importance of getting education first, or to our swimmers, who usually make these choices. Children can and will continue to be a primary source of personal meaning and salvation. But moving too quickly means that the door to education and careers will become ever harder to keep open. Some argue that those who have children early do so because they realize their futures are not very bright regardless. It is hard to say whether this is true or a rationalization young people make after the fact. But one thing is clear: Doing so seriously reduces one's life chances.

Although most young adults are delaying marriage, they are not delaying relationships or even living together. Dating and romance may look different today, but they are not obsolete. What is different today from past generations is the growing acceptability of living together. We see a decided split here in the trajectories of these relationships, however. Our swimmers see living together as a test run for marriage, while treaders see living together as a temporary arrangement, instigated by children or for financial reasons.

Cohabitation is very unstable in the United States, and unstable relationships are hard on children. Instability, however, is not a problem unique to cohabitation—it is also true of marriage. When the relationship is stable and committed, as well as unburdened by significant conflict or tension, living together can be a beneficial arrangement. It is stability that matters most, especially when children are involved.

Of course, there are those who will argue that it is marriage itself that matters most; that marriage is the glue that holds together the most fragile of relationships. But the group that moves quickly to marriage is also composed of those who are already on shaky ground. Their relationships and marriages are unstable for the same reasons they are vulnerable in other domains: They have less education, fewer resources, and fewer skills. For these young people, even solutions like mandatory marriage preparation or counseling are unlikely to be effective.

Given the rapid rise in cohabitation and its growing acceptability, we might consider adopting a model more typical in European countries, which takes the stigma out of cohabitation and treats it as a relationship that confers the same legal rights and responsibilities as marriage. This approach provides a set of civic protections aimed at strengthening long-term, committed relationships.

Is It All Bad?

So much media attention and public debate starts from the assumption that there's something amiss with young people today, that delays in the transition to adulthood are the beginning of the end for families and society. These changes do bring significant challenges and consequences for those who are treading, but there are also some great things about how this period of life is being shaken up. The rigid three-box life of education–work–retirement that men born in the first half of the last century marched through in lockstep is crumbling. New flexibilities expand opportunities and choices for life's path, which can be liberating. Likewise, the strings that tied mother's aprons tightly around their waists have been undone, allowing more choices and freedoms for women. Educational attainment has grown dramatically, and a college education is within reach for more youth. The social scripts that once signaled a single "right" time and order for all of life's transitions have all but disappeared.

As one young man from Michigan says, "I don't think there is one order that is going to work for everybody." That stereotype, he says, "puts pressure on people and makes people feel like if I don't do it this way that I've done it wrong." Or as this New Yorker put it: "It's hard living up to the expectations of being an adult. You should have a good job. You should have your own place. Should have a family." When those do not happen in that order, he says, people are quick to judge. "It's 'What's wrong with you?' What's wrong with you if you don't have a good job. What's wrong with you if you don't have a family.'" When the scripts are less set, the weight of expectations is lighter.

What *do* American parents and the public really want for young people? We surely don't want to turn back the clocks. At the end of the day, maybe what we really want is to be assured that young people will ultimately make it on their own—for their own welfare and that of our families and nation. And here, the news seems good: Most are pushing toward adulthood. They are seeking responsibility, negotiating autonomy, making commitments in education and work, nurturing connections with other people, finding ways to be involved in their communities, and expressing concern about the world around them.

But let's not forget the big ifs. As inequality continues to widen in our country, and as we still cling to independence and autonomy as a sign of success, the risks grow ever larger for growing numbers of youth whose families cannot offer, or lack access to, the kinds of supports that are necessary in this new era, supports that allow young people to swim rather than to tread furiously or even sink. Families cannot shoulder the burden completely. While some things about these years seem positive—young people have more time to figure out what they want to do in a job, more time to develop intimate relationships, more time to gain a sense of identity—the big picture is one of serious treading for many young Americans. This picture is remarkably absent in media portrayals and public views, where the focus is almost exclusively on young people with ample resources who are using these years to actively explore rather than those who are on their own without a net.

As we suggested at the beginning of this chapter, perhaps the best model for young people as they embark on the path to adulthood is no longer one of independence, but of interdependence. Going it alone may have worked in the past, but in today's highly competitive, highly interconnected, increasingly unequal, and longer life, it behooves young people to forge connections at every step of the way.

Young people need institutions and supports that foster responsibility and hope, that help them set goals and build the skills they need as adults in a fast-moving and fast-changing world. These will ease pressure on parents, particularly for those families that are unable to extend help because their resources are already stretched to the breaking point or because they simply don't have the knowledge and skills to help their children move forward in productive ways.

The changes underfoot in our society and the resulting need for better scaffolding as young people make their way into adulthood are sure to prompt intense political and public debate. But one thing is clear: The great shake-ups that are going on in the early adult years, as well as in other stages of life, are transforming American life, and their reverberations will be felt by everyone. These changes will demand new responses from families, governments, and society. Expecting young people to be "adult" by age eighteen or twenty-one, or even twenty-five, is no longer feasible, or even desirable. The status quo simply will not and cannot fit the world today and tomorrow, for there is now a new and extended period of life before us—one in which young people are no longer adolescents, but not quite adults.

Acknowledgments

This book could not have been written without the contributions and support of many individuals and organizations. The foundation of this book has been built from nearly a decade of research conducted or commissioned by the John D. and Catherine T. MacArthur Foundation Research Network on Transitions to Adulthood and Public Policy. It is therefore fitting to first acknowledge, with enormous gratitude, the MacArthur Foundation for its generous funding of the Network and its activities. At MacArthur, we are indebted to the staff members whose stewardship shaped the Network's vision and activities: Idy Gitelson and Craig Wacker, former and current program officers; Connie Yowell, director of education; and Julie Stasch, vice president of human and community development.

What an amazing experience it has been to share ten years of our professional careers and personal lives together as Network members. We have learned so much from our mentors, colleagues, and friends: Frank Furstenberg, chair (University of Pennsylvania), Gordon Berlin

(MDRC), Sheldon Danziger (University of Michigan), Connie Flanagan (Pennsylvania State University), Vonnie McLoyd (University of North Carolina–Chapel Hill), Wayne Osgood (Pennsylvania State University), Jean Rhodes (University of Massachusetts–Boston), Rubén Rumbaut (University of California–Irvine), Cecilia Rouse (Princeton University), and Mary Waters (Harvard University). We are also deeply grateful to Patricia Miller, Network administrator, for all she has done to nurture the promise and progress of the Network's activities.

Many of the Network's projects have also been conducted in collaboration with an extraordinary group of associate members. Our work has also benefited from their hard work and insights: Tom Brock (MDRC), Pat Carr (Rutgers University), Colleen Dillon (University of Washington), Mike Foster (University of North Carolina–Chapel Hill), Beth Fussell (Washington State University), Doug Hartmann (University of Minnesota), Jennifer Holdaway (Social Science Research Council), Maria Kefalas (St. Joseph's University), and Teresa Swartz (University of Minnesota).

In our decade together, the Network has commissioned some of the nation's best scholars to conduct research to inform particular topics and questions of interest. These efforts have culminated in the books *On the Frontier of Adulthood* (edited by Richard Settersten, Frank Furstenberg, and Rubén Rumbaut, University of Chicago Press), *On Your Own Without a Net* (edited by D. Wayne Osgood, E. Michael Foster, Connie Flanagan, and Gretchen Ruth, University of Chicago Press), and *The Price of Independence* (edited by Sheldon Danziger and Cecilia Rouse, Russell Sage Foundation). Together, these three books represent the scientific efforts of nearly ninety researchers across a wide variety of disciplines and fields. The story lines of our chapters are often anchored in their exceptional work. To all of you, we offer our heartfelt appreciation.

As we wrote this book, we also conducted fresh analyses and interviews to further expand and strengthen the storylines that emerged from the Network's projects. Many of these interviews were with professionals whose expertise was indispensable in interpreting, supplementing, or otherwise bringing to life some of our findings. We are grateful for their help. These individuals include Elizabeth Armstrong (Indiana University), Fran Goldscheider (University of Maryland), Rob

Ivry (MDRC), Joe Kahne (Mills College), Kim McAlexander (Oregon State University), Michelle Sandlin (Oregon State University), Robert Schoeni (University of Michigan), Dan Schwab (Oregon State University), David Shulenburger (Association of Public and Land-Grant Universities), Tom Watson (CauseWired Communications), and Kris Winter (Oregon State University).

One of the major projects of the Network involved conducting comprehensive, in-person interviews with nearly five hundred young adults from five distinct American sites. Facts and quantitative trends are important, but it is the lives of the young people that make those facts come alive. Without the hard work of the investigators at those sites, and of the young people who were interviewed, this book would not have been possible. The lives of these young people have given our stories a voice. We are truly in debt to the principal investigators and research teams at those five sites: Jacque Eccles, who directed the Detroit, Michigan, site; Pat Carr and Maria Kefalas, for the community in rural Iowa; Jeylan Mortimer and Teresa Swartz, for St. Paul, Minnesota; Rubén Rumbaut, for San Diego, California; and Mary Waters, for New York City.

As we wrote the book, we also interviewed many young people to better understand particular issues. For purposes of anonymity, their names cannot be mentioned here. But to these young adults, along with the other five-hundred who were interviewed as part of the Network's efforts: Thank you for the time you gave, and for the intimate details of your lives that you revealed. In sharing your stories with readers, we hope we will help enrich social conversation and political debate about young people and the future of our society. Your stories are ultimately about all of us.

We thank the Spencer Foundation for awarding Rick a visiting research fellowship in Chicago. Their generous support of an office for Rick and apartment for his family allowed us to work together for three months. Special thanks at Spencer are due to Liz Carrick, vice president; Susan Dauber, program director; and Michael McPherson, president. What an amazing gift of time, place, and memories that will always be treasured.

We are also grateful to Molly Trauten, a doctoral student at Oregon State University, for her research assistance. Molly was helpful on so many fronts—in searching literature, crunching data, analyzing interview transcripts, processing ideas, and reviewing chapters.

We also have many people to thank in the publishing world. Early in the journey came along our agent Joelle Delbourgo, of Joelle Delbourgo Associates. Joelle's long tenure in the business, and her razor-sharp questions and candid comments, helped strengthen the prospectus and early drafts of a few chapters. Her guidance has been invaluable throughout the entire process. At Random House, it was our deep pleasure to have had an opportunity to work with Toni Burbank, former vice president and executive editor, before she retired. The book benefited from the insights of editorial consultant John Paine. It also benefited from the wisdom of Philip Rappaport, former senior editor; Beth Rashbaum, senior editor; and finally Angela Polidoro, assistant editor at Bantam Dell. We also thank Laura Jorstad for her superb copyediting.

Each of us also has those we'd like to personally thank. From Rick— I am so very thankful to Dan Dowhower and our children, Maya Grace and Mario Nelson, for their love and laughter, and for their understanding when the unpredictable rhythms of writing have strained our lives and diverted my attention. When I open my eyes in the morning and put my head down at night, I am reminded of what truly matters in my life: you. I am also grateful to my parents, Richard and Diann, for teaching me this lesson, and for teaching me so many of life's most precious lessons, by living in ways that leave me inspired. I am also thankful for many dear friends, students, colleagues, and mentors who have listened with great interest and supported with great strength and patience. Thank you all for your kindness and generosity.

From Barbara—I could not have written this book without the constant support and silly puns of the love of my life, Rex. My dear friends Maria Kefalas and Pat Carr deserve a medal (or a lifetime supply of Guinness) for reading drafts and offering sage advice throughout the process. Having just written their own book, they knew firsthand the quiet panic of putting word after word on the page and hoping it makes sense to someone. I'm truly lucky to be surrounded by a fantastic group of friends, who all have my deep gratitude for listening to me complain and fret for more than a year. Cheryl, Bun, Brande, Lucy...thanks.

Your endurance is remarkable. My sister Sally had my back the entire way, as did everyone in my family. You can't grow up hoping to be a writer without parents who believe in you. And last but not least, my favorite barista, Mike, without whom I truly would not have made it.

—*Rick Settersten and Barbara Ray*

Notes

Introduction

1. In writing this book, we have relied principally on research conducted or commissioned by the MacArthur Research Network, but not exclusively so. Despite the wide scope of the Network's activities, we inevitably discovered topics that were not addressed (or not sufficiently addressed in ways that suited our unique themes and storylines). In these situations, we conducted primary research of our own or went beyond the Network to tell or augment the story, selecting what we judged to be the most fitting, compelling, and scientifically sound research. We have also not incorporated everything the Network has produced. For the individual cases discussed in this book, we used two strategies to conduct our own analyses of the Network's five hundred in-person interviews, which will be discussed momentarily. One strategy was to identify cases that fit the evidence from large, quantitative analyses and then use them to bring those findings to life. The second strategy, especially when the evidence wasn't as clear or strong, involved us wading through cases across sites, working up themes, and integrating them into our story lines. We also conducted additional interviews to gain fresh insights and updates into the changing experiences of young people (such as in

the economic downturn) or to probe more deeply particular topics of interest.

2. We are truly indebted to the principal investigators and research teams at those five sites: Jacque Eccles, who directed the Detroit, Michigan, site; Pat Carr and Maria Kefalas, for the community in rural Iowa; Jeylan Mortimer and Teresa Swartz, for Minneapolis–St. Paul, Minnesota; Rubén Rumbaut, for San Diego, California; and Mary Waters, for New York City.

3. Of course, in discussing larger categories of young people, such as "swimmers" and "treaders," we run the risk of overgeneralization. That is, we must recognize that young people in these categories are neither uniform as a group nor uniform as individuals. There are differences among swimmers and treaders, with some members of these groups functioning better than others. Similarly, individual swimmers or treaders may not swim or tread in all domains of life—and indeed, like most of us, they probably do better in some areas than others. Still, there are young people at the extremes—some doing very well across most domains and some doing very poorly—and for the remainder, it is the relative balance or main effect we care about.

4. Harry Holzer, Diane Whitmore Schanzenbach, and Greg Duncan, "The Economic Costs of Childhood Poverty in the United States." Discussion paper 1327-07 (Evanston, IL: Institute for Research on Poverty, Northwestern University, 2007).

Chapter 1

1. Kim Clark, "Solving the College Crisis," *U.S. News & World Report,* September 2009.

2. Gates Foundation, "Diplomas Count" (Seattle: Bill and Melinda Gates Foundation, 2008). These figures are calculated differently from the U.S. Department of Education, National Center for Education Statistics, 2008. The Gates method results in higher estimates. The U.S. Department of Education lists high school dropout rates among people sixteen to twenty-four years old (not enrolled in school and who have not earned a high school diploma or equivalent credential, such as a GED) as 9.3 percent overall in 2006, and 5.8 percent, 10.7 percent, and 22.1 percent for whites, blacks, and Hispanics, respectively. For data on graduation rates within six years, see Sara Goldrick-Rab and Josipa Roksa, "A Federal Agenda for Promoting Student Success and Degree Completion" (Washington, DC: Center for American Progress, 2008). The methods of calculating dropout rates vary across studies, and studies therefore often arrive at slightly different figures. For data on the share of young adults with bachelor's degrees, see Rubén

Rumbaut and Golnaz Komai, "Young Adults in the United States: A Mid-Decade Profile" (Philadelphia: MacArthur Network on Transitions to Adulthood, September 2007).

3. Rumbaut and Komai, "Young Adults in the United States."

4. US Department of Education, National Center for Education Statistics, *2001 Baccalaureate and Beyond Longitudinal Study* (Washington, DC: NCES, 2002), Table II.11.

5. "Urban Schools Are Aiming Higher than Diploma," *New York Times,* January 17, 2008, A24.

6. Melanie Guldi, et al., "Family Background and the Transition to Adulthood," in *The Price of Independence: The Economics of Early Adulthood,* edited by Sheldon Danziger and Cecilia Rouse (New York: Russell Sage Foundation, 2007).

7. National Association for College Admissions Counseling, "2009 State of College Admissions" (Washington, DC: NACAC, 2009).

8. Alexandra Robbins, *The Overachievers: The Secret Lives of Driven Kids* (New York: Hyperion, 2006).

9. Approximately 30 percent of African American students and 43 percent of Latino students feel that their parents could have done more in dealing with officials at their college or in helping to select college courses. In contrast, fewer than 17 percent of white students, who more often came from better-off families, shared these sentiments. Cooperative Institutional Research Program, "The American Freshman: National Norms for Fall 2007" (Los Angeles: Higher Education Research Center, UCLA, 2007).

10. Thomas Brock and Allen LeBlanc, *Promoting Student Success in Community College and Beyond* (New York: MDRC, 2005).

11. Goldrick-Rab and Roksa, "A Federal Agenda for Promoting Student Success."

12. Thomas Bailey, Dong Wook Jeong, and Sung-Woo Cho, "Referral, Enrollment, and Completion in Developmental Education Sequences in Community Colleges." CCRC Working Paper No. 15 (New York: Community College Research Center, Columbia University, December 2008).

13. Tom Brock, et al., "Opening Doors" (New York: MDRC, June 2008). See also William Doyle, "Community College Transfers and College Graduation: Whose Choices Matter Most?" (New York: Carnegie Foundation, 2006).

14. Ibid.

15. *Dropouts* are those who are not enrolled in school and who have not earned a high school diploma or equivalent credential, such as a GED. See the National Center for Education Statistics, *Digest of Education Statistics: 2007*

(Washington, DC: NCES, 2008). Some dropouts will, of course, go on to receive a GED. See also note 2.

16. Susan Jekielek and Brett Brown, "The Transition to Adulthood: Characteristics of Young Adults Ages 18–24 in America" (Baltimore: Annie E. Casey Foundation, 2005), available at www.prb.org/pdf05/TransitionToAdulthood.pdf.

17. Similar questions are now popping up in public and educational debates. See, for instance Charles Murray, *Real Education: Four Simple Truths for Bringing America's Schools Back to Reality* (New York: Crown Forum, 2008), and Rona Wilensky, "High Schools Have Got It Bad for Higher Ed—And That Ain't Good." *Phi Delta Kappan* 89, no. 4 (December 2007), pp. 248–259.

Chapter 2

1. For luck versus work, see Paola Giuliano and Antonio Spilimbergo, "Growing Up in a Recession: Beliefs and the Macroeconomy." NBER Working Paper No. 15321 (Cambridge, MA: National Bureau of Economic Research, 2009). For earnings differences, see Till von Wachter, et al., "Long-Term Earnings Losses Due to Mass Layoffs During the 1982 Recession." NBER Working Paper (Cambridge, MA: National Bureau of Economic Research, April 2009).

2. Jesse Rothstein and Cecilia Rouse, "Constrained After College: Student Loans and Early Career Occupational Choices." NBER Working Paper (Cambridge, MA: National Bureau of Economic Research, May 2007).

3. Ngina Chiteji, "To Have and to Hold," in *The Price of Independence: The Economics of Early Adulthood,* edited by Sheldon Danziger and Cecilia Rouse (New York: Russell Sage Foundation, 2007), p. 246. The mean among young adult households ages twenty-five through thirty-four was $7,065. Young adult households are those whose heads are ages twenty-five through thirty-four, which, at the low end, is a minimum of three years past the traditional age of college graduation.

4. National Center for Education Statistics, *Condition of Education* (Washington, DC: NCES, 2000).

5. Rothstein and Rouse, "Constrained After College."

6. In 1975, men with a college degree earned about $8,300 more (in 2002 dollars) on the job than a man with a high school degree. For women, the difference was $7,800. By 2002, that gap had widened to $17,000 for men and $16,000 for women—a little more than doubling in value. Sheldon Danziger, "Earnings by Education for Young Workers, 1975 and 2002." Data Brief No. 17 (Philadelphia: Network on Transitions to Adulthood, 2004). Likewise,

college graduates from more affluent backgrounds enjoy greater returns on college than do lower-income students, while first-generation college graduates have significantly lower returns than students whose parents have a college degree. See S. L. Thomas and L. Zhang, "Post-Baccalaureate Wage Growth Within Four Years of Graduation: The Effects of College Major, Quality and Performance." Paper presented to 2001 Annual Meeting of the Association for the Study of Higher Education, Richmond, VA.

7. New research by William Bowen, Matthew Chingos, and Michael McPherson, however, suggests there may be a wrinkle to consider with respect to the Network's findings: When extremely capable students are severely "undermatched" to the institutions they end up attending—for example, when a student who could have gotten into an Ivy League school goes to a community college—they are far less likely to finish their degrees. See *Crossing the Finish Line: Completing College at America's Public Universities* (Princeton, NJ: Princeton University Press, 2009). The Network's findings, in contrast, focus more on the margins—say, in choosing to attend a college or university one notch down, or in choosing a cheaper option from among institutions in approximately the same tier (hence, "The Mercedes Versus the Corolla").

8. Research indicates most students and families tend to overestimate the prices of college, underestimate the availability of student financial aid, and underestimate the value of college in the long run. This misperception, says a recent study, "plays an alarmingly large role in post-secondary decision making for many families, [but] especially among lower income groups." Canadian Council on Learning, "Are Low-Income Averse to Financing Post-Secondary Education by Borrowing?" Question Scans 06 (2006), p. 3. See also A. Usher, "A Little Knowledge Is a Dangerous Thing: How Perceptions of Costs and Benefits Affect Access to Education." Canadian Education Report series (Toronto: Educational Policy Institute, September 30, 2005); L. E. Gladieux and W. S. Swail, "Is College Affordable? Sorting Perception and Reality," *College Board Review* 189–190 (2000), p. 55.

9. Institute for Higher Education Policy (IHEP), "Promise Lost: College-Qualified Students Who Don't Enroll in College," available at www.ihep .org/assets/files/publications/m-r/PromiseLostCollegeQualrpt.pdf.

10. Brian K. Bucks, Arthur B. Kennickell, Traci L. Mach, and Kevin B. Moore, "Changes in Family Finances from 2004 to 2007: Evidence from the Survey of Consumer Finances," *Federal Reserve Bulletin* 95 (2009).

11. Danziger, "Earnings by Education for Young Workers, 1975 and 2002."

12. Lawrence Mishel, Jared Bernstein, and Sylvia Allegretto, *The State of Working America* (Washington, DC: Economic Policy Institute, 2008).

13. Edwin Park, Paul N. Van de Water, and Matt Broaddus, "Private Health

Coverage Declined, Became Less Secure in 2008: New Census Data Underscore Importance of Comprehensive Health Reform" (Washington, DC: Center on Budget and Policy Priorities, September 2008).

14. Mishel, et al., *State of Working America.*

15. Kaiser Family Foundation and Health Research and Education Trust, *Employer Health Benefits 2009 Annual Survey* (Washington, DC: Kaiser Family Foundation, 2009).

16. Helen Levy, "Health Insurance and the Transition to Adulthood," in *The Price of Independence,* edited by Danziger and Rouse. Levy finds that job instability and part-time work are the main reasons for lack of insurance coverage. Other reasons, such as pricing, also help to explain the gap, but none as dominantly as job instability and job-hopping. Young adults may find that the price of health insurance is not worth it, given that they are relatively healthy at this stage in their lives. Because insurance pools risk, the most healthy support the least healthy, and health insurance companies may not be pricing their product in a way that accurately reflects the "actuarial" risk of young adults—and thus young people view the cost as too high.

17. Interestingly, the dip in coverage for men is exacerbated by the decline in public coverage such as Medicaid, which for men ends at age eighteen. Low-income women with children are allowed to remain on Medicaid slightly longer, although not indefinitely. Levy, "Health Insurance and the Transition to Adulthood."

18. Kaiser Family Foundation, "Uninsured Workers in America." Kaiser Commission on Key Facts (New York: Kaiser Family Foundation, July 2004).

19. Chiteji, "To Have and to Hold."

20. In 2007, only 15 percent of all young adults had total debt burdens that consumed more than 40 percent of their income—considered onerous. This was the same or slightly lower than their parents, but higher than their grandparents. Brian K. Bucks, Arthur B. Kennickell, Traci L. Mach, and Kevin B. Moore, "Changes in U.S. Family Finances from 2004 to 2007: Evidence from the Survey of Consumer Finances," *Federal Reserve Bulletin* 95 (February 2009), pp. A1–A55.

21. Chiteji, "To Have and to Hold." In this scenario, based on 2001 data, "the Tricias" refers to the bottom 20 percent of earners. Income quintile groupings are based on census data on the distribution of income for the national population at large. The top earners are those in the top 20 percent.

22. Robert Haveman and Edward N. Wolff, "The Concept and Measurement of Asset Poverty: Levels, Trends and Composition for the U.S., 1983–2001." Working Paper (New York: Russell Sage Foundation, 2003). Asset poverty differs from income poverty in that it measures the ability of families or in-

dividuals to tap into their assets (other than income) to cover their basic needs for three months. Assets include home equity, stocks, bonds, net worth, savings, and any other income that is unearned. Even excluding home equity in the calculation between renters and homeowners, the asset poverty rates of renters are more than double those of homeowners.

23. U.S. Census Bureau, "Housing Vacancies and Homeownership, Annual 2008" (Washington, DC: U.S. Census Bureau, 2009), Table 17: Homeownership Rates for the United States, by Age of Householder and by Family Status: 1982 to 2008.

24. Bucks, et al., "Changes in U.S. Family Finances from 2004 to 2007," Table 13, p. A-40.

25. Bucks, et al., "Changes in U.S. Family Finances from 2004 to 2007." Lending Tree data show that 74 percent of young singles ages nineteen through thirty-four, 80 percent of young marrieds, and 56 percent of young families with children had savings or investments in 2007 (with a margin of error of about 10 percentage points).

26. Yoonkyung Yuh and Sherman D. Hanna, "Which Households Think They Save?" *Journal of Consumer Affairs,* forthcoming, as reported by Jennifer Saranow Schultz, "Young Adults May Be Saving After All," *New York Times,* December 21, 2009. See also Ron Lieber, "Americans Are Finally Saving: How Did That Happen?" *New York Times,* "Your Money" column, December 18, 2009.

27. Patrick Wightman, Bob Schoeni, and Keith Robinson, "Familial Financial Assistance to Young Adults." Working Brief (Ann Arbor: University of Michigan, January 2010).

28. Sheldon Danziger and Cecilia Rouse, *The Price of Independence.*

Chapter 3

1. Young adults ages eighteen through thirty-four in 2005 constituted 34 percent of the U.S. civilian workforce. Those eighteen through twenty-four made up 13 percent of the workforce; those twenty-five through twenty-nine, 10 percent; and those thirty through thirty-four, 11 percent. Rubén Rumbaut and Golnaz Komai, "Young Adults in the United States: A Mid-Decade Profile" (Philadelphia: MacArthur Network on Transitions to Adulthood, September 2007).

2. Carolyn Martin and Bruce Tulgan, *Managing the Generation Mix* (Amherst, MA: HRD Press, 2006).

3. Henry Farber, "Is the Company Man an Anachronism? Trends in Long-Term Employment in the United States, 1973 to 2006," in, *The Price of*

Independence: The Economics of Early Adulthood, edited by Sheldon Danziger and Cecelia Rouse (New York: Russell Sage Foundation, 2007).

4. Families and Work Institute, "Generation and Gender in the Workplace." Issue Brief (New York: American Business Collaboration, 2002), Table 6, p. 18.

5. Cone, Inc., *The Cone 2006 Millennial Cause Study* (in collaboration with Amp Insights) (Boston, Cone, Inc., November 2006).

6. Barbara Schneider and David Stevenson, *The Ambitious Generation: America's Teenagers, Motivated but Directionless* (New Haven, CT: Yale University Press, 1999).

7. This point is also reinforced by the recent work of John Reynolds, Michael Stewart, Ryan Macdonald, and Lacey Sischo, "Have Adolescents Become Too Ambitious? High School Seniors' Educational and Occupational Plans." *Social Problems* 53 (2006), pp. 186–206.

8. All data in the paragraph are from Lawrence Mishel, et al., *The State of Working America* (Washington, DC: Economic Policy Institute, 2008), Tables 3.27, 4.

9. Bureau of Labor Statistics, "Household Data Annual Averages, Table 8: Employed and Unemployed Full- and Part-Time Workers by Age, Sex, Race, and Hispanic or Latino Ethnicity" (Washington, DC: BLS, 2009).

10. Bureau of Labor Statistics, "Occupations in the Temporary Help Services" (Washington, DC: BLS, 2007).

11. Bureau of Labor Statistics, "Contingent and Alternative Employment Arrangements" (Washington, DC: BLS, February 2005).

12. Bureau of Labor Statistics, "Table 1. Median Years of Tenure with Current Employer for Employed Wage and Salary Workers by Age and Sex, Selected Years, 1996–2006" (Washington, DC: BLS, 2007).

13. Danziger and Rouse, editors, *The Price of Independence,* p. 10.

14. Robert Topel and Michael Ward, "Job Mobility and the Careers of Young Men," *Quarterly Journal of Economics* 107, no. 2 (1992), pp. 439–479.

15. Tom Smith, "Generation Gaps in Attitudes and Values," in *On the Frontier of Adulthood: Theory, Research, and Public Policy* edited by Richard Settersten, Jr., Frank Furstenberg, Jr., and Rubén Rumbaut (Chicago: University of Chicago Press, 2005).

Chapter 4

1. Child Trends, "Dating." Data Bank (Washington, DC: Child Trends, Spring 2008), available at www.childtrendsdatabank.org/indicators/73Dating.cfm.

2. See Laura Sessions Stepp, *Unhooked: How Young Women Pursue Sex, Delay*

Love, and Lose at Both (New York: Penguin, 2007) and Kathleen Bogle, *Hooking Up: Sex, Dating, and Relationships on Campus* (Albany: New York University Press, 2008).

3. Frank Furstenberg, What Happened to the American Family? (draft paper).

4. Michael Rosenfeld, *The Age of Independence: Interracial Unions, Same-Sex Unions and the Changing American Family* (Cambridge, MA: Harvard University Press, 2007).

5. Frances K. Goldscheider and Linda J. Waite, *New Families, No Families? The Transformation of the American Home* (Berkeley: University of California Press, 1993). See also Frances Goldscheider and G. Kaufman, "Do Men 'Need' Marriage More than Women? Perceptions of the Importance of Marriage for Men and Women," *Sociological Quarterly* 48 (2007), pp. 27–40.

6. Elizabeth Fussell and Frank Furstenberg, "The Transition to Adulthood During the Twentieth Century," in *On the Frontier of Adulthood,* edited by Richard Settersten, Jr., Frank F. Furstenberg, Jr., and Rubén Rumbaut (Chicago: University of Chicago Press, 2005), p. 32.

7. Andrew Cherlin, "American Marriage in the Early Twenty-first Century," *Future of Children* 15 (2005), pp. 33–55.

8. Suzanne Bianchi and Lynne Casper, "American Families," *Population Bulletin* 55 (December 2000), available at www.prb.org/Source/ACFAC41.pdf.

9. Wendy Manning, Monica Longmore, and Peggy Giordano, "The Changing Institution of Marriage: Adolescents' Expectations to Cohabit and Marry." Working Paper No. 2005-11 (Bowling Green, OH: Center for Family and Demographic Research, Bowling Green State University, 2005). These plans vary slightly by religion (far fewer from more religious backgrounds plan to live together), and by education. Among women ages twenty-two through forty-four in 2002, roughly 69 percent with a high school degree or less had ever lived together compared with 46 percent among college-educated women. U.S. Department of Health and Human Services, "Fertility, Family Planning, and the Health of U.S. Women: Data from the 2002 National Survey of Family Growth" (Hyattesville, MD: National Center for Health Statistics, 2006).

10. For more information see Pamela Smock, Lynne Casper, and Jessica Wyse, "Nonmarital Cohabitation: Current Knowledge and Future Directions for Research." Research Report 08-648 (Ann Arbor: Population Studies Center, University of Michigan, July 2008).

11. Centers for Disease Control, *Advance Data No. 323.* Table 3 (Atlanta: CDC, May 31, 2001).

12. The National Marriage Project, *The State of Our Unions: The Social Health of Marriage in America, 2007* (Piscataway, NJ: University of Virginia and

Rutgers University, July 2007), available at www.uvirginia.edu/marriage
projects/pdfs/ 2008update.pdf.

Chapter 5

1. For 1980 data, see Daniel T. Lichter and Zhenchao Qian, "Marriage and
   Family in Multiracial Society" (Washington, DC: Population Reference
   Bureau, 2005), available at www.prb.org/en/Reports/2004/Marriageand
   FamilyinaMultiracialSociety.aspx?p=1. For 2008 data, see U.S. Census Bureau, Current Population Survey, 2008 Annual Social and Economic Supple-
   ment, Table A1: Marital Status of People 15 Years and Over, by Age, Sex,
   Personal Earnings, Race, and Hispanic Origin, 2008.
2. Michael J. Rosenfeld, "Young Adulthood as a Factor in Social Change in the
   United States," *Population and Development Review* 32, no. 1 (March 2006),
   pp. 27–51. We combined Rosenberg's male and female data into one figure
   for both sexes.
3. D'Vera Cohn and Rich Morin, "American Mobility: Movers, Stayers, Places
   and Reasons" (Washington, DC: Pew Research Center, December 17, 2008).
4. Mark Granovetter, "The Strength of Weak Ties," *American Journal of Sociology* 78, no. 6 (May 1973), pp. 1360–1380.
5. Ibid. Pierre Bourdieu, "The Forms of Capital." In *Handbook of Theory and
   Research for the Sociology of Education,* ed. J. G. Richardson (New York:
   Greenwood Press, 1986).
6. Ibid.
7. Miller McPherson and Lyn Smith-Lovin, "Social Isolation in America:
   Changes in Core Discussion Networks Over Two Decades," *American Sociological Review* 71 (2006), pp. 353–375.
8. Nicholas Christakis and James Fowler, *Connected: The Surprising Power of
   Our Social Networks and How They Shape Our Lives* (New York: Little,
   Brown, 2009).

Chapter 6

1. Pew Research Center, "A Portrait of 'Generation Next': How Young People
   View Their Lives, Futures, and Politics." A survey conducted in association
   with the Generation Next Initiative (Washington, DC: Pew Research Center, January 9, 2007).
2. Ivar Frones, "Sense and Sensibility: An Essay on Changes to the Family, Life
   Course and Romance," *Family Today* 10 (2004), pp. 12–16.

3. National Survey of Student Engagement (NSSE), 2007. Available at http://nsse.iub.edu.

4. Tom Smith, "Generation Gaps in Attitudes and Values," in *On the Frontier of Adulthood,* edited by Richard Settersten, Jr., Frank Furstenberg, Jr., and Rubén Rumbaut (Chicago: University of Chicago Press, 2005).

5. Author computations, 2007 American Community Survey, U.S. Bureau of the Census. For additional data on other age groups (twenty-five through forty-nine; thirty through thirty-four) and split by gender, see Richard Settersten, Jr., and Barbara Ray, "What's Going On with Young People Today? The Long and Twisting Path to Adulthood," *Future of Children* 20 (2010), pp. 195–217.

6. For a parallel analysis of this case, see Teresa Toguchi Swartz, "Family Capital and the Invisible Transfer of Privilege: Intergenerational Support and Social Class in Early Adulthood," *New Directions for Child and Adolescent Development* 119 (2008), pp. 11–24. See also Teresa Toguchi Swartz, Douglas Hartman, and Jeylan Mortimer, "Transitions to Adulthood in the Land of Lake Wobegon," in *Coming of Age in America,* edited by Patrick Carr, Maria Kefalas, Jennifer Holdaway, and Mary Waters (Berkeley: University of California Press, forthcoming).

7. Barbara Mitchell, *The Boomerang Age: The Transition to Adulthood in Families* (Piscataway, NJ: Transaction Books, 2008).

8. Rubén Rumbaut and Golnaz Komaie, "Immigration and Adult Transitions," *Future of Children* 20 (2010), pp. 43–66.

9. Rubén Rumbaut and Golnaz Komaie, "Young Adults in the United States: A Midcentury Update" (Philadelphia: Network on Transitions to Adulthood, 2006). See also Rubén Rumbaut, *Legacies: The Story of Immigrant Second Generation in Early Adulthood* (Berkeley: University of California Press, 2001).

10. Katherine Newman and Sofya Aptekar, "Sticking Around: Delayed Departure from the Parental Nest in Western Europe," in *The Price of Independence: The Economics of Early Adulthood,* edited by Sheldon Danziger and Cecilia Rouse (New York: Russell Sage Foundation, 2007).

11. Lisa Belkin, "When Children Leave," *New York Times,* September 17, 2008 (online: Life's Work column), available at http://community.nytimes.com/article/comments/2008/09/18/fashion/18Work.html.

12. Mark Courtney and Darcy Hughes Heruing, "The Transition to Adulthood for Youth 'Aging Out' of the Foster Care System." In D. Wayne Osgood et al., *On Your Own Without a Net: The Transition to Adulthood for Vulnerable Populations* (Chicago: University of Chicago Press, 2005); Mark Courtney et

al., The Midwest Evaluation of the Adult Functioning of Former Foster Youth: Outcomes at Ages 23 and 24." Report. (Seattle and Chicago: Partners for Our Children, and Chapin Hall Center for Children, April 2010).

Chapter 7

1. Peter Levine, Connie Flanagan, and Richard Settersten, Jr., "Civic Engagement and the Changing Transition to Adulthood" (Washington, DC: Center for Information and Research on Civic Learning and Engagement, January 2009), available at www.civicyouth.org/?p=327.

2. But even for volunteering, the levels are not terribly high—from 44 percent in the 1970s to 50 percent in the 2000s. Ibid.

3. Paola Giuliano and Antonio Spilimbergo, "Growing Up in a Recession." NBER Working Paper No. 15321 (Cambridge, MA: National Bureau of Economic Research, 2009).

4. An estimated twenty-three million Americans under the age of thirty voted in 2008, or between 4 and 5 percentage points higher than in 2004, and an 11 percentage point gain over 2000. Center for Information and Research on Civic Learning and Engagement (CIRCLE), "Young Voters in the 2008 Presidential Election." Fact Sheet (Washington, DC: CIRCLE, December 1, 2008).

5. Of course, this number is also based on registered voters and doesn't include those who are eligible but not registered, which makes the true turnout far lower than half. Depending on the data source (National Election Pool exit polls, Current Population Survey), and on the equation used to generate the estimate, the rate for 2008 was somewhere between 49 and 53 percent. For more information, see CIRCLE, "Young Voters in the 2008 Presidential Election."

6. This seems at odds with our prior finding that people in their late twenties and thirties tend to be more scornful of politicians than those who are in their late teens and early twenties. Yet, as we will later show, the voting rates of most generations, even those whose rates have started relatively low, have eventually increased by the time they are in their early thirties—at least for major presidential elections. This is taken to be a sign of finally "settling in"—of paying significant taxes, buying homes and having children (and therefore developing new commitments to communities and schools), and the like. That is, delays in the traditional markers of adulthood therefore bring delays in civic commitments. Still, the voting rates of current cohorts of young adults are, despite the hoopla, lower than ever before.

7. Institute of Politics, "Fifteenth Biannual Youth Survey on Politics and Pub-

lic Service" (Cambridge, MA: Harvard University, Institute of Politics, October 2008).

8. According to a CIRCLE study, about 13 percent of young people can be classified "hyperinvolved," claiming ten or more (out of nineteen) different kinds of participation. At the other end are the disengaged—58 percent—who are unable to cite even two forms of civic or political participation. Of these, 28 percent (17 percent overall) have done none of them. Mark Lopez, et al., "The 2006 Civic and Political Health of the Nation" (Washington, DC: CIRCLE, October 2006).

9. Constance Flanagan, D. Wayne Osgood, Laine Briddell, Laura Wray, and Amy Syvertsen, "The Changing Social Contract at the Transition to Adulthood: Implications for Individuals and the Polity" (Philadelphia: Network on Transitions to Adulthood, March 2006).

10. Institute of Politics, "Fifteenth Biannual Youth Survey."

11. CIRCLE/Carnegie Corporation of New York, "The Civic Mission of Schools" (New York: Carnegie Corporation, 2003).

12. W. Lance Bennett, "Changing Citizenship in a Digital Age." In *Civic Life Online: Learning How Digital Media Can Engage Youth,* edited by W. Lance Bennett (Cambridge, MA: MIT Press, 2008), p. 5.

13. Amy K. Syvertsen, Laura Wray-Lake, Constance Flanagan, Laine Briddell, and D. Wayne Osgood, "Thirty-Year Trends in American Adolescents' Civic Engagement: A Story of Changing Participation and Educational Difference" (Philadelphia: Network on Transitions to Adulthood, 2008).

14. Michael Xenos and Kirsten Foot, "Not Your Father's Internet: The Generation Gap in Online Politics," in W. Lance Bennett, editor, *Civic Life Online*.

15. Institute of Politics, "Fifteenth Biannual Youth Survey"; National Survey of Student Engagement, "Promoting Engagement for All Students: The Imperative to Look Within" (Bloomington: Indiana University, 2008).

16. Allison Fine, "Social Citizens" (Washington, DC: Case Foundation, 2008).

17. CIRCLE, *2008 Civic Health Index* (Washington, DC: CIRCLE, 2009).

18. See Joseph E. Kahne and Ellen Middaugh, "Democracy for Some: The Civic Opportunity Gap in High School," in *Policies for Youth Civic Engagement,* edited by James Youniss and Peter Levine (Nashville: Vanderbilt University Press, in press).

19. National Conference on Citizenship, in association with CIRCLE and Saguaro Seminar, "America's Civic Health Index: Broken Engagement" (Washington, DC: National Conference on Citizenship, 2006).

Chapter 8

1. Patrick Wightman, Bob Schoeni, and Keith Robinson, "Familial Financial Assistance to Young Adults." Working brief (Ann Arbor: University of Michigan, January 2010).

2. Peter Gosselin, *High Wire: The Precarious Financial Lives of American Families* (New York: Basic Books, 2009).

3. Readers interested in cross-national perspective on differences in the protections and services offered to young people by governments can see Richard A. Settersten, Jr., "Social Policy and the Transition to Adulthood: Toward Stronger Institutions and Individual Capacities," in *On the Frontier of Adulthood: Theory, Research, and Public Policy,* edited by Richard Settersten, Jr., Frank Furstenberg, Jr., and Rubén Rumbaut (Chicago: University of Chicago Press, 2005).

4. Frank Furstenberg, Jr., editor, "Early Adulthood in Cross-National Perspective," *Annals of the American Academy of Political and Social Science* (London: Sage Publications, 2002); Settersten, et al., editors, *On the Frontier of Adulthood*.

5. Richard Settersten, Jr., "Passages to Adulthood: Linking Demographic Change and Human Development," *European Journal of Population* 23, nos. 3–4 (2007), pp. 251–272. We have not in this book taken up an examination of the particular personal meanings or markers that young people use to define the term "adult." This is the subject of other research using MacArthur interviews. It is also the focal point of a growing body of research in psychology led by Jeffrey Jensen Arnett and his colleagues on adolescence and "emerging adulthood." See, for example, Jeffrey Jensen Arnett, *Emerging Adults in America: Coming of Age in the 21st Century* (Washington, DC: American Psychological Association Press, 2006). For readers interested in understanding how young people build their identities, we also recommend the work of James Côté, *Arrested Adulthood: The Changing Nature of Maturity and Identity* (New York: NYU Press, 2000).

6. See an interview with Michael Kimmel at *www.guyland.net/interviews.htm*.

7. *Chronicle of Higher Education,* "The College of 2020: Students." Executive Summary. See: http://research.chronicle.com/asset/TheCollegeof2020Executive Summary.pdf.

8. For further discussion of how to build stronger partnerships between schools and employers, see Settersten, "Social Policy and the Transition to Adulthood."

9. Interested readers will find many good examples on the websites of the Center for Information and Research on Civic Learning and Engagement

(www.civicyouth.org), and the Corporation for National and Community Service (www.nationalservice.org), with which members of the Network have partnered on research and interventions.

10. See also Connie Flanagan and Peter Levine, "Civic Engagement and the Transition to Adulthood," *Future of Children* 20 (2010): pp. 159–180; Peter Levine, Connie Flanagan, and Richard Settersten, Jr., "Civic Engagement and the Changing Transition to Adulthood" (Washington, DC: Center for Information and Research on Civic Learning and Engagement, January 2009), available at www.civicyouth.org/?p=327.

Index

PHOTO: © KARL MAASDAM

RICHARD SETTERSTEN, PH.D., is Hallie Ford Endowed Chair and professor of Human Development and Family Sciences, and director of the Hallie Ford Center for Healthy Children and Families, at Oregon State University. He is also a member of the MacArthur Research Network on Transitions to Adulthood. A graduate of Northwestern University, Settersten has held fellowships at the Max Planck Institute for Human Development and Education in Berlin, the Institute for Policy Research at Northwestern, and the Spencer Foundation in Chicago. He is the author or editor of many scientific articles and several books, including *On the Frontier of Adulthood.* Besides MacArthur, his research has been supported by divisions of the National Institutes of Health.

PHOTO: © JULIA MARCUS

BARBARA E. RAY, as owner of Hiredpen, Inc., helps researchers and nonprofit organizations convey their work to broader audiences. She was the communications director for the MacArthur Research Network on Transitions to Adulthood, and has held positions as senior writer at the DHHS-funded Joint Center for Poverty Research, and as a managing editor at the University of Chicago Press journals division. For two years while living in the western Pacific, she was a travel writer and culture reporter. Most recently, she is the executive editor of the website Spotlight on Digital Media and Learning for the MacArthur Foundation. She blogs at mybarbararay.com. She is still not quite adult.